Strong Hermeneutics
Contingency and moral identity

Nicholas H. Smith

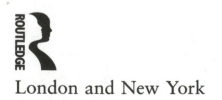

London and New York

First published 1997
by Routledge
11 New Fetter Lane, London EC4P 4EE

Simultaneously published in the USA and Canada
by Routledge
29 West 35th Street, New York, NY 10001

© 1997 Nicholas H. Smith
Typeset in Sabon by Routledge
Printed and bound in Great Britain by
Creative Print and Design (Wales), Ebbw Vale

All rights reserved. No part of this book may be reprinted or
reproduced or utilized in any form or by any electronic,
mechanical, or other means, now known or hereafter
invented, including photocopying and recording, or in any
information storage or retrieval system, without permission in
writing from the publishers.

British Library Cataloguing in Publication Data
A catalogue record for this book is available from the British Library

Library of Congress Cataloging in Publication Data
Smith, Nicholas H. (Nicholas Hugh)
  Strong Hermeneutics : contingency and moral identity / Nicholas H. Smith
Includes bibliographical references and index.
1. Ethics. 2. Hermeneutics. 3. Identity. 4. Contingency (Philosophy) I. Title.
BJ1031.S65 1997
170–dc2196–51763

ISBN 0–415–16431–1 (hbk)
ISBN 0–415–16432–X (pbk)

For my father and in memory of my mother

Contents

Preface

In recent years there has been a resurgence of interest in ethics across a number of philosophical traditions, including phenomenology, hermeneutics, deconstruction, critical theory and 'post-analytic' philosophy. At the same time, questions of identity have risen to prominence throughout the humanities and beyond. As awareness of the complexity and volatility of human identity grows, we are forced into a reckoning of its inner contingency. The implications for ethics of such a reckoning are profound. According to one view, whose broader cultural influence under the names of 'weak thought' and 'postmodernism' seems pervasive, identity is nothing but a concatenation of contingencies and our ethics should be reoriented to fit this basic fact. On another view, which also enjoys considerable currency, contingent identities are subject to universal but formal moral constraints, the reconstruction of which is the proper business of ethics. The argument of this book is that since both these views give a distorted picture of the relation between contingency and identity, neither can provide a proper framework for ethics. The book commends an alternative framework – a 'strong hermeneutics' – for thinking about these matters.

I have several acknowledgements to make. The book assumed its final form during my tenure of a research fellowship in modern European philosophy at Middlesex University. The Centre for Research in Modern European Philosophy at Middlesex provided an exceptionally hospitable environment in which to work. I have also had the good fortune to test my ideas at the 'Philosophy and the Social Sciences' summer schools held in recent years at Prague. I am indebted to Peter Dews and Axel Honneth for inviting me to participate in these rewarding events. Thanks are also due the Institüt für Hermeneutik at the Freie Universität Berlin, where I was able to make some late refinements to the manuscript. The book also profits from conversations had with Martin Löw-Beer and Hans Joas at this time. I would especially like to thank Bob Canon, Diana Coole, Peter Dews, David Frisby, Dudley Knowles, Christopher Martin, Shane O'Neill, Peter Osborne, Jonathan Rée and Hartmut Rosa for their comments on earlier versions of sections of the manuscript. I am also very grateful to the readers at Routledge (Jay Bernstein and David Ingram); the book would have had much less edge than it has were it not for their critical comments on the penultimate draft of the whole text. Thanks too to my commissioning editor, Tony Bruce, for supporting the project, and to my desk editor, Katherine Hodkinson, for overseeing production of the book so efficiently. Finally, I would like to express especially warm thanks to Valli Melchior for her abundant generosity and support.

Chapter one contains a considerably expanded version of a section of 'Charles Taylor, Strong Hermeneutics and the Politics of Difference', *Radical Philosophy* 68, Autumn 1994. Parts of chapter two originally appeared in 'Contingency and Self-identity: Taylor's Hermeneutics vs. Rorty's Postmodernism', *Theory, Culture and Society*, 13: 2, May 1996. I acknowledge both journals for permission to reprint this material.

Nicholas H. Smith
London

Introduction

In a cunning polemic, Freud rebuked his contemporaries for allowing a naïve human self-love to override reason when evaluating the new science of psychoanalysis.[1] Science had already dealt two grievous blows to human pride: Copernicus had displaced humanity from the centre of the universe, and Darwin had toppled *homo sapiens* from the summit of creation. Copernicus and Darwin damaged the human ego and were resisted for it. Psychoanalysis can expect a similar reception, Freud predicted, since it deflates the human self-image still further by proving 'to the ego that it is not even master of its own house', never mind the heavens or earth.[2] Freud thus transformed his opponents' most robust and precious asset – their sense of human identity – into a fragile and ruinous liability.

As Richard Rorty observes, Freud thereby anticipated a theme that would be repeated throughout the twentieth century: the 'decentering' of the human subject.[3] But the primary import of Freud's idea, according to Rorty, is the role it plays in extending the 'mechanization of the world view'. In the first stage of this process, Copernicus and Newton demonstrated that the cosmos did not instantiate divine principles of self-contained harmony, beauty and purpose. Rather, it has the intelligibility of a vast, pointless machine. After the Copernican revolution had disenchanted the heavens, it fell to the Darwinian revolution to disenchant life: for a picture of life as an edifying hierarchy of perfected forms, Mendel and Darwin substituted the image of a purposeless series of fortuitous combinations of mutation and circumstance. Henceforth, neither the cosmos nor life could credibly be interpreted as a realm of meaning in relation to which human beings could find reassurance about their *own* moral identity. By extending the 'mechanization of the world view' to the mind, Rorty suggests, Freud completed an irreversible process of disenchantment and demythologization: he uncovered the last veil of moral meaning hiding the naked contingency of human identity.

So just as Freud ingeniously threw his opponents onto the defensive by redescribing their motives, Rorty forces critics of the unlimited reach of the mechanized world view into an impossible position. If ideas of intrinsic moral meaning are invariably associated with a mythical, pre-scientific outlook, we are licensed from the outset to dismiss the thought that there may be *limits* to contingency. Without even needing to contest the issue of limits, Rorty can move straight on to consider the *consequences* of framing the human self-image in terms of radical contingency. For if scientists have learnt to make sense of the world without any reference to its moral meaning, Rorty asks, are we not bound to learn to see *ourselves* as the chance outcome of processes devoid of any inner significance, as bearing the stamp not of purpose and meaning but a 'blind impress'? Rorty considers Freud and Nietzsche to be the great educators here, and he sees his own work as continuing their project of treating '*everything* – our language, our conscience, our community – as a product of time and chance'.[4]

In advocating such an absolute subjugation of meaning to contingency, Rorty is by no means an isolated figure. Two particularly noteworthy trends of contemporary thought share a similar conviction. On the one hand, there is the more Nietzschean, materialist strand of post-structuralism, which subjugates meaning to the dynamics of elemental forces and desires.[5] On the other hand, the 'blind impress' may be conceived on the model of a structure, as in deconstruction; or as a system, as in recent systems theory.[6] The close affinity of Rorty-style pragmatism, deconstruction and systems theory, in respect of their affirmation of absolute contingency, is well illustrated in Herrnstein-Smith's *Contingencies of Value*, a book that combines these approaches in an all out attack on the idea that normativity as such is intelligible only as a transcendental or categorial limit to contingency.[7]

The thesis that the demands of morality are intelligible only on the presupposition of transcendental limits to contingency is of course a defining characteristic of Kantian thought. For Kant, sense can be made of moral meaning by reflecting on the formal presuppositions of rational action. It behooves the rational agent to universalize the maxims on which he or she individually acts, and this principle of universalizability can be invoked to circumscribe a domain of morally valid norms as opposed to contingently occurrent facts. In Kant, the intrinsic dignity of the moral subject is assured by practical reason. But Kant also construed the *sense* of moral order as testimony to a less fragile source of reassurance: the existence of a loving God. For many contemporary neo-Kantians, however, Kant's basic strategy for dealing with contingency does not need such a metaphysical foundation. Moreover, Kant's outlook can also shed its subject-centred, individualist character, they think, if the procedure by which a norm is justified includes *others* as much as oneself. The most ambitious and systematic theory of this kind is undoubtedly the 'discourse ethics' of Karl-Otto Apel and Jürgen Habermas.[8]

But while Habermas has been highly critical of the advocates of unlimited contingency, he also shares a lot of ground with them.[9] For instance, like Rorty, Habermas presents his view as the rightful heir to an unvanquishable tradition of scientific discovery. According to the self-understanding of that tradition, which discourse ethics incorporates into itself, modern science owes its success to a series of differentiations, including the separation of matters of objective truth from sources of value-orientation. Consequently, those who question the differentiation theses built into discourse ethics can be charged with pitting themselves against more than two centuries of cognitive maturation. With the stakes set so high, is it not unwise, perhaps even intellectually irresponsible, to pursue an alternative paradigm for thinking about categoric limits to contingency, if indeed such limits can coherently be thought at all?

Nevertheless, it is precisely such a third path, diverging both from the postmodernist thesis of radical contingency and Habermas's Kantian response to it, that I shall be exploring in this book. Neither the postmodernist nor the Habermasian approach, in my view, gives an adequate account of the relationship between contingency and moral identity. Moreover, their shortcomings have a common root. For both show an excessive reluctance to address fundamental questions of *ontology*. The thesis of radical, unqualified contingency, though often underpinned by a mechanistic ontology of nature, effectively suppresses the kind of ontological thinking that takes its departure from fundamental predicaments of human existence. Once the spell of quietism concerning an ontology of the human is broken, the affirmation of absolute contingency, I argue in chapters two and seven, is unsustainable. On the other hand, Habermas's Kantian strategy for establishing limits to contingency, as I argue in chapter six, is debilitated by a kind of blinkeredness that artificially keeps ontological issues out of view. To be sure, both postmodernism and discourse ethics see virtue in their minimization of ontological presumption. But we may ask whether the modesty they avow might not be excessive, or even 'false'. The modesty will be excessive if it can be shown that the ends served even by their own favoured mode of philosophical discourse can be met with a 'thicker' set of ontological commitments. But more tellingly, it will be *false* modesty if ontological commitments are *required* for meeting those ends, assuming they can be met at all. A conclusion of this sort is reached in chapters two and six, but also in chapter four, where we deal with the relation between contingency and normativity in Habermas's work prior to his elaboration of a discourse ethics.

The resources needed for a satisfactory understanding of the relationship between contingency and moral identity are provided by what I shall call 'strong hermeneutics'. Strong hermeneutics marks a departure from the thesis of radical contingency in that it considers human existence to be intelligible only on the assumption of certain limits to contingency. However, contrary to the Kantian approach followed by discourse ethics, it construes this transcendence not so much as a formal requirement of rational action as a substantive condition for a mode of being. The limits of contingency excavated by hermeneutic reflection do indeed halt the expansion of the 'mechanization of the world view'. But they are not for that reason inconsistent with the great demystifying achievements of Copernicus, Darwin and Freud.

Let me now give a chapter by chapter run down of the book's argument. Chapter one lays down the framework for the debates that follow. It begins with a synopsis of the 'Enlightenment' view – which I call, following Ernest Gellner, 'Enlightenment fundamentalism' – that there is no room for beings with a moral identity in the kind of world which, as a result of its 'mechanistic' mode of legitimating beliefs, a proper science *has to* find. To use Gellner's formulation, cognition and identity stand in insoluble conflict. On the one hand, modern science establishes that genuine knowledge practices succeed by separating meaning from being, by exposing the knower to the intrinsic meaninglessness of the world of objects and events. On the other hand, human beings *need* beliefs that place them in a realm of unconditional significance. So while Enlightenment fundamentalism regards genuine cognitive practices to be subversive of any belief in the reality of significance, it concedes that having that belief has hitherto been constitutive of the human orientation towards the world.

Now this tension between cognition and identity, or between knowledge and meaning, is reflected in a series of notoriously unstable oppositions commonly taken to characterize Enlightenment thought. Nature and culture, reason and purpose, means and ends, intellect and sensibility, object and subject; all stand paradoxically both with and against each other. But Enlightenment fundamentalism considers the instability of these dualisms – of which the subject–object relation is philosophically paradigmatic – a price worth paying for its uncompromising acknowledgement of the maturation of human cognitive powers. Cognitive maturity finds expression in an objectified conception of nature and a conception of reason unembellished by purpose and sentimental resonance. Hence, at the heart of Enlightenment fundamentalism there is a *rationalist affirmation* of the contingencies inflected in the subject–object relation. As conceived within the Enlightenment fundamentalist's outlook, the demands of reason and nature are both non-negotiable and empty as sources of orientation for the *contingently* acculturated, purposeful human subject.

As is well known, hermeneutic thought rose to prominence historically as part of the Romantic reaction to the Enlightenment. Contemporary hermeneutics can also be characterized as arising from dissatisfaction with the Enlightenment fundamentalist view concerning how things stand with moral identity in a world whose contingency is shown up by genuine cognition. But it is important to recognize the diversity of ways in which the Enlightenment view can be challenged hermeneutically. The rest of chapter one attempts to convey a sense of this variety by distinguishing between 'weak', 'strong' and 'deep' hermeneutics. That strand of contemporary hermeneutics most closely allied with postmodernist sensibilities – what I call 'weak hermeneutics' – urges a *radicalization* of the Enlightenment's acknowledgement of contingency. For weak hermeneutics, whose chief representatives here are Nietzsche and Rorty, the rationalist character of Enlightenment fundamentalism demonstrates its failure of nerve in the face of contingency. On this view, Enlightenment fundamentalism forgets that it too is part of the meaningless, disenchanted world that science discloses. If it were to be more reflexive about this fact, if it were to build into itself an acknowledgement of its own contingency, it would take on a more sceptical, ironic, ontologically 'weak' character. Hence weak hermeneutics has considerable affinities with Enlightenment fundamentalism. This point is foregrounded by strong hermeneutics, which sees weak hermeneutics as perpetuating rather than overcoming the underlying pattern of thought embedded in Enlightenment fundamentalism. According to strong hermeneutics, Enlightenment fundamentalism is best challenged by questioning the assumption that the oppositions between reason and purpose, and between nature and meaning, can be reconciled only at the cost of a reckless metaphysics that ignores the cognitive achievements of modernity. Strong hermeneutics, whose outstanding contemporary representatives are Hans-Georg Gadamer, Charles Taylor and Paul Ricoeur, seeks to achieve reconciliation by way of ontological reflection on the structure of human existence.

A third counter-position to Enlightenment fundamentalism – that represented by a deep hermeneutics – is then introduced by way of a brief review of Habermas's dispute with Gadamer. Gadamer's philosophical anthropology, according to Habermas, suffers not so much from metaphysical excess as from its inability to comprehend how certain manifestations of 'unreason' *foreclose* access to the purposes that bestow meaning on a human life. By contrast to mere hermeneutics, 'depth' hermeneutic reflection allegedly has the theoretical support needed to make such manifestations intelligible as non-contingent symptoms of disturbance in the deep structure of self-formative processes. More specifically, in his early work Habermas argues, by way of a Hegelian reading of Freud, that crises of identity and their reflectively mediated resolution provide unique insight into a deep-rooted human need for recognition. While even in his early work Habermas inclines to the view that deep hermeneutic reflection actually moves beyond the orbit of hermeneutics as such, in terms of the framework for debate set out here, we must be careful not to exaggerate his difference with Gadamer on *this* issue. For strong and deep hermeneutics converge on the fundamental thesis that, due to the existence of deep-seated anthropological interests, contingency does not exhaust human identity.

However, the rift between Habermas and strong hermeneutics widens in his later work. As I have already suggested, in his programmatic writings on discourse ethics Habermas argues that the specific claim of norms to *moral* validity transcends contingency in a much more radical way than that specified by deep-rooted anthropological interests. Now, Habermas takes up Kant's notion that the moral point of view must be autonomous, that is to say, independent of the regularities of nature and the accidents of history. In other words, Habermas maintains that the normativity of the moral is strictly unconditional. But just for this reason, he thinks, it has to be separated off from the concrete conditions of identity formation. This differentiation can be achieved in a manner that does not collapse back into Enlightenment fundamentalism, on Habermas's view, because of certain surprising and far-reaching consequences of tracing back the principle of morality to the pragmatic presuppositions of discourse. That is to say, discourse ethics derives the limits of contingency imposed by the moral point of view from normatively charged but formal features of language use. From the fact that human actions are linguistically mediated, so Habermas argues, it is possible to reconstruct the universal applicability of the moral demand. Since the psychological contingencies of desire and the historical contingencies of cultural allegiance can be made *accountable* to this demand, discourse ethics considers itself capable of grounding a rational *critique* of actually existing cultures and traditions. If at this point discourse ethics is *contrasted* with hermeneutics, the latter can suddenly appear stiflingly conservative, as if a critique of actually existing traditions and cultures were impossible from the hermeneutic standpoint. The onus is then on strong hermeneutics to dispel that appearance. If it succeeds, as I believe it can, it will have removed a considerable obstacle to its acceptability.

With this framework in place, we turn in more detail to the competing hermeneutic and discourse ethical accounts of the contingency of the self, language, and value. Chapter two contrasts and assesses the conceptions of selfhood proposed by Taylor and Rorty. On Rorty's view, which as we have seen arises from a Nietzschean reading of Freud, the self is no more and no less than a 'tissue of contingencies', a fluctuating network of accidentally associated beliefs and desires. To think of the self as having no essence, Rorty believes, is to renounce all those reassuring illusions of self-possession that have traditionally underpinned judgements of good and bad, of moral approbation and condemnation. But the disillusionment only undermines morality in a troubling way, Rorty suggests, if we eschew Freud's counsel, and continue to think of chance as 'unworthy of determining our fate'. However, it is questionable whether the self, even on Rorty's own account, is as contingent as it seems. For, as I argue here, Rorty's model tacitly presupposes that certain kinds of characterization – what Taylor calls 'strong evaluations' – are *non-contingently* applicable to the self. And to the extent that the self cannot but be described in strongly evaluative terms, the self is not, in fact, contingent 'all the way down'. Furthermore, Rorty's view gains what appeal it possesses not so much from its contrast to the idea that the self is constituted by an atemporal, contingency-transcending moral essence as from its opposition to practices of moralizing that take *no* account of the contingencies of character formation and the local contextual determinations of action. But opposition to this 'blame-centred' construction of moral identity, I suggest, is best made on strong hermeneutic grounds. In this and other ways, Rorty's insistence on radical contingency leaves him curiously inarticulate on just the matters that most pressingly motivate his weak hermeneutic stance. The chapter then moves on to discuss Ricoeur's recent work on self-identity, which challenges the Nietzschean 'humiliation' of the human subject on a number of different levels.

Whereas chapter two considers the non-contingency of the general applicability of the concept of strong evaluation, chapter three deals with the question of the contingency of its *particular* application. For even if it can be shown that background, strong evaluative frameworks are inescapable for human beings – that it is a non-contingent fact about human beings that they are oriented in the way described by Taylor's philosophical anthropology – does it not remain a contingent fact that one finds oneself oriented against *this* particular background framework, bound to *this* historically specific culture? How does the acknowledgement of contingency at this level affect the intelligibility of moral identity? Strong hermeneutics responds to these questions by offering a 'narrative' model of practical reasoning and a 'realist' reading of strong evaluative discourse. That is to say, while one must indeed find oneself 'thrown' into a given, contingently occurring culture, this does not exclude the possibility of rational change in one's identity. On this view, the claim to rationality, like the claim to realism, of identity-conferring values has been occluded by orthodox but profoundly inappropriate 'criterial' models of reason and reality. Drawing on recent debates in analytical philosophy, the 'realist' self-understanding of strong hermeneutics is then examined. The focus then turns to whether, despite avowals to the contrary, this realist spirit betrays a hostility to pluralism and self-critique. Does hermeneutic realism entail conservatism after all? The chapter concludes by pointing to ways in which strong hermeneutics can deliver a negative answer to this question.

In chapter four, as I mentioned above, we turn to the thematization of contingency and the intelligibility of moral identity in Habermas's depth hermeneutics. The chapter begins by recalling the neglected significance of Hegel and Freud in Habermas's initial conception of critical theory. We are reminded here that critical theory, understood as depth hermeneutics, models itself in the first instance on the young Hegel's critique of Kant's explication of the origins of the moral demand. According to the Hegelian model, moral subjectivity is an achievement reached in the context of a struggle for recognition. Moral identity is rendered intelligible through the avenging force of a suppressed 'ethical totality' or 'damaged intersubjectivity': it shows its structure *indirectly* through the unforeseeable consequences of unsatisfied and suppressed needs. This 'fateful' causality, operating behind the backs of subjects, points to 'quasi-anthropological' limits to the contingency of self-formative processes. However, according to

Habermas's Hegelian reading of Freud – one which takes a very different course to Rorty's Nietzschean interpretation – these limits cannot be established simply by way of an objective, scientific theory of human nature. Rather, they are presupposed in a *practice* of self-reflection that combines general principles of normal human development with auto-biographical, subject-specific, affectively loaded insight. There then follows a discussion of the suitability of this conception of self-reflection as a paradigm for regaining moral identity by overcoming contingency. I argue that while the model is more apt than some critics have assumed, it is questionable whether it owes its power to a departure from the orbit of hermeneutics.

In his later work, Habermas construes the normative implications of the dialogical constitution of subjectivity differently. In a manner that reflects his growing distance from hermeneutics, Habermas becomes gripped by the conviction that the key to the intelligibility of moral identity lies hidden in the deep structure of language *use*. Language use, for Habermas, comes in two fundamentally distinct kinds. On the one hand, there is communicative action, which is action oriented to reaching an understanding with another; and on the other hand there is strategic action, in which language is used as an instrument conditioned by some externally defined goal. While Habermas acknowledges that language is commonly used in both these ways, he argues that one type, communicative action, is 'originary'. Forms of linguistic action that are not oriented to consensus reached by understanding, Habermas claims, are parasitic on the originary communicative mode. Only communicative action, in other words, is *sui generis* language use. Now this claim has drawn extensive criticism from what I have been calling a weak hermeneutic perspective. In chapter five, after summarizing Habermas's basic thesis, I rehearse these objections and divide them into two types. On the one hand, there are those with a deconstructivist accent that take issue with Habermas's way of *privileging* consensual over strategic use. On the other hand, there are considerations of the kind put by Lyotard for *reversing* the priority; that is, for making strategic language use originary. I argue, however, that neither Habermas nor his weak hermeneutic opponents are fully successful in making their case. I conclude with the strong hermeneutic suggestion that the stalemate between them arises from a misleading presupposition of both parties – that language should be considered primarily under its *pragmatic* aspect at all.

The relationship between strong hermeneutics and Habermas's discourse ethics is examined in a more systematic fashion in chapter six. We shall see how, in order to get going, Habermas's theoretical programme has to invoke certain fundamental distinctions concerning the autonomy of moral norms, the scope of practical reason and the tasks of philosophy. But there are, I think, good hermeneutic grounds for questioning their propriety. In particular, the notion that an autonomous moral domain is a suitable object of rational reconstruction – in the same manner in which, say, grammatical competence may be – is deeply problematic. As a corollary, the division of labour Habermas imposes on philosophical reflection to accommodate the hypothesis that moral competence is reconstructible arguably distorts its subject-matter. In his more recent writings, Habermas has revised his theory in order to obviate problems of the kind noted here, but we are still led to the conclusion that his account of the intelligibility of the moral demand remains skewed by an unwarranted suspicion of the conservative bias and metaphysical burden of strong hermeneutics. Moreover, if these revisions were allowed to develop unhampered by such prejudices, I suggest, if they were permitted to unfold according to their inner logic, discourse ethics would soon find itself back on clearly recognizable hermeneutic ground.

In chapter seven, my claim that strong hermeneutics provides the basis for a critical ethical outlook without metaphysical excess is put to the test by examining how it might make sense of the problem of ecological responsibility. The signal failure of Enlightenment fundamentalism to render ecological responsibility intelligible on a more than prudential, utilitarian basis has undoubtedly pushed many philosophers and social critics in the general direction of hermeneutics. But which kind of hermeneutics is best equipped to succeed where Enlightenment fundament- alism fails? Drawing on Stephen K. White's account of the significance of postmodernism for political theory, weak hermeneutics is found wanting on account of insurmountable problems it generates with its notion of 'world- disclosure'. But once construed in strong hermeneutic terms, powers of linguistic disclosure, by pointing to an affectively potent yet cognitively apt sense of the 'otherness' of nature, do indeed have a role to play in renewing and broadening our conception of responsibility. This ambitious, though admittedly rather formally articulated suggestion, is backed by an interpretation of Heidegger's later writings. In advancing it I do not mean to propose that philosophical criticism in the field of ecological politics is exclusively of hermeneutic provenance. For responsible ecological politics is not just a matter of sensitive world-disclosure. It also requires a sound sense of the structure and imperatives of democratic action-coordination. On the latter issue, Habermas's theory remains instructive – if incomplete.

1 The variety of hermeneutics

As the theory of interpretation in general, hermeneutics has a long, complex history. In a tradition that is conveniently earmarked as running from Schleiermacher through Dilthey and Heidegger to Gadamer and Ricoeur, hermeneutics shows continuity through considerable diversity in content. But I shall not, to any serious degree, be dealing with the variety of hermeneutics in this historical sense.[1] Nor, despite my ambition to contribute something worthwhile to the field, shall I be concerned primarily with the multiple manifestations of hermeneutics in current literary, cultural and art theory.[2] Rather, I shall use the term 'hermeneutics' to stand for various patterns of contemporary philosophical argument occasioned by reflection upon the bearing of contingency on the intelligibility of moral identity.

According to the framework set out here, there are three major tributaries of hermeneutic thinking. Each can be regarded as co-emerging in opposition to elements of the view that I shall call, following Gellner, 'Enlightenment fundamentalism'.[3] After a brief exposition of this view, alive today in the work of thinkers like Gellner and Hans Albert but with roots going back to Descartes and Kant,[4] I offer a schematic outline of the different paths subsequently taken by hermeneutics. In the chapters that follow, these strong, weak and deep varieties of hermeneutics – and offshoots of them that claim to move beyond the horizon of hermeneutics as such – are brought into debate on matters concerning the contingency of self, culture and value.

BEFORE HERMENEUTICS: ENLIGHTENMENT FUNDAMENTALISM

Enlightenment fundamentalism – as loosely defined by Gellner and followed, with refinements, here – can be understood as a philosophical *apologia* for a sociological fact. Following Weber, the Enlightenment fundamentalist maintains that the becoming modern of a society and its characteristic ways of understanding the world involves an irreversible process of disenchantment. From the Weberian perspective, the transition to modernity appears as an evolution from traditional modes of thought and action like religion, revelation and myth, to rational enlightened modes like science and technology. Enlightenment fundamentalism then imports *philosophical* significance to the phenomenon of disenchantment by construing it as definitive of the maturation of human rational capacities. According to the Enlightenment fundamentalist, science and technology are not merely the *prevailing* form of reason in modern times; they do not just chronologically succeed religious and mythic ways of seeing the world. Rather, they give the lie to those orders of significance which, as supposedly revealed through myth, dogmatic metaphysics and religion, *ground* human identity in its pre-mature phases of cognitive development. In other words, Enlightenment fundamentalism construes disenchantment as conceptually as well as historically compelling. Denuded of natural and traditional orders of meaning by genuine cognition, says the Enlightenment fundamentalist, we are bound by reason, and not just by historical circumstance, to acknowledge the truth of the contingent basis of human existence. Though the yearning for ontological significance lingers, human beings are doomed *de facto* and *de jure*, in Gellner's words, 'to suffer a tension between cognition and identity'.[5]

The Enlightenment fundamentalist's reasons for finding the tension between cognition and identity conceptually as well as empirically compelling run as follows. Cognition *emerges* in opposition to identity as an ideal with its own distinct normative content. This 'ethic of cognition', as Gellner calls it, has two basic components: first, that 'anything must be true before it can significantly claim other merits'; second, that truth *be* merited in virtue of satisfying maximally risky criteria of epistemic legitimacy.[6] The first principle implies that different kinds of value can be ascribed to beliefs, that one of these is truth, and that the ethic of cognition prioritizes the truth-value ('truth') of beliefs over other evaluable properties they may have. Besides being evaluable in terms of their truth, belief-systems may serve to reinforce tradition, to edify the past, or maintain social order. The ethic of cognition requires that the accountability of beliefs be independent of such purposes: authority, tradition and faith ought not to 'fill out the world'.

This step towards disenchantment is consolidated by the way in which the ethic of cognition attempts to differentiate that function of language responsible for the felicitous description of the world from functions that are adventitious to the world-descriptive capacity of language. Enchantment is a symptom of cognitive immaturity because it arises, as Gellner puts it, from the 'systematic conflation of descriptive, evaluative, identificatory, status-conferring and other roles of language'.[7] It is a consequence of a vocabulary sufficiently 'thick' to perform each of the different linguistic functions simultaneously. According to Enlightenment fundamentalism, such conflation allows language that is really just the expression of a particular cultural or moral code to gain the appearance of objectively describing the world. The autonomy and primacy of truth affirmed by the ethic of cognition, Gellner suggests, serves to alienate 'man the knower' from the 'citizen and the moral being'.[8]

Enlightenment fundamentalism considers the differentiation of descriptive and evaluative functions of language to testify to the ethic of cognition's respect for rules. Rules command consistency and symmetry, like cases are treated alike in accordance with them, they do not admit of idiosyncratic variation. This is how the Enlightenment fundamentalist makes sense of his aversion to ideas like revelation and the miraculous. Such notions require room for the *exceptional* case. But the ethic of cognition demands the levelling of *all* legitimate explanations. For Enlightenment fundamentalism, genuine cognition issues from a procedure of legitimation that subjects all explanations to public and repeatable testing. That which is legitimate by way of belief becomes, ideally, that which is *mechanically* testable: like a machine, genuine knowledge is 'an artifact which can be reproduced at any time, in any place, in any society, provided the same specified materials are used and put together in a publicly specifiable way'.[9] Just as Enlightenment fundamentalism insists that procedures of explanation must follow an orderly, rule-governed method, so it demands that the concepts by which they are articulated must be such as to be applicable in a strictly ordered, non-idiosyncratic way. The order, regularity and symmetry imposed by rules on the behaviour of objects and concepts disenchants them by ruling out spontaneity and idiosyncrasy. Thus the *cognized* world loses the meaning discharged by the kind of concepts that find application in the *inhabited* world.

Gellner observes that the loss of spontaneity that Weber captured in his image of modern, bureaucratically organized society as an 'iron cage' also extends to the modern scientific conceptual organization of the world. A language of genuine cognition is gained at the expense of a vocabulary in which human identity can be expressed: the concepts 'in terms of which identities are forged and life is lived' are submitted to an irreversible form of 'intellectual erosion'.[10] To adopt a formulation from John McDowell, modern science develops conceptual capacities that are directed to the kind of intelligibility that is proper to the realm of *law*, precisely by separating that intelligibility from the kind that is proper to *meaning*.[11] But since human beings do fall within the realm of law, an Enlightenment fundamentalist like Gellner can see no alternative to the view that 'we should set about saving whatever is worth saving in our conception of ourselves, by reconstructing it in terms of conceptual apparatus that is already unproblematically naturalistic'; that is, suitable for characterizing the realm of law as such.[12] This is just the constraint required by the mechanistic baseline of legitimate explanation, which thus issues, Gellner believes, in the modern 'certainty of reductionism': 'that everything is an unedifying something else'.[13]

The second component of the ethic of cognition generates disenchantment in a similar manner. In order to maximize the extent to which beliefs are held in virtue of their truth, and to minimize the degree to which non-assertoric functions of language serve to influence the content of belief, the norm of cognition demands of truth claims that they pass a maximally rigorous selection procedure. It *may* be the case that traditions and common sense are the vehicles of truth content, but the ethic of cognition biases the burden of proof by invoking criteria of legitimacy that are minimally dependent on particular cultural contents. It also insists that since it is better to hold beliefs that are true rather than false – and this independently of the consequences of holding them – there is an obligation to maximize the chances of arriving at the truth, and this means following a procedure for reaching them that minimizes the risk of error. We are obliged, that is, to be able to legitimate beliefs in as stringent a manner as possible. For the Enlightenment fundamentalist, modern epistemology from Descartes, Hume and Kant to Popper and contemporary empiricism, more or less successfully clarifies how this obligation is best met. Much more important than its explanations of cognitive success and its possibility are modern epistemology's 'recommendations for the proper conduct of our intellectual life'.[14] For Enlightenment fundamentalism, the worth of epistemology lies in the series of 'cultural injunctions' it elaborates, including, most crucially, the validation imperative to place all beliefs and practices *sub-judice*. From this perspective, for instance, Locke's famous description of philosophy as the 'handmaiden to science' reflects his view that the emerging empirical sciences of his time did faithfully satisfy the requirements of proper intellectual conduct.

The Enlightenment fundamentalist acknowledges the need for enchantment. He recognizes the real desire for meaning in a chaotic universe of harsh, relentless contingency. But he refuses to succumb to it, choosing instead to affirm the honour and dignity of the knowing subject. He does this in awareness of the fact that, in the final analysis, his own position is bereft of foundation: his Enlightenment is, ultimately, a fundamentalism. In this respect, the Enlightenment fundamentalist contrasts himself favourably with others who fail to resist the seduction of meaning. Indeed, it is in this desire for re-enchantment that Gellner finds the primary motivation for hermeneutic philosophy. According to Gellner, hermeneutics represents a failure of nerve in face of the contingencies and predicaments bequeathed by the irrefutable success of the norm of cognition. Gellner aims to demonstrate this thesis by way of an explication of the duplicity at work in the key hermeneutic concept of the 'lifeworld'.

As Gellner sees it, hermeneutics aims to restore identity and moral self-reassurance by separating off or *bracketing* the world in which humans live and endorsing it, as it were, from within. It is in the service of such re-enchantment that Gellner sees the significance of the lifeworld. The lifeworld provides both the resources for human identity formation and the field of expression of human identities. It becomes problematic, Gellner contends, with the differentiation of the languages of cognition and life, which he in turn identifies with the discontinuity between the vocabularies of science and the everyday. Gellner urges that, because the modern lifeworld is partly *constituted* by this discrepancy, the hermeneutic attempt to bracket it from the cognized world is forlorn. In so far as we are under the sway of the norm of cognition, we must recognize the 'interim status' of common sense understandings, since they are properly regarded merely as objects of possible 're-validation' by science. The claims of the lifeworld thus stand in perpetual threat of possible reconceptualization according to apparatus suitable for rendering them intelligible within the realm of law. This lack of congruence is evidenced, Gellner states, by the well-founded preference for the 'idiom for which we have greater *cognitive* respect' – namely, science and technology – even when dealing with problems of the gravest *practical* consequence.[15]

Again following Weber, Gellner traces the disintegrative effect of cognition on the lifeworld back to the expansion of instrumental rationality. According to Gellner, the lifeworld has traditionally consisted of a repertoire of practically oriented beliefs characterized by relative rigidity, stability and immunity from the challenges of recalcitrant experience. It is the taken-for-granted, *sui generis resource* for the legitimation of personal and social identities. As Gellner sees it, instrumental rationality is at work wherever hypotheses are constructed to discover the most efficient means to a particular end. By bringing everything under the sway of the hypothesis, and hence, in principle, opening up anything to instrumental, calculative reasoning, the ethic of cognition destabilizes the orienting function of the lifeworld. Through its neutral, homogeneous, mechanistic mode of legitimation, it transforms the lifeworld into a 'bundle of hypotheses', one in which instrumental rationality is at home. In this way it erodes the old frameworks of identity expression. But since the lifeworld had functioned as a *sui generis* resource of legitimation exempt from instrumental reason, its reduction under the hypothetical gaze needs to be compensated for. Demanded in areas that were previously exempt from it, instrumental reason falls short just where it is needed most.[16]

Hermeneutics acknowledges the phenomenon described here, but finds Enlightenment fundamentalism an inadequate basis for comprehending it. The varieties of hermeneutics take the *problem* of intelligible moral identity in a context of contingency as their common point of departure. They agree with Enlightenment fundamentalism that the old idea of pre-critical metaphysics that human identity is grounded in an objective cosmological order is finished. They also share the Enlightenment fundamentalist scepticism about absolute, trans-cultural substantive normative claims. Enlightenment fundamentalism goes wrong, hermeneutics claims, in its scientism. Putting it at its briefest, the scientism to which weak hermeneutics reacts is the urge to commensurate, to reduce rationality to rule, to aspire towards closure as the end of inquiry.[17] Beyond this, strong hermeneutics attacks the scientistic anthropology of disengagement, according to which human reality is ideally to be *finessed* of evaluative significance. Deep hermeneutics reacts primarily to the scientism of 'technocracy': the ideologically entrenched view that the only rational cognitive interest is in prediction and control. All three forms are vehemently critical of the persistently foundationalist nature of Enlightenment fundamentalism. And each proffers a powerful indictment of the epistemological paradigm of philosophy inspired by Descartes. But we need to look closer at these different kinds of hermeneutics to see why the mere negation of scientism or foundationalism does not of itself suffice to demarcate a distinctive philosophical position.

WEAK HERMENEUTICS: NIETZSCHE, RORTY AND POSTMODERNISM

Enlightenment fundamentalism opposes culture-dependent, reason-deficient, subjective identity to culture-transcendent, rationally replete, objective cognition. The strategy of weak hermeneutics is not so much to reconcile cognition and identity at a higher level as to down-play the philosophical significance of that which separates them. Weak hermeneutics turns against the very idea of an objective order that can secure *either* cognition *or* identity: cognition, as much as identity, is swamped by contingency. For weak hermeneutics, the privilege Enlightenment fundamentalism confers on science, the praise it bestows on reason as mechanical algorithmic rule-following, and the respect it holds for mainstream post-Cartesian epistemology, betray its residual attachment to just that kind of metaphysical thinking it avows to replace. In each case, weak hermeneutics accuses Enlightenment fundamentalism of stopping short of the thoroughgoing acknowledgement of contingency that would mark the final break with the foundationalist project. Hence weak hermeneutics seeks a *radicalization* of the anti-metaphysical, de-divinizing thrust of Enlightenment fundamentalism. It takes the ethic of cognition at its word *as* an ethic in order to relativize and de-rationalize its claims. It suggests that, as a matter of consistency, partisans of the ethic of cognition should drop the notion of culturally transcendent truth. But weak hermeneutics goes further than such logical objections by insisting that the *aspiration* to pursue an external order of truth is actually detrimental to proper intellectual conduct. Following Nietzsche, weak hermeneutics models proper intellectual conduct on self-creation and self-transformation that has itself 'no other end'. In having 'no other end', weak hermeneutics dispenses with the idea of a human identity *guided* by an order toward which the powers for self-creation may be properly or improperly directed.

Weak hermeneutics is 'weak' in virtue of its radical withdrawal from ontological commitment. The defining characteristic of ontological weakness issues from the way its epistemological, ethico-political and metaphilosophical convictions are shaped by the acknowledgement of contingency. The epistemological case for weak hermeneutics typically runs as follows: all knowledge is interpretation; interpretations are always value-laden; values are ultimately expressions of some heterogeneous non-cognitive faculty, process or event (such as the mechanics of desire, history or the will to power); therefore truth claims are ultimately expressions of that non-cognitive faculty, process or event. The following passage, taken from a synopsis of the project of 'weak thought' as advocated by G. Vattimo, nicely illustrates this kind of reasoning:

> everything we encounter in our experience is no more and no less than an *interpretation* – things in the world are always interpreted into the terms of our own subjective values, and thus *the only world that can ever be known is a world of difference* (that is, a world of interpretations).[18]

The conception of knowledge operative in weak hermeneutics thus has affinities with 'perspectivism' – the doctrine, espoused most influentially of course by Nietzsche, that knowledge is either relative to the historically contingent point of view of the knower, or reducible to the acognitive, pre-discursive forces and mechanisms that constitute that point of view. Weak hermeneutics branches into several sub-tributaries depending on which force or mechanism is held to be constitutive.[19] Whatever it be, weak hermeneutics questions the legitimacy of the distinction between 'genuine knowledge' and 'mere interpretation' that is so central to the Enlightenment fundamentalist. The lack of certainty, consensus and finality that ordinary use of the term 'interpretation' connotes – and that provokes the Enlightenment fundamentalist's contempt for the non-scientific – are taken by weak hermeneutics as ineliminable characteristics of *all* knowledge. Furthermore, uncertainty and disagreement are construed as betraying the stubborn presence of historically contingent contexts and pre-discursive forces behind all human attempts at describing the world. Given this weak epistemological base, a weak ontological superstructure looks unavoidable: if all we can *know* about reality depends on the perspective from which it is interpreted, must we not assume that reality itself can only *be* how it seems to us fallible interpreters?

Weak hermeneutics avows *humility* in the face of this question, partly on account of the absence of historically invariant criteria of truth. But there is a more important reason. To call something 'real', weak hermeneutics maintains, is not just to *express* one's own particular perspective, it is also to make an *honorific gesture* about it. Thus while the gesture may be cognitively empty, it nevertheless serves a function: to privilege the claimant's own perspective and to exclude others. At this point, the epistemological considerations blur into ethico-political ones. For the non-realist conclusion of weak hermeneutics' epistemological argument is embraced as part of a broader affirmation of the nihilist project of the transvaluation of 'the higher' – namely, of the true, the real and the good. The idea that truth, for instance, should be regarded as the highest aim of intellectual conduct – and thus as an expression of what is higher in life – is questioned by weak hermeneutics on account of its *subordinative* function. If, as weak hermeneutics has it, the quest for truth subordinates difference – be it the difference of perspectives, the difference of subjectivities or the difference of power-struggles – its transvaluation as an honorific signifier is demanded precisely in the name of such differences. And if truth is rejected as the proper goal of intellectual conduct, *a fortiori* it is rejected as the goal of a properly conducted philosophical criticism.

So weak hermeneutics replaces the Enlightenment fundamentalist idea of science as the cognitive grasp of an objective order with the notion of science as one amongst many equally contingent perspectives and practices. It claims to make no sense of the idea that there is an order of truth beyond these perspectives and practices to which they might fail or succeed to correspond. But the distinctiveness of this strategy against Enlightenment rationalism lies not so much in its questioning the possibility of cognition. If it were, it would be no more than a traditional form of scepticism. Rather, the challenge of weak hermeneutics lies in its counter-position to the Enlightenment fundamentalist's aspiration towards truth. We have seen how weak hermeneutics can question the validity of the aspiration, but what about its alternative?

When Nietzsche presages weak hermeneutics with his famous description of truth, the norm of cognition, as 'worn out metaphors which have become powerless to affect the senses',[20] he is primarily contrasting and subordinating one norm to another. The challenge to the norm of cognition has force in virtue of this contrast, but it is difficult to specify the source of this other norm. Nietzsche variously refers to it as 'life' and 'will to power'. His suggestion is that so-called truths are antagonistic to life, where 'life' connotes a vital force of creative energy, a flux of sensuous particularity which resists the conceptual categorization conditioning claims to truth. On Nietzsche's view, life expresses itself in metaphor, and more generally, in art. Nietzsche thus seems to be proposing a norm of 'expression', though not the expression of a subject about which there can be a truth, but rather of a deeper impersonal reality that manifests itself through the artistic creation of humans. Although Nietzsche himself sometimes *conflates* truth with self-creation or 'a will to overcome that has in itself no end',[21] his will-to-power metaphysics is arguably adventitious to the central challenge his opponents must address: is it necessary to reject the norm of truth and the ethic of cognition for another norm that is external and *antagonistic* to it, and which must be thought of as having 'in itself no end'? The force of this question turns on the relationship between rationality and the ethic of cognition. If, as Enlightenment fundamentalism inclines to assert, rationality is exhausted by instrumental calculation, then a critique of the ethic of cognition must invoke an 'other of reason', not only because it is defined in terms of its antagonism to truth, but because it has no other end, no other standard against which the rational critique of contingency can begin.

Weak hermeneutics does not regard this absence of foundational standards as something in need of correction; it is not understood as a sign of failure, incompletion or unfulfilled responsibility.[22] On the contrary, the demand for foundations drives the ambition of the philosophical tradition weak hermeneutics aspires to overcome. The foundationalism of previous philosophy, it is alleged, encourages an intolerance of 'otherness' and the 'incommensurable'.[23] Weak hermeneutics can take the form of strategies for circumventing or subverting that demand for answerability to reason through which, it is believed, power and control is exercised. The goal of these postmodern strategies is to make space in thought for that which is allegedly non-assimilable to reason: diversity, heterogeneity and difference. Reason, weak hermeneutics maintains, is not only bankrupt in the face of difference as such, but the very enemy of it, since for something to be called to reason is for it to be subsumed under a concept, and thus for its difference to yield to an enforced principle of unity. The task of weak hermeneutic thought, accordingly, is not the justification or clarification of difference, but, to borrow Derrida's expression, the 'intensification of its play'.[24] For the weak hermeneutic postmodernist, reason is, and ought to be, the slave of difference.

So weak hermeneutics disavows previous philosophy's conception of itself as the 'guardian of reason' whose role it is to ground culture, to give it a foundation, to police it for epistemic and semantic transgression. While traditionally it may have seemed that some transcendence of contingency was necessary to ground the highest ideals of freedom and democracy once and for all, to weak hermeneutics the ideals and the tradition are irreconcilable. This view is proposed by John D. Caputo, who coins the term 'radical hermeneutics' to describe contemporary post-Nietzschean philosophies which cultivate 'an acute sense of the contingency of all social, historical, linguistic structures'.[25] Rather than speaking prescriptively of grand emancipatory interests that transcend fate – or the critical projects such interests might ground – radical/weak hermeneutics 'speaks only of a series of contingent, ad hoc, plans devised here and now to offset the exclusionary character of the prevailing system'.[26] In this way weak hermeneutic philosophy redefines its task and its relationship to culture in order to avoid the tradition's discredited foundationalism. To borrow Rorty's formulation, 'weak' hermeneutic thought comprises 'philosophical reflection which does not attempt a radical criticism of contemporary culture, does not attempt to refound or remotivate it, but simply assembles reminders and suggests some interesting possibilities'.[27]

STRONG HERMENEUTICS: GADAMER, TAYLOR AND RICOEUR

Weak hermeneutics deflates the philosophical significance of the separation of cognition and identity by a *levelling down* of cognition to the contingent status Enlightenment fundamentalism correctly assigns to identity. Its endorsement of the normative status of cognition functions to relativize and de-rationalize *all* ontological claims. Strong hermeneutics, on the other hand, undertakes a *levelling up* of identity-expressive, normative beliefs to cognitive status. It takes seriously the nature of the ethic of cognition as an ethic, not in order to dismiss it from the space of reasons and truth, but in the conviction that the space of reasons and truth can be made manifest in the rendering perspicuous of an ethical horizon. Strong hermeneutics takes the norm of cognition as one horizon of self-interpretation amongst others, its status as a cultural injunction is affirmed, but it is also allowed to admit of truth. It rejects two views which are central to Enlightenment fundamentalism: first, that the systematic differentiation of descriptive and evaluative linguistic functions does necessarily constitute a cognitive advance; and second, that beliefs merit rational acceptability to the degree to which they transcend their culture-specific content. For strong hermeneutics, interpretation is the living house of reason, not its tomb. Strong hermeneutics objects to the devaluation of interpretation which Enlightenment fundamentalism carries out in the way it construes the role of rules; its mechanistic constraint on the language of explanation; and its concept of rationality. Though strong hermeneutics shares some of these objections with weak hermeneutics, differences in the alternative conceptions of language, science and reason emerge from them. I will now briefly consider each domain of criticism in turn.

We have seen that the Enlightenment fundamentalist is impressed by the orderly, algorithmic, symmetrical, repeatable – in short, 'rule-like' features of scientific concepts and practices of legitimation. He takes this as a justifying consideration for the claim that our trust in scientific knowledge is of an unparalleled, privileged kind. As an initial response, hermeneutics demands of Enlightenment fundamentalism a reason for overturning the prima facie propositional (truth-evaluable) status of grammatically well-formed indicative sentences, *whatever* their conceptual content.[28] At a very general level, hermeneutics can expose serious difficulties facing the view that the rule-governed peculiarity of natural scientific discourse lies in the fact that 'like cases are treated alike'. The Enlightenment fundamentalist must claim either that what counts as the 'same' instance of the correct application of a concept is fixed in advance of and independently of practices of explanation, or that rule-boundedness is itself an expression of those practices. The Enlightenment fundamentalist is unhappy with the former position since it seems to hark back to pre-critical metaphysics.[29] It is a view, however, which the analogy between a culture-neutral baseline of explanation and the operation of an ideally decontextualized machine tempts him to take. If, on the other hand, the Enlightenment fundamentalist holds that rule-boundedness is an expression of modern practices of natural science, then the defender of hermeneutics will want to know why other discourses do not make the grade for fact-stating. The argument may then be pressed that the special fact-describing function arises in virtue of the degree of rigour in rule-following required by legitimate participation in the scientific language game. But as seen by hermeneutics, this argument only establishes that discourses exhibit differences along a continuum of rule-boundedness, a continuum which covers various degrees of consensus regarding what counts as rule-bounded, and what counts as a fact. The relative flexibility of the criteria which govern the correct application of evaluative concepts – and to that extent their idiosyncrasy – also serves to confirm their resistance to arbitrary usage. But if, as hermeneutics insists, we take resistance to be the tell-tale sign of fact-stating in scientific discourse, then no reason has been given yet for thinking the same does not hold for evaluative discourse.

At this point the Enlightenment fundamentalist might take a different tack. For it is open for him to reply that the symmetry and lack of idiosyncrasy that is required of the behaviour of concepts which feature in genuine cognition is elucidated not so much by their rule-boundedness, nor by the public and repeatable verification procedures of the theories containing them, but by something akin to the idea of *primary qualities*.[30] Primary qualities are those properties or powers the existence of which is not wholly contingent upon the existence of beings (like humans) who are disposed to be affected by them in the form of experience. They are distinguished from secondary properties which exist solely in virtue of such dispositions. If the world contained no beings with the idiosyncratic sensory (or linguistic) constitution of humans, it would contain no secondary qualities; whereas the existence of primary qualities is quite independent of such idiosyncrasy. The crux of the distinction, however, comes from the further supposition that human nature is prone to the error of *projecting* what is relative to the idiosyncrasy of the human enquirer onto the world as it exists – so to speak – absolutely.[31] Hence there issues an epistemological and indeed ethical requirement to disengage from these human idiosyncrasies; to gain a perspective on the world from a vantage point which is neutral with respect to the peculiar significance it has for humans; to give an absolute account of reality on which there would be (in principle) universal agreement between all enquirers who had successfully managed to overcome their naïve, partial, idiosyncratic standpoints. Such an account would be written in a language of primary quality concepts, and only explanations couched in them would qualify as genuinely cognitive. Instead of following Gellner's own formulation of the norm of cognition, the Enlightenment fundamentalist now declares: *Don't project!*

At this point weak hermeneutics challenges the coherence of the primary/secondary quality distinction and of the very idea of an absolute account of reality. The claim of strong hermeneutics, on the other hand, is that while the absolute conception *does* have a proper scope of application, insuperable difficulties face it when *overextended*. For strong hermeneutics, the shortcomings in the Enlightenment fundamentalist's diagnosis of the tension between cognition and identity result from just such overextension.[32]

One of strong hermeneutics' chief disputes with Enlightenment fundamentalism lies in its commitment to non-absolute patterns of explanation. Modern scientific explanations, guided by the claim to an absolute account of reality, seek to improve upon naïve everyday explanations by identifying facts independently of idiosyncratically human reactions to them. But by taking this neutral stance, by disengaging from the reactions which typically 'accompany' the understanding of a phenomenon, it is possible that we can lose our grasp of the phenomenon which needs explaining. In the case of moral phenomena, the assumption of the neutral stance can *disable* us from arguing competently about them. This suggests that the method of rescinding from moral 'prejudices' or the horizon of meaning of the inhabited world does not necessarily give better insight into the domain of reality under consideration.[33] So the absolute description, rather than giving us the really true story (Gellner's 'certainty of reductionism'), actually loses from view some aspect of reality requiring explanation. If that is the case, it would be irrational to pursue absolute descriptions in this domain.

But in order to be able to say this, strong hermeneutics needs a richer concept of rationality than Enlightenment fundamentalism provides. The model of rationality favoured by strong hermeneutics derives from the idea of perspicuous articulation.[34] A perspicuous articulation will be well-ordered and consistent, it will give an account which clearly distinguishes one kind of case or phenomenon from another, in formulations that are consistent internally and with each other. I have a rational grasp of something if I can articulate it in a perspicuously ordered, *a fortiori* consistent account. Likewise, an action merits the ascription 'rational' if it is consistent with achieving some more or less clearly defined objective which gives it its point, and it is irrational if it frustrates the achievement of that goal. But the criterion of consistency does not exhaust the concept of rationality; consistency is a necessary but not a sufficient condition of a rational account, or a rational action. For strong hermeneutics, the canons within which an account is consistent, and the objectives that are consistently met by means of action, can also be more or less rational. For canons and objectives often appear as rivals, and in virtue of this, they are assessable against each other. The demand of rationality *may* be to adopt a disengaged, neutral perspective, but where the disengaged perspective issues in inarticulacy, reason calls for an alternative approach. This has two crucial implications for the concept of rationality. First, it leads us to think of standards of rationality in terms of *contrasting* degrees of perspicuity possessed by available vocabularies, rather than in terms of some neutrally describable ideal standard. Second, it encourages us to think of truth as the *disclosure* made manifest by a perspicuous articulation, rather than as a relation of correspondence between an object and some external means of representation.

For strong hermeneutics, the most glaring inarticulacy in Enlightenment fundamentalism is its failure to render perspicuous the nature of the ethic of cognition as an ethic. Enlightenment fundamentalism considers the adoption of a disengaged, neutral stance towards the world a desirable characteristic of human beings – it considers it *better* for human beings to hold beliefs from that perspective and in that attitude – but it neglects to account for the possibility of making such characterizations correctly at all. It is just such 'desirability-characterizations' that constitute a human identity in the strong hermeneutic sense. Strong hermeneutics thus regards the ethic of cognition as an expression of identity, one that is deeply embedded in modern culture, but which undercuts itself when applied to itself as an identity. The tension between cognition and identity diagnosed by Gellner then looks more like something *internal* to the modern identity itself.[35]

So much for the manner of the strong hermeneutic response to Enlightenment fundamentalism. It is now time to summarize its key differences with weak hermeneutics. In contrast to its weak cousin, strong hermeneutics is realist in orientation, having an agenda set firmly in the orbit of ontology. Strong hermeneutics takes its point of departure not from *the epistemological fragility of foundational truth claims*, but from the *conditions of possibility of actual interpretive practices*. These conditions include the historical embeddedness and linguistic mediation of the interpreting subject upon which weak hermeneutics insists, but their range is furthered by a recognition of the capacity of language to disclose domains of reality which constitute the independently subsisting subject-matter of competing interpretations. Reality is what is disclosed by the better of competing interpretations, and the property interpretations 'compete' over, for want of a better expression, is truth. To conceive truth in this way is thus to propose a shift in epistemological gravity from *foundations* to *transitions*: disclosure, unlike correspondence, can only ever occur in relationship to a concealer and something concealed, hence what counts as truth becomes intelligible in terms of a *movement* from one account or interpretation to another.[36] From this perspective, epistemological considerations of the kind that motivate weak hermeneutics are misplaced, since in trumping the ontological presuppositions of best available accounts, they contravene the conditions of competent interpretive practice.

While the liberation of ontology from the fetters of foundationalist epistemology is of great consequence for the philosophy of nature, it is most radical in its implications for the status of the human sciences. As we just noted, this is because the language that features in the best accounts of human affairs is typically charged with significance; a vocabulary of significance is required as a condition of interpretive competence in this domain. But we have also just seen that, according to strong hermeneutics, the competent, articulate interpreter honours the ontological commitments entailed by the best available account *over and above* any more general epistemological or metaphysical considerations.[37] Since in practical matters the best accounts are articulated in concepts invested with significance, and the investment of significance imparts evaluative force, the ontology incumbent upon the interpreter in this domain will also be evaluatively laden: it will be, that is to say, a *moral ontology*. Conversely, if truth is understood as a matter of disclosure between contrasting interpretations, and the favoured interpretation is articulated in a vocabulary of evaluative significance, then the truth of the matter will also be describable in evaluatively significant terms. For strong hermeneutics, such a moral realism is the 'default' position for participants in interpretive practices a competence in which requires the use of terms of significance. In so far as we are unable to conduct ourselves competently as self-interpreters in a language shorn of such terms, it is the default position for us all.

Supported by such epistemological considerations, strong hermeneutics proposes an alternative philosophical agenda to weak hermeneutics and it adopts a quite different orientation by way of metaphilosophical critique. The agenda for strong hermeneutics is set by the concerns of a 'philosophical anthropology'.[38] Philosophical anthropology, in the sense undertaken by strong hermeneutics, is the attempt to elucidate the basic constitution of human subjectivity, where the human subject is understood as a being whose own being is a matter of self-interpretation. The fact that the subject is a self-interpreting being means that it can only be understood through its modes of mediation and externalization, rather than in an immediate conscious self-presence. Ricoeur lists three levels on which the self-understanding of the subject is mediated: signs, symbols and texts.[39] To say that the subject's self-understanding is mediated by signs is to acknowledge the fact – brought home by Wittgenstein in the *Philosophical Investigations* and by Hegel in the *Phenomenology of Spirit* – that human perception and desire – indeed all modes of meaningful human experience – are *articulated* by or like a language.[40] On account of the linguistic mediation of human subjectivity, philosophical anthropology branches out into philosophy of language. But not all signs contribute equally to meaning, nor do all signs make their semantic content manifest in equally accessible ways. The existential predicaments of human subjectivity are typically expressed symbolically and indirectly. While strong hermeneutics acknowledges the diversity of language use and the context-specificity of symbolisms to cultures, traditions, individuals and particular creative acts, it is not afraid in principle of positing a 'common symbolic ground' of subjectivity in general.[41]

But the necessary contextualization of symbols within larger semantic units, and the conflict of interpretations to which symbols are necessarily prone, do lead Ricoeur to explore a third level of mediation of the subject, that of the text. For Ricoeur, the subject can only hope to understand itself if it is able to read itself properly as a text. The challenge facing hermeneutics, accordingly, is to reconstruct what Ricoeur designates the 'work of the text'. There are two dimensions to this task, both of which Ricoeur attempts to execute by way of systematic reflections on the function of narrative and metaphor.[42] On the one hand, hermeneutics should clarify the 'sense-making' operations of the text, the internal dynamics that structure the text as a work. On the other, it must provide an account of the 'reference' of the text. In pursuing the latter goal, Ricoeur's hermeneutics deviates sharply from the trajectory taken by weak hermeneutics. For Ricoeur is convinced that metaphorical statements and narrative plots function not for their own sake – for the self-celebration of the creative act – but 'to bring into language an experience, a way of living in and of Being-in-the-world that precedes it and demands to be said'.[43] Ricoeur's insistence on a '*Being-demanding-to-be-said*' gives his account of narrative and metaphoric reference an 'ontological vehemence' wholly foreign to weak hermeneutics.[44] In aiming 'to restore to the work its ability to project itself outside itself in the representation of a world that I could inhabit',[45] hermeneutics as envisaged by Ricoeur returns from its long detour through the theory of interpretation to take up again the challenge of practical self-transformation.

The intimate link between hermeneutics and practice is perhaps even more emphatic in Gadamer and Taylor. Like Ricoeur, Gadamer and Taylor seek to clarify and draw out the implications of the insight that human beings are inescapably beings for whom things matter. All three explore the sources of significance that shape the identity of such beings and the conditions under which such sources (and the identities which depend upon them) are opened up or closed off. More than Gadamer, Ricoeur and Taylor urge a collaboration between philosophy and the social sciences, and both are critical of the disciplinary autonomy claimed on behalf of modern Western philosophy.[46] Such isolationism, strong hermeneutics suspects, helps hide the distorted conceptions of subjectivity propagated by the Cartesian philosophical tradition. In this respect, strong and weak hermeneutics converge. Both distance themselves from the notion of a unified subject transparently present to itself in reflective consciousness. But whereas weak hermeneutics takes the non-self-transparency of the self to signal the futility of all attempts at uncovering a unifying principle of subjectivity, strong hermeneutics draws the opposite conclusion; that we need to think about the truth and unity of the self-interpreting subject all the more.[47] For Taylor and Gadamer, the unity in question is essentially *practical*. According to Taylor, the living subject cannot but understand itself in a vocabulary of discriminations of significance and worth – what he calls 'strong evaluation' – even when making the philosophical claim that such a vocabulary lacks application. For Taylor, the post-Cartesian traditions of rationalism and empiricism are incapable of grasping their own underlying moral purpose. In this respect, Taylor thinks, modern philosophy reflects a broader inarticulacy in modern culture about the moral sources that sustain it. Taylor's gambit is that a philosophy that returns us to articulacy might also reactivate the sources within us. In stark contrast to Rorty's weak hermeneutics, then, the aim of Taylor's strong hermeneutics is precisely to *remotivate* the culture of modernity by recovering contact with those goods which, partly as a result of the obfuscation of philosophy, have become lost to it. The goal of strong hermeneutics, to use Taylor's formulation, is one of 'retrieval . . . to uncover buried goods by way of rearticulation – and thereby to make these sources again empower'.[48]

DEEP HERMENEUTICS: EARLY HABERMAS AND CRITICAL THEORY

It is in their common insistence on the priority and inescapability of the question of being, on the ontological irreducibility of background horizons of significance, and on the truth-disclosive, self-transformative function of the fusion of such horizons, that Gadamer, Taylor and Ricoeur share allegiance to strong hermeneutics. According to the framework set out by Habermas in *Knowledge and Human Interests*,[49] such a model of hermeneutics marks an advance on Enlightenment fundamentalism in the greater reflexivity it shows towards cognitive achievements. The achievements of the empirical sciences, hermeneutics points out, are bound up as much with the practical interest in reaching understanding within a community of interpreting enquirers as with a technical interest in controlling nature. For Habermas, hermeneutics correctly identifies a foreshortening of cognitive interests at work in Enlightenment fundamentalism. His point, however, is that in strong hermeneutics this special reflexivity does not go far enough. For a foreshortening of cognitive interests is also at work, Habermas claims, in the hermeneutic recourse to *tradition* as the horizon of self-understanding and the stock of practical wisdom. According to Habermas, the possibility of subjecting inherited horizons of meaning and capacities for self-understanding to systematic criticism points to a further cognitive interest, unacknowledged by hermeneutics, in *emancipation*.

The main thrust of hermeneutics, as Habermas saw it, was to show that the capacity for 'monological' technical control is no more subject to cognitive development than the irreducible 'dialogical' practical capacity for reaching an understanding. But the irreducibility of the emancipatory interest only comes to view once attention is drawn to the non-contingency of symptoms of disturbed deep structures of self-development. It is the task of critical theory, paradigmatically through ideology critique and the kind of reflection undertaken in psychoanalysis, so to draw our attention, and *in that very process*, to contribute towards emancipation from those disturbances. Hence the famous controversy between Gadamer and Habermas – which centres expressly around a constellation of methodological claims concerning the scope and function of 'hermeneutic reflection' – is at the same time a dispute about the relationship between contingency, the intelligibility of moral identity and the foundations of philosophical critique. I shall now offer a brief overview of the central contentions of that debate as they impinge on these issues.[50]

For Gadamer, hermeneutic reflection is, in the first instance, reflection upon what it is in virtue of which an interpreter is capable of reaching an understanding of an initially unfamiliar (because historically or culturally distant) text. The first principle that hermeneutic reflection reveals, according to Gadamer, is that the interpreter cannot help but bring to the text anticipations of its meaning – anticipations which are not the interpreter's own invention and hence not utterly contingent upon the subject's powers of self-constitution. The interpreter does not suddenly appear before the text as a *tabula rasa*, the text is always approached *from* somewhere. Gadamer chooses to call this 'somewhere' 'tradition' and he designates these anticipations 'prejudices'. These pre-reflective prejudices, and the tradition which carries the interpreter to the text, are the interpreter's access to it. It is mistaken, therefore, to think of prejudice and tradition as something that merely cannot be avoided, as an inevitable but regrettable incursion of contingency into ideally pure procedures of rational understanding. Rather, they are a positive condition of the interpreter's possibility of reaching any understanding at all. Further, the text itself both carries and is carried by tradition. Consequently, the point of departure for hermeneutic reflection is the concrete historical positioning of interpreter and interpreted – what Gadamer calls the 'hermeneutic situation'. The interpreter is always situated in his or her attempt to reach an understanding, a task that is only intelligible by virtue of the prejudices that are shaped by a tradition within which both interpreter and interpreted always find themselves.

A second principle hermeneutic reflection reveals is that the understanding sought on the part of the interpreter is reached through a procedure of dialogue with the text that is interpreted. The kind of understanding the interpreter seeks is 'dialogical' in that it involves the reaching of an agreement, with the person who speaks through the text, concerning the subject-matter of the text. But in order to avoid misconstruing the nature of this agreement as the coincidence of self-transparent psychological contents, and to give due weight to the traditions and prejudices along which subjectivity is always carried, Gadamer coins the phrase 'fusion of horizons' to describe the phenomenon of reaching a common accord. In the fusion of horizons, the truth of the subject-matter about which understanding is sought discloses itself. Furthermore, it is the function of the language of interpretation to disclose such truth. Interpretation, then, aims at truth which is disclosed through a fusion of the horizons between interpreter and interpreted by way of a genuinely dialogical interaction between the carriers of tradition. Consequently, the goal of interpretation is properly conceived as the broadening of the horizon of the interpreter, and thereby an enriched self-understanding. This is a third and crucial principle brought to hermeneutic reflection: the understanding sought has a *productive*, practical character. As well as being pushed *from* somewhere – the anticipations and prejudices which inform and guide a tradition – the interpreter is also pulled *towards* an expanded horizon that cannot be anticipated prior to a dialogical interaction with the text. Through the process of interpretation as it is revealed to hermeneutic reflection, both interpreter and interpreted are mutually transformed in a non-arbitrary, practically efficacious, truth-disclosive manner.

Now Gadamer holds that the position of the interpreter, the hermeneutic situation, is paradigmatic for the understanding of human interaction as such. Consequently, in its scope hermeneutic reflection has a claim to 'universality'. All human understanding, Gadamer insists, contains a substratum of prejudice that resists reflective rationalization. Gadamer proposes a general 'rehabilitation' of the concepts of prejudice, tradition and authority, which he thinks have been negatively polarized against the abstract ahistorical conception of reason favoured by Enlightenment fundamentalism. As we saw, according to that model, rational thought and action is *defined* in opposition to the recognition of authority and tradition. But this ideal of rationality, Gadamer claims, breaks with the principle revealed by hermeneutic reflection that understanding only issues from within or between tradition(s), and that without prejudices, the human enquirer would be without any 'windows' to the world. But if it is accepted that the goal of understanding is a truth of some sort, then truth itself needs to be divorced from a method which, if followed, would guarantee it 'monologically'; that is, independent of the contingencies of tradition and history. There can be no such guarantee if the means by which understanding is reached is dialogical, for there can be no telling in advance what the outcome of the dialogue will be. Indeed, for Gadamer, the scope of hermeneutic reflection is none other than the scope of language itself. And the scope of language is universal: it covers all meaningful human activity in its 'world-disclosive' aspect.

It is this last claim which provokes Habermas's challenge. While he finds much that is acceptable in Gadamer's hermeneutic insights – particularly his emphasis on the linguistic, participatory, dialogical character of reaching an understanding, and the limits of grasping the meaning of social action from the point of view of a scientific observer – he is unable to accept the contention that hermeneutic reflection is universal in its scope. Habermas's main worry is that by assigning universality to hermeneutic reflection, Gadamer forfeits the critical potentialities of reflection. For so long as reflection is bound by the traditions and prejudices of the hermeneutic situation, it remains hostage to structures of domination and relations of power that are legitimated *through* these traditions and that are opaque to hermeneutic reflection within them. Against Gadamer, Habermas insists that it is indeed possible to break out of the linguistic tradition that defines the hermeneutic situation. In the debate with Gadamer, Habermas appeals to the 'scenic understanding' achieved in psychoanalysis as a paradigm case of hermeneutic transcendence. In his early work, Habermas calls this kind of reflection 'depth hermeneutics'.

The scenic understanding achieved in the dialogue between the analyst and the analysand, it is claimed, retrieves the meaning of an initially incomprehensible 'text': the symptoms of the patient. It does this by appeal to *theoretical* assumptions about psycho-sexual childhood development. By resort to the theory, the analyst can reconstruct an 'original' traumatic scene in the patient's early life history that explains the distorted evolution of the patient's ego-identity. A correct understanding of the patient's behaviour is thus conditioned by a knowledge of the causal genesis of the systematic discrepancy between 'latent' meaning and 'manifest' intention. The crucial point for Habermas is his claim that such knowledge is discontinuous with the language of everyday, traditional horizons of understanding. For in the former case, understanding is guided by theoretical, methodologically non-naïve assumptions with real explanatory power. The phenomenon of systematically distorted communication is only intelligible if the dialogue situation is not assumed as always already built into contingently given traditions, but is postulated as an ideal, normative standard in a *theory of communicative competence*. For Habermas, psychoanalytical self-reflection acquires its explanatory power in virtue of *combining* hermeneutical interpretation of apparently incomprehensible behaviour with empirical scientific insight into the causal origin of that incomprehensibility.

As we shall see in chapter four, this condition is extremely demanding if not incoherent. But however difficult, the defender of deep hermeneutics will argue that something like the condition specified by Habermas must be met – on pain of hermeneutic idealism. Interpretations, at least of this kind, are not *sui generis*. They have a 'material' or 'empirical' base. Habermas then takes the charge of linguistic idealism further. Proposed as the means by which the basic structures of social reality are disclosed, hermeneutic reflection risks abstracting – in an idealist manner – linguistically constituted traditions from the systems of organized force that provide their material context. The most extreme manifestation of this idealist tendency is the assimilation of the mechanisms of power to a linguistic hermeneutic horizon. But idealist assumptions may also be operative in Gadamer's refusal to *pre-empt corruption* of the medium of hermeneutic reflection by structures of coercion. For to be bound by the manifest contingencies of the traditions and pre-judgements that make up the lived hermeneutic situation is also to be vulnerable to latent effects of residual domination. For Habermas, Gadamer's hermeneutics is idealist to the extent that it does nothing to accommodate this *possibility*, even if it is innocent of the more excessive idealism of conflating horizons of self-understanding with the social totality.

Avoiding idealism is one of three poles that set the parameters of Habermas's notion of deep hermeneutics. First, by insisting upon the interpretation-dependence of the human subject, it shows, in sympathy with strong and weak hermeneutics, the unsuitability of the human being as an object of the technical cognitive interest. Second, it must do this without collapsing into the doctrine that there are *only* interpretations – that is, it keeps its distance from weak hermeneutics. It achieves this by opening up a space for the critique of systematically distorted self-interpretations, by way of the supposition of a cognitive interest in emancipation from sources of misery operating non-contingently 'behind the back' of hermeneutic reflection. In doing so, it claims to move beyond the immanence of strong hermeneutics.

But while the problems of idealism associated with tradition-bound understanding are quite straightforwardly identifiable, finding a way of transcending the given horizon of self-interpretation is not so easy. Habermas's depth hermeneutical reading of Freud is one such proposal, but it will play only a minor role in Habermas's later reflections on the problem. The motivation behind deep hermeneutics is to correct deficiencies in given horizons of self-interpretation as repositories of explanation and critique. A corrective is necessary because otherwise, Habermas fears, supra-linguistic causes of disturbance in self-formative processes remain hidden and criticism remains vulnerable to the ideological *effect* of such disturbance. On the latter ground, as Ricoeur famously put it, a deep hermeneutics of 'suspicion' can be contrasted to a strong hermeneutics of 'retrieval'.[51] Habermas's own suspicion is provoked by the lack of distance between critic and tradition required for a hermeneutics of retrieval of the kind urged by Gadamer. For Habermas, hermeneutics thus has an intrinsically conservative philosophical orientation: it excludes *ex ante* that possibility of transcendence necessary for bringing inherited horizons of meaning to account.

BEYOND HERMENEUTICS: DISCOURSE ETHICS

The guiding idea of deep hermeneutics is that actual horizons of self-interpretation can hide or distort the virtual order of normativity that gives foundation to the very critique of scientism that originally motivates strong hermeneutics. But whereas in his early writings Habermas takes this hidden order to be a presupposition of modes of emancipatory, theory-laden, deep hermeneutic reflection, the claim advanced in his later work is that it can be reconstructed as an ideal presupposition made by participants in actual discourse. The philosophical project of reconstructing and grounding the validity basis of normative claims in obligations immanent to participation in discourse as such has been called 'discourse ethics'.[52]

Discourse ethics seeks to consolidate the conviction that the norms which regulate the conduct of individuals and groups stand or fall by a rationally binding principle of morality. It maintains that such a principle of morality, if it is to be rationally binding, must hold independently of two sets of contingency. On the one hand, it must not depend on the empirical contingencies of what, as a matter of brute psychological fact, happens to satisfy people's wants. Discourse ethics, in line with strong hermeneutics, is thus to be distinguished from all kinds of psychologism in moral theory – in particular from egoism, hedonism and utilitarianism. On the other hand, discourse ethics expresses commitment to the view that moral validity holds independently of the historical contingencies of the customs, habits and traditions which happen to prevail in any given society at any given time. Discourse ethics is thus opposed to the varieties of historicism in moral theory – namely, to different formulations of the view that moral principles are valid only relative to some particular historical context or some specific cultural community. With its insistence that there is a universal moment to moral legitimacy, it considers itself as standing opposed to strong and weak hermeneutics.

The strategy of discourse ethics is to reconstruct the universal constitution of the moral point of view in terms of presuppositions that cannot but be made by participants in an unavoidable form of activity – what Habermas calls communicative action. According to Habermas's argument, from the conditions that are naïvely assumed to obtain whenever discourse is entered into, the non-contingency of the moral demand can be brought to clarification. For Habermas, this is the demand that the norms which organize the social world be just. But in a plural social world – one in which there are many, potentially conflicting visions of the proper ends of individual and collective life – the accountability of norms to a criterion of justice can only be made plausible as a procedure for testing normative claims. Under such conditions, the rationality of the moral point of view is secured by separating it from the content of any particular vision of the good life. The moral point of view, so considered, is impartial and universalistic. Only with the separation of this point of view from particular identity-forming traditions, Habermas believes, can the conviction be upheld that the contingent norms and institutions of actually existing societies are accountable to reason.

But this separation of the right from the good, of normative questions concerning just principles of social interaction from evaluative questions regarding the proper ends of conduct, and of a moral domain from the sphere of the ethical, invites the objection that far from moving beyond hermeneutics, discourse ethics in fact signals a *return* to just those dualisms that characterized Enlightenment fundamentalism. How justified is this suspicion? Certainly, Habermas agrees with Gellner that the systematic differentiation of descriptive, prescriptive and evaluative linguistic functions ushers in the cognitive achievements of modernity.[53] They are also at one in thinking that the terms of acceptability of belief thereby take on an increasingly formal and reflexive character.[54] In chapter six, I will argue that strong hermeneutics rightly has serious misgivings about these commitments. But by way of bringing this introductory chapter to a close, I would like to comment briefly on the differences between Habermas's and Gellner's defence of the Enlightenment project. For the fact is that discourse ethics, though Kantian in inspiration, by no means constitutes a simple return to hermeneutically naïve Enlightenment fundamentalism.

Unlike Enlightenment fundamentalism, discourse ethics deploys a concept of the lifeworld without embarrassment. A lifeworld, as Habermas puts it, is a horizon of 'more or less diffuse, always unproblematic, background convictions'.[55] Beliefs, assumptions, definitions and expectations present themselves in an unthematized, intuitive, pre-given way in the lifeworld horizon. Problematic beliefs and situations are '*encompassed* within the horizons of a lifeworld', but the lifeworld as such, Habermas writes, 'cannot become problematic, it can at most fall apart'.[56] The lifeworld as a whole is immune from total revision. It is encountered by subjects as a pre-given, pre-interpreted reality the limits of which 'cannot be transcended'; for the lifeworld, on Habermas's account, is that 'transcendental site where speaker and hearer meet'.[57] In employing the lifeworld concept in this way, Habermas is exploiting a function which the notion has always served: to signal the exhaustion of foundationalist epistemology. From Husserl to Habermas, the idea of the lifeworld is a philosophical tool constructed for the purpose of *saving cognition from the reductio which issues from sceptical demands for foundational justification*. In other words, it serves to redeem reflexive justificatory practices from the incoherence into which they collapse when pushed beyond their proper scope of application. Gellner himself acknowledges that the unbounded application of the principle of validation threatens to undermine all cognitive claims by infinite regress, but recommends that we resign ourselves to this predicament.[58] However, in rejecting the lifeworld concept *tout court*, he leaves himself no room to make such an acknowledgement. And this refusal is a consequence of a misunderstanding of the philosophical motivation behind the concept.

Contrary to Gellner's presumption, the lifeworld need not be a safe haven for philosophers on the run from the world-machine. This is particularly clear in the use Habermas makes of the concept. Habermas is careful to distinguish world concepts that are the referential presuppositions of redeemable validity claims from the lifeworld concept that represents the context which conditions the meaning of those claims. According to Habermas's theory, I can raise claims with presuppositional reference to an objective world ('the totality of objects and states of affairs'), what he calls a social world ("the totality of legitimately regulated interpersonal relations') and a subjective world ('the totality of experience to which a speaker has privileged access and which he can express before a public').[59] These 'worlds' are the ontological correlates of claims that can be validated by appeal to the irreducible criteria of truth, rightness and sincerity or truthfulness respectively. The lifeworld, on the other hand, plays no such ontological role; speakers and hearers cannot refer to it in the way they can to the objective, social and subjective worlds. Hence knowledge of the objective world does not compete with the lifeworld as it does in the scenario depicted by Gellner.

Another significant departure from Enlightenment fundamentalism is signalled by Habermas's notion of a *rationalized* lifeworld. To say that a lifeworld can possess degrees of rationalization is to propose a thesis concerning the scope made available for communicative action. With this concept Habermas can capture both the thought that traditionally sanctioned stocks of knowledge are put at risk under the requirement for validation, and the idea that any particular validation is encompassed by a background totality of taken-for-grantedness that cannot be bracketed at will. This move makes room for a conception of rationalization that goes beyond the opening up of entrenched identity-expressive beliefs to instrumental reason. It also sheds a very different light on the significance of instrumental rationality for the tension between cognition and identity.

A lifeworld becomes rationalized, in Habermas's sense, 'to the extent that it permits interactions which are not guided by normatively *ascribed* agreement but – directly or indirectly – by communicatively *achieved* understanding'.[60] A communicatively achieved understanding is one which is reached purely on the basis of the better argument, whereas an agreement is normatively ascribed if it is accepted habitually or uncritically – say, on the basis of some unchallenged convention, authority or tradition. I will offer a more detailed discussion of Habermas's concept of communicative action in chapter five. For the moment, what matters is the sense in which the conception of rationalization for which communicative action is the vehicle differs from and promises to improve upon Gellner's thesis concerning the erosion of the lifeworld by instrumental rationality. From the point of view of Habermas's theory, the privilege which Gellner accords to scientific method (the ethic of cognition) corresponds to a *foreshortening* of the rational potential of communicative action. Communicative reason finds its criteria 'in the argumentative procedures' for redeeming 'validity claims geared to intersubjective recognition'.[61] From the discourse ethical point of view, Gellner's exposition of these procedures is much too narrow. Not only does it fail to account for the possibility of criticizable – but non-truth-evaluable – validity claims, but it does so by undercutting the role of everyday, uncoerced dialogue as the idiom of validation. Once the latter is taken as paradigmatic, then the human capacity for 'making true statements and implementing plans' loses its privilege, and the space emerges for replacing an ethic of cognition with a more fundamental communicative ethic oriented by the norm of mutual *recognition*.

In short, Habermas thinks that the fundamental error of Enlightenment fundamentalism can be traced back to the central flaw in Weber's 'disenchantment thesis': a false opposition between the identity-consolidating, cosmically embodied reason built into religion and metaphysical world views on the one hand, and an identity-draining instrumental rationality built into modern forms of action and scientific knowledge on the other.[62] He replies in his post-depth hermeneutic phase by way of reconstructing the demand for justification in a manner that drops the priority Enlightenment fundamentalism cedes to truth. If the first component of Gellner's version of the cognitive ethic is dropped, and cognitive worth is attributed to redeemable validity claims *other* than truth-claims, then a corresponding shift in our conception of the idiom of validation (the second component) is required. Here Habermas substitutes procedures of argumentation operative in everyday communication for the mechanistic idiom of validation. If the demand for justification is dissociated from its positivistic construal as mechanism – if it is radicalized to cover the claims of the lifeworld themselves – then the invocation of the lifeworld can in turn be divorced from the motivation for re-enchantment. The effect on the lifeworld of different kinds of rationality would also need to be distinguished and the tension between cognition and identity diagnosed by Gellner retheorized. It is by virtue of such a radicalization of the validation imperative that Habermas's position marks a break with Enlightenment fundamentalism.[63]

After introducing the basic theoretical orientation of discourse ethics, I devoted the remainder of this section to showing that despite important areas of convergence between Habermas's and Gellner's projects, discourse ethics by no means signals a mere regression to Enlightenment fundamentalism. On the other hand, Habermas's project stands or falls with the viability of his notion of a non-instrumentally rationalized lifeworld and a correspondingly expanded conception of rationality the criterion of which transcends and makes accountable the contingency of means–ends relations. That is to say, it remains an open question whether, despite its incorporation of complex notions of communicative reason and a rationalized lifeworld, discourse ethics ultimately fares any better than Enlightenment fundamentalism on the basic problem of moral identity. It might be that discourse ethics shares too much with Enlightenment fundamentalism to deal adequately with the question of how ethical life can transcend contingency. More specifically, the concepts of communicative reason and a rationalized lifeworld have force only on the assumption that Habermas's analyses of the proceduralization of reason and the threefold differentiation of the validity claims, their respective 'worlds' and spheres', have genuine application. On the hermeneutic view, by this point many of the obstacles facing the intelligibility of moral identity are *already* in place.

As we shall see in chapter six, for strong hermeneutics the contingency of means–ends relations is of itself destructive of moral identity, the proper sense of which can be recovered only by way of a more substantive conception of ethical rationality and a less rationalistic conception of ethical substance.

2   Strong hermeneutics and the contingency of self

In important respects, the recognition of contingency serves to define the theoretical outlook and practical momentum of hermeneutics. Inquiry is hermeneutic if, in contrast to the negation of contingency ideally achieved by an objective or transcendental consciousness, it is undertaken with reflexive awareness concerning the concrete historical, and hence contingent, positioning of the inquirer. Similarly, in opposition to the idea that the correct grasp of a matter can be gained by following neutral methodological or procedural rules, hermeneutics insists that what counts as a sound understanding cannot be fixed in advance of the contingencies of real engagement. In addition to informing these well-known epistemological features of hermeneutics, the concept of contingency also serves to structure its ontological commitments. *Dasein*, the self-interpreting animal that is the subject at least of strong hermeneutics, is a being whose existence precedes its essence, since in its existence it cannot but interpret itself, and its essence depends on how, contingently, it does its interpreting. That there is a rich plurality of self-interpretations also gives practical momentum to hermeneutics. By acknowledging the contingency of our own self-interpretations, we are encouraged to learn from the self-interpretations of others and discouraged from making *a priori* judgements on their worth. In the light of these considerations alone, it is indisputable that the concept of contingency organizes all kinds of hermeneutic thinking at a deep level.

Just how deeply depends on the particular kind of hermeneutics in question. Weak hermeneutics, we have seen, is a philosophy of radical, unconditional contingency. This is what makes it so well-suited to postmodernists. If, following Bauman's nice formulation, we characterize postmodernity as 'the age of contingency *für sich*, of self-conscious contingency',[1] and if we consider postmodernism as a crystallization of and contribution to this self-consciousness, then we can usefully call a conception of self-identity which acknowledges and affirms its utter contingency 'postmodernist': to think of the self as contingent all the way down, by further bringing contingency to self-consciousness, is to contribute to the ushering in of postmodernity and provides the basis of a normative orientation fitting for a postmodern world. Given this definition, Richard Rorty's reflections on the self as nothing but a 'tissue of contingencies' seem to fit the bill for a postmodernist theory perfectly.[2] Moreover, the conception of selfhood proposed by Rorty comes packaged with a model of moral deliberation designed precisely for the purpose of bringing the self's doings and its ethical orientation in line with a recognition of its own contingency.[3] As we would expect from our discussion so far, the accent of Taylor's strong hermeneutic reflections on self-identity is rather different. Taylor weaves together distinctive notions of identity, strong evaluation and the good, which in turn situate his theory within the framework of a philosophical anthropology. Thus while Rorty and Taylor share common ground in rejecting the metaphysical notion of a truth to the self which is there 'waiting to be seen', the latter regards this as an insight of *hermeneutic ontology* quite at odds with the *naturalistic ironism* the former inherits from Freud and Nietzsche.

The strategy I will adopt for considering the difference between Taylor and Rorty on self-identity will be to focus on the extent to which an unqualified acknowledgement of contingency is consistent with the logic of one of the fundamental terms of Taylor's hermeneutics – the concept of strong evaluation. After a brief outline of Taylor's conceptualization of identity, strong evaluation and the good, I examine an argument Taylor offers for establishing the necessity, or non-contingency, of the applicability of the concept of strong evaluation to human affairs, and *a fortiori* its place in practices of critical reflection. With the focus on how it relates to strong evaluation, Rorty's theory of the self is then considered, and the challenge it represents to Taylor's strong hermeneutics assessed. The rest of the chapter is devoted to Ricoeur's account of self-identity. Like Taylor, Ricoeur opposes the Nietzschean dissolution of selfhood on ontological grounds. Moreover, the course of Ricoeur's reflections on a hermeneutics of the self is shaped by a distinction between 'idem' and 'ipse' identity that helps us to locate more precisely the scope of the self's contingency. Ricoeur's contribution to an ontology of the Same and the Other also points forward to themes taken up in the chapters that follow.

TAYLOR'S PHILOSOPHICAL ANTHROPOLOGY

A philosophical anthropology is made up of those irreducible categories that are held to have, or are presupposed as having, general application to human reality. It raises and provides answers to questions concerning the kind of being human beings are. As a theorist of hermeneutics, Taylor's first principle of philosophical anthropology is that human beings are the kind of being for whom their own being is open to question. As a theorist of *strong* hermeneutics, Taylor puts forward a second principle that this question must be answered by reference to a *moral* identity, one whose content has the intelligibility of an *ideal*. The core claim of Taylor's philosophical anthropology is that it is 'not just a contingent fact' about a human being that it is 'a being for whom certain questions of categoric value have arisen' on which it has 'received at least partial answers'.[4] In other words, his strong hermeneutics proposes limits to the contingency of self as a condition of its intelligibility.

If one were to pinpoint a single core idea around which Taylor's hermeneutics is organized, it would be that a person is a being for whom things matter. This is what makes the identity of a person – a self-identity – different to the identity of other kinds of being. For while the identity of other kinds of being might be fixed by a set of physical properties which uniquely individuates an object through processes of change, explanations of the actions of persons must take into account interpretations of what matters to the person. Thus the identity of a person is peculiarly dependent on self-interpretations. Indeed for Taylor, the identity of the self, rather than being a set of neutrally describable individuating facts, just is what interpretations disclose as mattering. 'We are selves', Taylor writes, 'only in that certain issues matter for us'.[5] Interpretations serve to disclose what these issues are. Self-interpretations cannot be qualitatively neutral, since interpretive disclosure always takes place by way of articulating a contrast. Mattering, Taylor informs us, is only intelligible as a background of qualitative discrimination; if everything mattered the same, if anything mattered, nothing would. What matters makes a difference, its articulation requires qualitative distinctions between the worthwhile and the worthless, the significant and the trivial, the fulfilling and the vacuous. For Taylor, the identity of a person is intelligible in virtue of the capacity to make such distinctions, and a person's being matters, is good life rather than 'mere' life, to the degree to which it can be interpreted as actually or potentially worthwhile, significant or fulfilling.

So that which makes the life of a person or group of persons worthwhile, significant and fulfilling, is that which defines the good life for that individual or group. Taylor identifies three different strata to the good life that correspond to three analytically separable axioms of moral intuition.[6] First, a good life will be meaningful or fulfilling; we refer to a life lacking in this dimension as in a certain sense 'wasted'. Second, a course of life can possess various degrees of dignity. Like a meaningless life, a life lacking dignity lacks goodness, but the person who leads it is subject to a different kind of reproach. Third, forms of individual or collective life have obligations to others. The censure falling on cases of unfulfilled duties and obligations to others, or the violation of their rights, is of a different order again. But it is not *so* different as to constitute a leap out of the domain of the good altogether. Taylor thus rejects the Kantian distinction between the right and the good, and the neo-Kantian differentiation of the moral and the ethical domains. For Taylor, the 'moral' domain of rights and obligations represents *one dimension* of the culturally specific conception of the good to have emerged in Western modernity, not a normative sphere whose autonomy (as the realm of the universalizable) moderns 'have come to see'. From this point of view, the categorical imperative of respecting the other as an end in itself is worth following only in so far as it is anchored in an understanding of what it is to be a fully human agent. In each of the three strata, Taylor contends, the good must be defined contrastively, and definitions of goods taken together make up a framework that furnishes human beings with an orientation for acting for the best, or living to their full potential.

According to a basic insight of Taylor's hermeneutics, the good is a matter of the kind of interpretation he calls 'strong evaluation'. In many circumstances, objects are evaluated and choices are made on the basis of what one happens to desire. In a café, about to choose breakfast, I weigh up the bacon roll and the muesli, and evaluate in accord with my matter of fact preference. At stake in a weak evaluation is the satisfaction of *de facto* desire; satisfaction of *de facto* preference (or its likelihood) is the measure of evaluation. In other circumstances, however, the process of evaluation is not exhausted by this kind of measuring. As opposed to a weak evaluation, strong evaluation employs qualitative distinctions concerning the worth of alternative desires, and indeed of alternative courses of action and ways of living. The measure of evaluation in such cases is not mere preference, but an *independent* standard of worth against which the value of *de facto* desire satisfaction may be questioned. In the café, for instance, you may really fancy the bacon roll, but you may not choose it because you acknowledge a standard which holds independent of your fancies – a conception of the proper relation between humans and animals which forbids, where the relationship is improper, the partaking of meat. In this case, the process of evaluation involves the adoption of a stance to which your brute desires and appetites are accidental.

One evaluates strongly, then, in so far as one evaluates by appeal to a standard which is not contingent upon one's *de facto* desire. But as has already been indicated, there is a further decisive element to Taylor's view that strong evaluations have the kind of intelligibility that is suitable to aspirations rather than desires. This is the conceptual linkage between the stand that one adopts as a strong evaluator and one's 'identity'. The person who craves for the bacon roll but also acknowledges the force of the strong evaluation, for instance, refuses the meat because she would think of herself as a worse kind of person for choosing it – precisely the kind of person in contrast to whom, in this respect, she defines herself. This is a thought which couldn't occur to her if she were merely weakly evaluating. For in the case of the strong evaluation, the stand which is adopted tells us something about what matters to the person – in this case a proper relationship between humans and animals – and that quite independent of brute appetites one may happen to experience. The background conception of a proper relation between humans and animals stands independently of her *de facto* desires, yet allegiance to it also provides her with an 'identity', it contributes towards her conception of her 'self'.

It is this sense of 'identity' and 'self' that is conceptually tied to strong evaluations. As a person is a being for whom things matter, so a particular person's identity is what particularly matters for that person, and in both senses of 'particularly'. In the first sense, I am specifically this person rather than that, according to Taylor's view, because I take this kind of life to be fulfilling and that kind of life to be empty, or because I interpret this course of action as right and that action wrong, or because I find this species of motivation admirable but that species contemptible. In the second sense, what I find fulfilling or empty, right or wrong, admirable or contemptible, is no small matter, but is of particular or *fundamental* significance to me as a person. In answering the question of identity, I am forced to take a stand. We will see in a moment that it is crucial for Taylor's view that anyone can always be asked about what really matters to them, about what motivates their actions, what gives them their point, and that in answering the question of identity one must take a stand in a space which only a framework of strong evaluation makes available.

A self-identity that is constituted against a background framework of strong evaluations is in an important sense non-contingent, since matter of fact desires stand accountable to an *independent* source of worth. But what if the very *applicability* of the concept of strong evaluation were contingent? If evaluative frameworks of the kind highlighted by Taylor were optional, then it would seem to be merely a matter of choice, of contingency, whether strong evaluations feature in self-descriptions. With this issue in mind, let us turn now to an argument Taylor gives for establishing that 'doing without frameworks is utterly impossible for us ... that the horizons within which we live our lives and which make sense of them have to include these strong qualitative distinctions'.[7]

The argument turns on a phenomenological account of what a life would be like under conditions in which a horizon of strong evaluative distinctions were unavailable. To be without the sense of orientation which the background otherwise provides is how Taylor interprets the phenomenon of an 'identity crisis'. To suffer an identity crisis is to be incapable of telling why a life should be led one way rather than another; it is to be without any sense of discernment between the more or less worthwhile; it is to lose contact with the frameworks within which some life possibilities appear to take on more significance than others. The meaning of such possibilities becomes 'unfixed, labile, or undetermined': indeed, the very *intelligibility* of a meaningful possibility is threatened. As a result, the person in an identity crisis feels a kind of vertigo before the question of identity. The person has access to no resource by which to answer it. But this does not make the question go away. On the contrary, the force of the identity crisis is just that the question of what is really of more or less importance, worthwhile or fulfilling *demands* an answer even if we are not in a position to give one. Taylor infers from this that frameworks furnish 'answers to questions which inescapably pre-exist for us'; namely, questions about our identity or the strong evaluations that define where we stand. Only upon the supposition that the question of our identity arises independently of our ability to answer it, Taylor argues, does the possibility of *failing* to answer it make sense. Moreover, this failure is experienced both as a lack and as an unbearable lack. Taylor describes the experience as one of an 'acute form of disorientation', 'a terrifying emptiness', which presupposes the *absence* of a stand from which to take one's orientation, and implicitly a 'fullness' of being or personhood that depends on it.[8]

Since, as Taylor puts it, 'the condition of there being such a thing as an identity crisis is precisely that our identities define the space of qualitative distinctions within which we live and choose', it follows that these distinctions themselves are *not* something we can choose on the basis of matter of fact desires and preferences. They are therefore not subject to the contingency such choice would represent. This conclusion is opposed to what Taylor calls the 'naturalist' view that strong evaluations are dispensable for human beings; that frameworks of evaluative contrasts are an optional, contingent extra for human agency. Naturalism is refuted, Taylor argues, because it 'defines as normal or possible a human life which we would find incomprehensible and pathological'. The absurdity of naturalism rests in its assertion of the contingency of something which it is impossible *to live* a recognizably human life without. And it is this *existential* impossibility of living without an orientation to the good that shows the non-contingency of the applicability of the concept of strong evaluation.[9]

To be sure, this argument rules out contingency only at a very general level. It claims to show that there is a non-contingent relationship between self-interpretation and an orientation to the good, but it does not say anything about the content of the good. *That* a self-interpreting animal is non-contingently oriented against a background framework of strong evaluation does nothing to contradict the contingency of *how* a person is so oriented. On the contrary, Taylor's hermeneutics crucially presupposes the absence of the kind of metaphysical foundation which would fully close the self off to contingency. That a life oriented towards authenticity, family life, national liberation or universal social justice is strongly evaluable is contingent upon a historically specific cultural horizon, but on Taylor's view, that a life is oriented against the background of *some* such horizon is inescapable: 'Horizons are given'.[10]

RORTY, NIETZSCHE AND FREUD

To this point, Taylor's reflections on self-identity serve as a reminder of how an over-investment in contingency can lead to absurdity at the level of ontology – that is, on questions concerning the kinds of being self-interpreting animals are. Rorty's theory of the self is more Nietzschean in inspiration. For Rorty, ontological reflection becomes *de trop* with the demise of foundationalism. He maintains that there is nothing *ontologically* interesting about the self. On Rorty's view identity crises, which on Taylor's account serve to disclose the ontological peculiarity of self-interpreting animals, can be considered in terms of a causal process, explicable as a phenomenon like any other in the natural, physical world. Such a naturalistic kind of explanation could account for why identity crises are suffered in the space of a whole range of questions; from the weighty and existential to the everyday and trivial. Drawing on Freud, Rorty invites us to question whether the phenomenon of crisis Taylor describes is only intelligible under the presupposition of the lack of a horizon of strong evaluations. He then wants to persuade us to respond normatively to the contingency of selfhood with an unreserved yea-saying. In making the former point Rorty speaks as a Freudian naturalist; in the latter as a Nietzschean ironist.

Taylor claims that there is a certain kind of unintelligibility to a life led without a framework of strong evaluation, and therefore that there is a certain kind of non-contingency to a life led with one. This view, we have seen, is proposed in opposition to 'naturalism', which amounts to the doctrine that, rather than being a transcendental condition of human agency, frameworks of strong evaluation are an optional extra for human beings. Taylor's critique of naturalism is explicitly directed against utilitarian and 'emotivist' conceptions of the self.[11] But as a version of naturalism, Rorty's postmodernism is more challenging than these spin-offs of empiricism. Like Taylor, Rorty is anti-empiricist both about the self and about value. He is critical of Hume's 'mechanization of the self' and he rejects the idea of a pre-linguistic realm of the evaluable. Taylor and Rorty converge on the thesis of the irreducibility of interpretation. Nevertheless, Rorty construes self-interpretations not, *pace* Taylor, transcendentally and ontologically, but naturalistically and pragmatically. Furthermore, it is just the attitude of affirmation towards the contingency implied by such a construal that characterizes normative orientations in a postmodern culture.

As a naturalist, Rorty maintains that there would be nothing more to say about the self once its *de facto* desires, beliefs, hopes etc., were fully accounted for. There are, however, constraints on what particular desires and beliefs can be ascribed to a *person*. Following a cue from Donald Davidson, Rorty holds that to ascribe a particular desire or belief to a person is always to ascribe it as part of an internally coherent and prima facie plausible set or web of desires and beliefs. The self must be understood *holistically*: the particular desires and beliefs which make up a person are intelligible by virtue of fitting with others into a whole. But often there is a lack of fit. For a thoroughgoing naturalist, this would be the case where the desirability-characterizations Taylor calls strong evaluations stand opposed to matter of fact desires. It also holds between what are called 'unconscious' and 'conscious' desires and beliefs. To render the lack of fit between the unconscious and the conscious self intelligible might therefore point the way to a naturalized self which, holistically understood, can dispense with, while account for, the logic of strong evaluation. If successful, Rorty would made good his striking remark that '*holism takes the curse off naturalism*'.[12]

How are phenomena of radical incoherence by way of desire and belief intelligible given the supposition that a person is an internally coherent cluster or web of desires and beliefs, the parts of which are only ascribable to a person in so far as they are ascribable to such a coherent whole? Since it is an incoherence of agency which poses the problem of intelligibility, Rorty rejects the empiricist theoretical strategy of reducing the incoherence to a person-neutral (say, neural or endocrinal) mechanism. Rorty's move, rather, is to posit *another* self, or what he calls a 'quasi-self' or 'person-analogue', as constituted by another net of desires and beliefs of which the prima facie incoherent desire or belief is reinterpreted as a coherent part. Again as a naturalist, Rorty insists that each of these quasi-selves 'is a part of single unified *causal* network'.[13] This causal network is the product of the very particular and idiosyncratic contingencies of the person's upbringing. In the course of a person's natural history, Rorty argues, several internally coherent but mutually incompatible nets of desire and belief are formed, only one of which is normally available to introspection at any one time. This much, Rorty proposes, is to be learned from Freud. But according to Rorty's reading, there is a lesson about moral reflection to be drawn from Freud's conclusion – one which signals a challenge to Taylor's view on the relationship between the self and the good.

As we have seen, Taylor's concept of identity turns on the idea of strong evaluation. His thesis is opposed to the naturalist levelling of qualitative contrasts in modes of being. Now Rorty is also opposed to a certain *kind* of levelling: that which is perpetrated by *reductive* theories of agency. Rorty does not think that the meaning of qualitative contrasts can be reduced to some homogeneous operation like ego-utility maximization, 'qualia' association, evolutionary benefit, or the like. As we have seen, Rorty is as implacably opposed to empiricism as Taylor. The levelling proposed by Rorty is of a quite different sort: not the reduction of the self to some inarticulate mechanism, but its *decentering*. According to Taylor's view, *de facto* desires, motivations and actions await assessment as higher rather than lower, admirable as opposed to base, truly worthwhile rather than superficial. The stand which one takes in the light of these characterizations *centres* the self. From this centre, judgement can be passed on the marginal and the superficial. Now Rorty can claim that his view is able to accommodate generic distinctions of this kind, but rather than hierarchically opposing a true or authentic self to a *de facto* net of desires, he would prefer to construe the former just as a *different* self (or network of desire and belief). In response to the objection that this move would transform strong evaluations into weak or *mere* preferences, Rorty might say they are 'mere' only in the incoherent sense in which networks of desire are 'mere' persons. According to this revisionary account, it would follow that qualitative contrasts or strong evaluations would be better construed as involving contrasts between different selves, rather than between 'the self' and '*de facto*' desire. What Taylor calls 'the self' would then be understood not as what stands independently of *de facto* desire, but rather as another pattern or web of desire and belief which stands *alongside* dispersed sets of desires and beliefs. It only seems otherwise, to extend Rorty's reasoning, because usually – that is, when not engaged in moral deliberation – just one of these 'quasi-selves' is open to introspection. Accordingly, what counts as more or less worthwhile will vary between the different nets of desire and belief (or quasi-selves) which make up any particular person. And this means that the question, inescapable on Taylor's view, of what counts as of *fundamental* importance drops out of focus.

For the postmodernist, the question only has a focus where the point of moral reflection is understood as unearthing the 'essence' of personhood, the 'core' self or the 'truly' human. And this is how the role played by strong evaluations might now be viewed. From the postmodernist perspective, strong evaluations now look disingenuous as answers to the question 'where do I stand?' For given the multiplicity of quasi-selves which make up the person, what 'this is where I stand' means will turn on which 'I' is asking the question. Further, the postmodernist might urge, the question is loaded in favour of Taylor's view in virtue of the fact that only a certain kind of 'I' *will* ask the question: it will be raised by a reflective self with access to a certain language of self-interpretation. It is also the self which defines the essence of the human *as* self-interpretation, as addressing the interpretative question of identity. Against this, Rorty favours the view, which he takes to be encouraged by Freud, that we 'see ourselves as centerless, as random assemblages of contingent and idiosyncratic needs rather than as more or less adequate exemplifications of a common human essence', even if that essence is taken to be self-interpretation.[14] For the anti-essentialist in this sense, 'all possible purposes compete with one another on equal terms, since none are more "essentially human" than any others'.[15]

So far I have been reconstructing Rorty's challenge to Taylor as a naturalist, but this thought leads us to the alternative model of the self and moral reflection he offers. As a pragmatist, Rorty insists that the *de facto* desires, hopes and beliefs of a person are never in fact *fully* accounted for. For they are ever open to reinterpretation and redescription. One can pragmatically adapt to the contingencies of selfhood by self-creation through self-redescription. The point of moral reflection would then take a corresponding turn: it would shift from the grounding of an identity ('where I stand') to the exploration of the different, hidden 'quasi-persons' which make up a self. Rather than searching for one's 'true centre', moral reflection would be directed towards becoming 'acquainted with these unfamiliar persons'. The question 'who am I?' need not then be 'where do I stand?', but 'who causes me to have my strong evaluations?' The task would be to reconcile in conversation what splits us up 'into incompatible sets of beliefs and desires'. If we think of strong evaluations as analogous to the voice of conscience, discriminations between the significant and trivial will be taken as part of '*just* another story', like Freud shows us that the story of the superego is on a par with the stories told by the ego and the id. In abandoning the idea of a single story holding them all together, so the idea of an overriding narrative of a life *quest* loses its hold.[16] The idea of a unifying, self-perfecting quest should be dropped in favour of *ad hoc* narratives tailored to the contingencies of individual lives. Such small narratives are 'more plausible because they will cover *all* the actions one performs in one's life, even the silly, cruel, and self-destructive actions'; they will be without 'heroes or heroines'.[17]

To refrain from asking Taylor's question of identity requires that a different attitude be adopted to the self, and conversely that the self is better thought as something for which a different attitude is apt. For the pragmatical postmodernist, maturity involves substituting recognition of chance as 'not unworthy of determining our fate' for the aspiration to see things 'steadily' and 'whole'.[18] From a conception of ourselves as 'tissues of contingencies' can be derived an imperative to self-creation. According to Rorty, such a pragmatic attitude would encourage us to become more 'ironic, playful, free, and inventive in our choice of self-descriptions'. If there were to be no longing for a centre, if I were to take an ironic attitude toward myself before the question of identity, the anxiety of being without an orientation would be relieved. Indeed, it *ought* to be relieved, not only because the idea of a centred self is deluded, but because it is a hang up from a foundationalist culture which has lost its use.

STRONG HERMENEUTICS AND THE POSTMODERN SELF

I now want to consider whether, and if so at precisely what point, Rorty's reflections on selfhood show that contingency trumps strong evaluation and the notion of self-identity associated with it. First there is the question of whether Freud undermines the link between identity and strong evaluation. We have seen how Freud's splitting of the self might change the force of the distinction between the admirable and the contemptible, the higher and the base. But how seriously does this impinge on Taylor's strong hermeneutic position? On the one hand, it is a recurrent feature of hermeneutic thought – which Taylor's work shares – that the disengaged, controlling, disciplining, instrumental stance of the self, which according to Rorty is represented by the Freudian ego, is criticizable by appeal to more spontaneous, playful action orientations. In so far as unconscious impulse can be thought of as the source of such orientations, then it would simply be a mistake to identify the generically 'lower' with unconscious motives, and in this respect Taylor's position is unthreatened. Still more pertinently, Taylor emphasizes how, for the purpose of exploring and realizing contact with *moral sources*, modernist art struggles to articulate the irreducibly multilevelled nature of human life 'against the presumptions of the unified self'.[19] In the 'Post-Schopenhauerian world', he writes, 'there is no single construal of experience which one can cleave to without disaster or impoverishment'.

On the other hand, however, Taylor's justification for the inescapability of horizons of strong evaluation does turn on the *conscious* state of the person in an identity crisis: strongly evaluated motives must be conscious, as must be the 'stand' by which, for Taylor, the self wins back its identity. At this point, the postmodernist can wedge the objection that the self-interpretative question of identity *presupposes* a reflective and consciously situated 'I' for whom the question is inescapable. In other words, at the level of transcendental justification Taylor is open to the charge that the question of identity is only inescapable for a certain kind of self; that of a reflective subject whose self-interpretation is of fundamental concern. There does then seem to be a tension between Taylor's justification of the inescapability of frameworks and the aesthetic *means* by which, under conditions of modernity, the moral sources empowering an orientation to the good are capable of being disclosed.

But the implications for selfhood and moral deliberation which Rorty draws from the Freudian insight concerning the contingency of the consciously situated 'I' are also problematic. Take Rorty's insistence that Freud enables us to relativize discriminations between the significant and the trivial – of the kind which strong evaluations perform – to stories constructed in an *ad hoc*, pragmatic manner, to suit the particular contingencies of a person's self-development. For Rorty, such 'small narratives' have the advantage of covering *all* one's actions, even those which are silly and trivial. Rorty is surely right in refusing to exclude such actions from the domain of selfhood. Part of the attraction of his view lies in clearly reminding us of the bad metaphysical urge, brought to our attention by Derrida, to construct a pure essence out of exclusions of a negative which is simultaneously denied any constitutive significance.[20] Rorty seeks above all else to avoid such a metaphysical distortion of self-identity. But perhaps even more than this, his view gains its appeal from its opposition to practices of 'moralizing' which are insensitive to the particular life-histories of agents, to what Bernard Williams calls 'the institution of blame'.[21] Blame, according to Williams, corresponds to the sanction required for binding individuals together within 'the system of morality' – morality grounded as Law. To think of the moral demand as the demand of the moral law, Williams suggests, encourages two fictions: that there is a common reason for acting which all agents implicitly or explicitly recognize; and that the act of conformity with the law is the achievement of a purely autonomous will. These two fictions underpin 'moralizing' allocations of blame, which tend to focus narrowly on an action or omission perpetrated by an isolated, ideally autonomous and responsible moral subject. In turn, the two fictitious principles underlying the practice of blame can encourage people 'to misunderstand their own fear and resentment...as the voice of the Law'.[22]

Williams's line of thought will be pursued in chapter four, where its affinity with the young Hegel's critique of the Kantian transcendence of contingency will be explored. Admittedly, his conclusion that the fictions underpinning the institution of blame arise from the attempt to expunge luck from processes of character formation seems at first sight to lend support to Rorty's view. But there are several problems with Rorty's turn to Freud for the purpose of clarifying the source of objections to the institution of blame. First, while Freud does discourage us from thinking of selfhood in terms of an obligation-centred moral psychology that marginalizes many aspects of character vulnerable to chance, the point of the psychoanalytical narrative is to uncover the significance behind what is only *apparently* trivial. But this significance-disclosing *transformation* of the meaning of actions requires that it is already accepted that what the general psychoanalytic theory covers is of fundamental concern – namely, the roots of psycho-sexual development in early childhood experience. Clearly, in so far as their potential for articulating discriminations regarding the worthwhile and the worthless in a life-history goes, stories in this domain are not on a par with all others. The new language of self-interpretation may enlarge the scope for significance, but it does not undermine the distinction between the significant and the trivial.

Second, the morally charged distinction between the significant and the trivial is presupposed in the conditions of acceptability of the 'small narrative'. One only *begins* the 'conversation' with other quasi-selves because some particular feelings *do* assume a highly significant role in the leading of one's life. As we will see in chapter four, Habermas shows in his 'depth-hermeneutic' interpretation of Freud that the acceptability conditions of the psychoanalytically informed self-redescription are grounded in a 'passion for critique'.[23] If the psychoanalytical process is to issue in productive, self-transformative self-renarration, the patient has to assume moral responsibility for the content of the illness, in the sense 'that the ego of the patient recognize itself in its other' – namely, the misery-inducing feelings and actions – and 'identify with it'. This passion for critique is a passion for change *for the better*. Note that the 'criteria' of self-transformation cannot simply be pragmatic. Although Rorty implies that the shift to new vocabularies of self-enlargement is as contingent and pragmatic as the life-histories they tell, this either leaves the question of why one particular narrative is preferable to another unanswerable, or if pragmatic criteria are appealed to, it leaves the question unanswered, since the question of what counts as useful is internal to the vocabulary of self-interpretation, and is thus begged by appeal to pragmatic considerations.

Furthermore, as Jay Bernstein notes, the acknowledgement of otherness required of Habermas's passion for critique defies pragmatic criteria in that it situates and constitutes the self in a network of mutual dependency.[24]

From Taylor's strong hermeneutic perspective, the crucial point is that one can acquire 'self-enlargement' not only through exploratory conversation with one's 'quasi-selves', but also through *critical* conversation with them. By going some way down the road to contingency, Rorty opens up possibilities for exploration; but by going *all* the way down that road, he closes off possibilities for critique. For Taylor, 'quasi-selves' are criticizable because their contrasting orientations are strongly valued. For itself to be *affirmed* as good, 'self-enlargement' must exercise its pull in contrast to something less humanly fulfilling – in Rorty's case, for example, the life of the self-responsible, duty-bound 'Kantian man'. In contrasting the two types of moral reflection and character type, Rorty is exploiting a qualitative contrast. Indeed, there are points at which Rorty comes very close to Taylor's hermeneutic position. That Rorty shares with Taylor an acceptance of the importance of self-interpretations is evident in his assertion that a self (a network of desires, hopes and beliefs) becomes 'richer and fuller' by developing richer and fuller ways of formulating its hopes and desires. The main technique of self-enlargement and development is the 'acquisition of new vocabularies of moral reflection'. By this phrase, Rorty means 'a set of terms in which one compares oneself to other human beings', for example as 'magnanimous', 'decent', 'cowardly', 'epicene'. These terms feature as answers to questions of identity like 'What sort of person would I be if I did this?' Rorty asserts further that the availability of a richer language of moral deliberation makes us 'more sensitive and sophisticated than our ancestors or than our younger selves'. But to talk of a relative deficiency in 'sensitivity' or 'richness' is to acknowledge that the *move* from one language or self to another is explicable on the basis of reasons. It is therefore tantamount to an acknowledgement of limits to the contingency of self-identity.

There are, then, views Rorty espouses which are compatible with the self's orientation to the good and the potentially rational basis of the transitions it undergoes as a result of dialogue with others. Both these aspects of the self signal a limit to its contingency. At other moments, however, as if afraid of lapsing into essentialism, he turns his back on hermeneutic ontology and opts instead for a postmodern ironism. Rorty's 'ironism' is motivated by idea that the claim that one is *really* more (or less) sensitive, decent, magnanimous, etc. than one's former self, presupposes commitment to an 'essence' of the self – an absolutely non-contingent ideal of personhood – which one can fail or succeed in realizing. But as will now be clear, ironism is not the only alternative to Platonism. Indeed, the lack of credibility enjoyed by the latter suggests that the real appeal of Rorty's vision comes not from its contrast to essentialism, but from its opposition to the institution of blame. Yet we have seen that the coherence of Rorty's critique of the institution of blame depends on it being interpreted through the resources of strong hermeneutics.

Of course, Rorty's ironism is driven by normative as well as theoretical considerations. He thinks that self-conscious contingency offers a suitable point of departure for practical deliberation in a postmodern liberal culture. Conceptions of self-identity which fail to acknowledge contingency are ultimately self-mutilating, he argues, in that they close off possibilities for self-redescription. But from the hermeneutic point of view, this salutary reminder of the dangers of essentialism gains rather than loses for being anchored in an ontology of the human. The capacity for self-creation would then be understood as part of a more *general* process of undamaged self-formation; one which satisfies, for instance, a 'given' human need for recognition.[25] Evidence from sociological and psychoanalytical studies also suggests that it is precisely the *scarcity* in resources of identity-carrying horizons of significance that, at least in part, makes the leading of life unbearable in actually existing 'liberal' culture.[26] In such a situation, it might be more appropriate to regard moral deliberation as aiming at the retrieval and renewal of moral sources rather than as a perpetual, ironic reminder of the contingency of them.[27]

If these points are sound, the postmodernist rhetoric of radical contingency backfires. Taylor's hermeneutic claim that it is a non-contingent fact about self-identity that it emerges against a background of qualitative contrasts is not undermined by Rorty's reflections on the contingency of selfhood; indeed, in some ways it might even be strengthened by them. Where Rorty does go for unqualified contingency – in his ironism – he feeds on opposition to an essentialist conception of the self which relies implicitly, so I argued, on a double hermeneutic insight. The first moment takes into consideration the kinds of being self-interpreting animals are; the second takes seriously, rather than ironically, the conditions which enable such animals to improve upon their self-interpretations. Both place limits on the contingency of self-identity.

These two problems with Rorty's ironism mirror more general misgivings about postmodernist theory that are often voiced. When Taylor sets out to defend hermeneutics, he acknowledges the need to dissociate it from the kind of relativism which, for its opponents, is the only and impossible alternative to their own view. Taylor's point is that hermeneutic theorists have over-invested in contingency, mistaking the ethnocentric rationality of anti-hermeneutic theories for the force of reason in matters of cultural value as such. A similar over-investment is involved in the conflation of essentialist theories of the self with hermeneutic ontology. Taylor believes that hermeneutic theorists have been too ready to assume there is no compatibility between the force of reason and the practical imperative of fostering an open, non-dogmatic attitude to irreducibly diverse horizons of self-interpretation. Hermeneutic theories employ genealogical tools to account for changes in background horizons of significance. When used appropriately, so strong hermeneutics maintains, they can issue in a 'language of perspicuous contrast' that give rational compulsion to one of rival self-interpretations. But little has been said so far about how this view can be supported. For even if the postmodernist were to concede that a self-identity is not contingent in the sense of being arbitrarily situated against a background framework of strong evaluation as such, he or she might still insist that the stand which defines a self-identity is contingent to a *particular* framework. The postmodernist may feel on firmer ground with the claim that the proper space for thinking about contingency lies not within frameworks but between them. According to this interpretation of the relation between contingency and self-identity, there is nothing that has the force of *reason* on matters of cultural value. We will explore the strong hermeneutic argument to the contrary in the next chapter.

RICOEUR ON SELF-IDENTITY

But before moving on to that problem, I would like to attend to other levels of reflection at which strong hermeneutics blocks the dissolution of self-identity into a bundle of contingencies. I shall do this by considering the account of self-identity offered by Paul Ricoeur in *Oneself as Another*.[28] Like Taylor, Ricoeur steers a course between the 'exaltation' of the 'I' perpetrated by philosophies of the subject on the one side, and the 'humiliation' of the self announced in Nietzschean thought on the other. Instead of modelling the self either on the 'Cogito' of the former or the 'Anticogito' of the latter, Ricoeur proposes a 'hermeneutics of the self' that takes its departure from the multiple and irreducible ways of raising and answering 'who?' questions.[29]

Ricoeur has four questions in mind: 'who is speaking?', 'who is acting?', 'who is narrating himself or herself?', and 'who is the subject of moral imputation?' The corresponding *multiplicity* of ways of analysing 'who-ness' registers the contingency of self-identity: the self who speaks, the self who acts, the self who narrates himself or herself, the self who is the subject of moral imputation – each comes to view in the light of contingently occurring grammatical structures and the fortuitous reproduction of traditions of philosophical inquiry. Furthermore, for Ricoeur the grammatically dispersed senses of self cannot be gathered together under a metaphysical principle of unity. He supposes there to be no common substrate in which these different 'whos' inhere; no pure essence which lends them the same intelligibility. The fact that a hermeneutics of the self is forced into a detour through contingently available traditions of reflection activated by contingently occurring grammatical structures also means that it can have no claim to being a foundational science. It has no aspirations to the supreme authority putatively commanded by the Cogito. *Within* 'who-ness', hermeneutics acknowledges, there is a steady flow of contingency.

But between who-ness and *what-ness*, contingency ebbs away. On Ricoeur's account, there is an *irreducibility* of 'who?-questions' to 'what?-questions' that begins with grammar but points forward to insurmountable, non-contingent modalities of the self's existence. According to Ricoeur, the grammatical pressures keeping the 'who?' and the 'what?' apart are hidden by an equivocality in the word 'identity'. On the one hand, one's identity is that which makes one the same, it signifies permanence in time, and it has that which differs, the changing and the variable, as contraries. This sense of identity, Ricoeur observes, corresponds to the Latin term *idem*. On the other hand, there is the sense of identity that corresponds to the Latin *ipse*, one that is preserved in the English word 'ipseity'. Synonyms for ipse-identity or ipseity include individuality and selfhood. Ipseity signifies *my*self, my selfhood in contrast to sameness. The distinction will prove crucial for avoiding misunderstanding over the level at which contingency intervenes in self-identity. First, it enables Ricoeur to distance the idea that there may be limits to the contingency of self-identity from any notion of an hypostatized, 'unchanging core of the personality'.[30] But more generally, it means that the existentially significant constraints on contingency operating at the level of ipse-identity by no means entail an ontology of 'the same' or the 'self-identical' (in the sense of idem-identity).

Ricoeur's hermeneutics of the self has an epistemology that supports the fine balance it pursues at an ontological level between contingency and non-contingency. Its first noteworthy feature is the warrant it claims to being a unified doctrine. We just noted that for Ricoeur, the polysemy of the 'who?' suggested by the multiplicity of who?-questions forbids the positing of any substantive unity to selfhood. But Ricoeur also takes it to allow him to speak of *some* kind of unity – namely, an 'analogical' unity to the different dimensions of human action.[31] The point of this epistemic qualification is to respect the plurality of discourses on the self, and the legitimacy of different levels of reflection, without leaving the reintegration of the dispersed discourses merely to chance. Relatedly, while the ontology that comes into view by way of hermeneutic reflection is not supported by demonstrative proofs – while it does not enjoy the certainty of the Cogito – nor, on Ricoeur's view, is it merely arbitrary. For it can offer an 'attestation' of its truth, a ground for *trust* that might suffice for overcoming, but never eliminating, suspicion. Like Taylor, Ricoeur maintains that the truth of a hermeneutics of the self has a vital practical-existential moment: the truth disclosed about the self at the same time *empowers* it. The attestation provided by a hermeneutics of the self, Ricoeur writes, is 'fundamentally an attestation *of* self'; the trust it secures 'a trust in the power to say, in the power to do, in the power to recognize oneself as a character in a narrative, in the power, finally, to respond to accusation in the form of the accusative: "It's me here"'.[32]

In order to show how Ricoeur's analyses of the polysemy and irreducibility of the self that answers to who?-questions complement and enrich the strong hermeneutic account of the self we found in Taylor, it will suffice to consider in a little more detail these two ways of avoiding confusion over the self's contingency.[33] We shall turn first to Ricoeur's critique of Parfit's theory of personal identity. This is of special interest to us since it is here that Ricoeur most clearly articulates the folly of subsuming ipse-identity to idem-identity.[34] Second, we shall reflect briefly on Ricoeur's sketch for an ontology of the self understood as the subject of moral imputation. What, we ask, does *conscience* tell us about self-identity as a mode of being? Besides bringing us back to the relationship between strong hermeneutics and Nietzsche and Freud, this issue – which takes us to the frontier of strong hermeneutic research – also anticipates key themes in the chapters that follow.

First, Ricoeur's critique of Parfit. Taking up the problem of personal identity as it occurs in Locke and Hume, Parfit considers the meaning that can be given to the idea that the self has an identity that endures through time.[35] By appeal to what criteria can we say that a person has the *same* self at different times? Only two criteria for identity seem to be available: either the person has the same mental properties – that is, shows uninterrupted psychological continuity; or the person possess the same physical properties – that is, displays bodily continuity. Parfit then invites us to consider a number of fantastical 'thought-experiments' – involving scenarios of tele-transportation, brain-transplantation, and the like – that function to expose the deep paradoxes to which these criteria lead. Parfit's thought-experiments seem to show that personal identity is much less permanent and much more indeterminate than our ordinary thinking supposes. On the evidence of his thought-experiments, Parfit concludes that self-identity is radically contingent. Furthermore, like Rorty, Parfit maintains that the incoherence of the pre-reflexive sense of self – as enduring and relatively determinate – is less disturbing from the moral point of view than at first appears. But whereas on Rorty's account the *conjunction* of morality and contingent self-identity gives us a better view on the former, Parfit's reasoning goes in the opposite direction. On Parfit's view, it is the *disjunction* of morality and identity that enables us to see morality as that which really matters. Far from supporting morality, belief in the existence of selves that endure through time is, according to Parfit, an illusion that at best distracts from and at worst positively hinders the satisfaction of moral demands. Speaking now as a radicalized utilitarian, Parfit concludes that morality is objectively satisfied when the totality of pleasurable mental events is maximized, irrespective of particular lines of continuity between them. Moral reason surpasses contingency by factoring the self out of its calculations.

Now there are several features of Ricoeur's response to Parfit that help to illuminate the strong hermeneutic understanding of self-identity and the contingency proper to it.[36] First, there is his criticism of Parfit's way of setting up the problem of identity. Parfit starts out by opposing his own view to 'the non-reductionist thesis'. According to Parfit's definition, the non-reductionist thesis asserts that there is some 'further fact' to personal identity than physical or psychological continuity. Physical and psychological continuity, on Parfit's understanding of them, are constituted by *impersonal* events. After defining the non-reductionist thesis in this fashion, Parfit proceeds by ruling out possible candidates for the 'further fact' non-reductionism supposedly requires. On Parfit's view, the paradigm for such a 'further fact' is Cartesian spiritual substance. However, Ricoeur maintains that non-reductionism appears *too late* in Parfit's argument to impose itself in a credible form. For even before the question of a further mental/spiritual fact arises, non-reductionism as Ricoeur advocates it takes issue with the neutralization of the *body* into an impersonal event. A better formulation of the non-reductionist thesis would therefore assert that the very 'factual character of an event' – bodily *or* mental – stands in intrinsic relation to a 'phenomenon of mineness'.[37] Parfit's reductionist thesis *assumes* that mental and bodily events share the same mode of intelligibility as the happenings of disenchanted nature. It conflates the intelligibility conditions of selfhood with the causal conditions of a sub-class of objectivized events. It is only against the background of this conflation that it becomes feasible to dissociate 'belongingness to me' from the criterion of identity, and then to hypostatize it as an extraneous 'further fact' – one extraneous and contingent to the 'basic fact' of psychological continuity. In other words, the 'further fact' preserved by Ricoeur's strong hermeneutic version of the 'non-reductionist thesis' is *ipse-identity*. But it only makes sense to call this a *further* fact if one has already accorded *idem-identity* ontological privilege.

It is this reductionism – the reduction of ipse to idem-identity – that now appears as the key presumption of the philosophical discourse on personal identity from Locke to Parfit. A hermeneutics of the self along the lines envisaged by Ricoeur would constitute a very different kind of discourse on account of its recognition of the irreducibility of both idem and ipse dimensions of identity. And as we shall see presently, it opens up the prospect of a renewed articulation of the predicaments facing self-reflection in terms of the *dialectic* at play between idem-identity and ipseity.

The second of Ricoeur's criticisms that interests us concerns Parfit's method. We noted that Parfit tests presumed conditions of self-identity by applying them to imaginary scenarios of a kind often found in science-fiction. These thought-experiments allegedly show the deeper contingency of the identity-conditions we naïvely presume to hold of necessity. Now Ricoeur agrees that fiction provides a suitable laboratory for testing intuitions about selfhood, as well as for bringing home the contingency of much that we take for granted about the self. On the other hand, he maintains that Parfit's use of science-fiction stories – Ricoeur calls them 'technological fictions' – leads him to posit contingency *at the wrong level*. In literary fiction, the contingencies of selfhood are played out against a

background of non-contingent worldly embodiment. For all their exploration of contingency, literary fictions 'remain imaginative variations on an
invariant, our corporeal condition experienced as the existential mediation
between the self and the world'.[38] In this respect they differ fundamentally
from the technological fictions invoked by Parfit. For whereas literary
fiction testifies to the universal and insurmountable existential predicament
of being-embodied, technological fictions – by means of imaginative devices
like tele-transportation – assign a merely contingent, optional status to
corporeality. In doing so, the latter evince not a sense of reality, but a
'technological dream'. Again, Ricoeur interprets this as a symptom of the
neglect of the idem–ipse relation that began with Parfit's framing of the
identity problem. For the technological fictions that make up such a large
part of the discourse on personal identity 'are variations with regard to
sameness' – that is, with regard to permanence in time – while the fictions
of literature, by virtue of their exploration of the interplay between *plot* and
character, concern selfhood 'in its dialectical relation to sameness'.[39]

It is this dialectical relation of selfhood to sameness that Ricoeur
attempts to fill out in his account of narrative identity. In a first step,
Ricoeur focuses on the identity of narrated actions and events. A story is
not just a contingent assemblage of actions and events, it involves their
synthesis by way of emplotment. Actions and events connected by
emplotment undergo a 'configuration' of concordance and discordance:
they unfold according to a certain order or necessity, but they occur
unexpectedly, with a meaning that becomes fully intelligible only
retrospectively, at the end of the story. 'The interconnection of events
constituted by emplotment', Ricoeur observes, allows permanence in time
to be integrated with 'diversity, variability, discontinuity and instability'.[40]
In a second step, he proposes that the connectedness of narrated actions
and events can be transferred to the identity of the character who
performs them. That is to say, it is to emplotment that the character owes
his or her intelligibility. Ricoeur reasons further that *self-identity* as
narrative identity should also be intelligible as a 'configuration' of
concordance and discordance; as a singularity possessing the unity of a
temporal totality punctuated and threatened by unforeseeable and
surprising circumstances. For a self to possess narrative identity is for it
to be subject at once to processes of 'sedimentation' and 'innovation'. In
the course of a life-history, many things – dispositions, habits, the person's
character – will remain more or less unchanged, and will allow for the re-
identification of a person as the 'same'. This is how sameness, idem-
identity, appears as a pole of narrative identity. But at the same time, the
character traits that anchor one's identity may be transfigured through
being narratively redeployed. In some cases, this may even result in a
'liberation' of the narrating self from the very behaviours that most
obviously and stubbornly identify it. There are circumstances, in other
words, in which narrative redeployment – a possibility written into

narrative identity as such – results in 'self-recovery', or the sublation of idem-identity to ipseity.[41]

Ricoeur's account of narrative identity, of the 'who' that recounts himself or herself in a story, addresses the self's temporal dimension; but it proceeds in close proximity to reflection on the moral dimension of the self. For there is a mode of permanence in time that attaches itself to the 'who?' of moral imputation – namely, self-constancy. To display constancy in friendship, or to keep one's word, is not just to exhibit the sameness of character. Rather, on Ricoeur's account, it is a matter of one's selfhood or ipseity. This sense of my self-identity is clearly bound up with my relation to others: as a subject of moral imputation I have to answer to another for my actions across time. By thus making moral imputation internal to ipseity, Ricoeur's view signals a third and decisive departure from Parfit's. For Parfit, we saw, the notion of self-identity has no place in ethics since it gives a false picture of the agent's relation both to time and morality. But having already introduced the dialectic of idem and ipse, Ricoeur can now agree that in a non-trivial sense identity – in the sense of idem-identity – is not what matters, without concluding that the satisfactions of selfhood and morality are incommensurable. Nor can they be, Ricoeur suggests, if we are to preserve the intuition that something matters only if we can speak of it mattering *to* someone, if we can ask 'to whom' it matters. From the hermeneutic point of view, the question of 'what matters' arises *within* selfhood; it is 'incorporated into the defence of selfhood in its confrontation with sameness'.[42]

Ricoeur is proposing, then, that the philosophical significance of the moral claims of others on the self can be articulated in terms of an ontology of selfhood. In order to lend plausibility to this idea, he must indicate the site where selfhood and otherness enter into an original, ontologically significant moral dialectic, and he must indicate how his representation of that dialectic relates to and improves upon previous ontologies operating at the level of the 'great kinds' of the 'Same' and the 'Other'. Let me conclude the chapter by reflecting briefly on the strategy Ricoeur adopts for taking hermeneutics forward on these issues.

For Ricoeur, the moral claim of the other on the self can be considered to announce itself in an ontologically primordial way in conscience. The voice of conscience, for Ricoeur, is the self speaking *as another*. But from a philosophical point of view, the authenticity or trustworthiness of this voice cannot simply be assumed; the voice has to *earn* its trust. We cannot rely on common sense to interpret its meaning. In no small part, this is a consequence of the suspicion rightly cast over the phenomena of 'good' and 'bad' conscience by Hegel and Nietzsche. Hegel's *Phenomenology of Spirit* sounds a 'warning shot' to conscience by attacking its role in the 'moral view of the world'.[43] By at once dismissing and condemning natural desire, by dictating that duty be done while making it impossible to satisfy, the moral view of the world gets caught up in contradiction and hypocrisy. If conscience is to be trusted, it has to be interpreted in different, less moralizing terms. Added to this source of suspicion there is what Ricoeur describes as the 'thunderbolt' struck by Nietzsche in the *Genealogy of Morals*.[44] Like Hegel, Nietzsche attacks the moral conception of the world by means of which 'bad conscience' falsely reassures itself. But unlike Hegel, he undertakes a genealogy of conscience that traces back its dynamic to an archaic, pre-moral struggle for power. Freud's genetic explanation of conscience in terms of the internalization of parental and ancestral authority-figures in the superego can be seen as substantiating the Nietzschean approach.

Now Ricoeur sees his hermeneutics of the self as providing a platform for Hegel's and Nietzsche's suspicion, as well as for Freudian talk of the superego, *at the same time* as according ontological weight to the metaphor of 'the voice' of conscience. Hegel and Nietzsche, for their part, by exposing the contradictions and hypocrisy of the moralizing interpretation of conscience, earn their place in a hermeneutics of the self. But their critique of this misinterpretation should not be taken to legitimate the *demoralization* of conscience. The demoralization of conscience loses something that Ricoeur considers to be essential to its phenomenology – namely, that the modality of the voice of conscience is *injunction*. Accordingly, an acceptable hermeneutics of the self will interpret the phenomenon of listening to the voice of conscience as signifying 'being-enjoined by the Other'.[45] The critique of conscience fits this interpretation as soon as it is seen to be directed not against injunction as such, but against a distorted and impoverished model of its voice – namely, the verdict of a court. The real lesson to be learned from Hegel and Nietzsche, Ricoeur suggests, is the folly of a narrow, legalistic paradigm of conscience. But as an alternative to this paradigm, Ricoeur proposes not a 'demoralized' model, but one that incorporates the force of moral prohibition, of duty and indebtedness, within a broader ethical injunction '*to live well* with and for others'. Furthermore, Ricoeur contends, it is largely to Freud that we owe our appreciation of the profundity of the generational dimension of the linked phenomena of injunction and indebtedness. According to Ricoeur, the genetic approach to conscience followed by Freud need not *compete* with an ontological one. For at least two considerations militate against the self-sufficiency of Freud's account: first, the empirical modes of identification that make up the superego seem to presuppose an ontological disposition for being-affected in the mode of injunction; and second, that without independent support the series of internalizations layering the superego regresses *ad infinitum*. If it is the case that genetic explanations cannot give an exhaustive account of the phenomena of injunction and indebtedness, the Freudian *reduction* of conscience is unwarranted, and Freud's anthropological insight can be retained within the framework of a hermeneutic ontology.

Having made space for an ontological account of conscience, Ricoeur uses his synthesis of attestation and injunction to situate himself in relation to the tradition of ontological reflection on the 'great kinds' of the Same and the Other. Especially noteworthy here is the way Ricoeur presents his hermeneutics as a corrective both to Heidegger and Levinas. The ontological account of conscience in Heidegger's *Being and Time*, Ricoeur maintains, ultimately faces the same shortcomings as Nietzsche's radical demoralization of conscience, albeit raised to a higher level. Considered from an ontological point of view, Heidegger thinks, conscience does not admonish or warn of wrong-doing. Rather it represents a call for *Dasein* to exist authentically, to realize its ownmost possibilities, prior to and independently of particular moral or ethical commitment. 'Ontology', in Heidegger's sense, 'stands guard on the threshold of ethics'.[46] The Other features as the unsurpassable 'thrownness' of being-in-the-world that counterpoises the resoluteness of *Dasein*. But Heidegger's account will not do as an account of conscience because, like Nietzsche's, it conceals the moment of alterity proper to the phenomenon of being-enjoined. Like many critics of Heidegger, Ricoeur objects that so long as resoluteness is cut off from the demands of others, it lacks any determinate moral or ethical content. Consequently, conscience itself risks losing all moral or ethical significance. Levinas sees this too, and seeks to correct it by jointly affirming the absolute priority of ethics over ontology and the primacy of the Other over the Same. But Ricoeur finds Levinas's alternative inadequate on two counts. First, it divorces injunction from attestation, leaving a voice that 'risks not being heard', a self unaffected 'in the mode of being-enjoined'.[47] The Other, in other words, must be sufficiently present *in* the self to matter to it. This is precisely why Ricoeur's hermeneutics incorporates being-enjoined into the structure of selfhood. Ricoeur's second objection concerns Levinas's presumption that the Other to the Same is an other person. At this point, Ricoeur does not propose an alternative paradigm for otherness. Rather he appeals for pluralism in view of indeterminacy at this level of inquiry, which represents the *interface* between ethics and ontology. Ultimately, Ricoeur concludes, philosophy may not be able to say 'whether this Other, the source of the injunction, is another person ... or my ancestors ... or God – living God, absent God – or an empty place. With this aporia of the Other, philosophical discourse comes to an end'.[48]

Ricoeur may be right in thinking that philosophy is incapable of unifying or ordering into a hierarchy these different senses of otherness by means of a single ontological principle. Nevertheless, the issue of *what it means* for other persons, tradition, being or nothingness to function as reflexively accountable sources of injunction lies at the heart of the strong hermeneutic agenda. For Ricoeur, 'the source of injunction' both makes a moral demand on the self and enables the self to realize its full potentiality. This is just another way of expressing his basic idea that, in the final analysis, being-enjoined must be comprehensible as a structure of selfhood. As such, it corresponds closely to Taylor's notion of a moral source. A moral source, in Taylor's sense, constitutes good things as good at the same time as empowering the realization of the good. But its empowering force, its potential to motivate good action or 'living well', depends on the self's proximity to it – a moral source can be close or distant, potent or dormant. Three connected questions then arise: How is the Other intelligible as a moral source? In what sense is the Other *qua* moral source answerable to reason? What sense can be made of the idea, which seems to follow from our premises, that moral sources may even be *activated* by philosophical reflection?

These questions, it seems to me, appear at the frontier of philosophical discourse rather than, as Ricoeur suggests, the other side of it. In addressing them, I will call upon two sources of the hermeneutic tradition that are unfortunately absent from Ricoeur's discussion. First, there is Hegel's work before the *Phenomenology of Spirit*. As we shall see in chapters four to six, Habermas especially has drawn attention to the young Hegel's insights regarding the moral dialectic of self and other, insights he attempts to integrate first into his depth hermeneutic reading of Freud and later his theory of communicative action. For Habermas, following the young Hegel, the Other as the source of moral injunction has to be conceived *intersubjectively*. But, following Taylor, the second strand of hermeneutic thinking I want to draw upon – Heidegger's work after *Being and Time* – does not take other selves to be paradigmatic for otherness. In chapter seven, I explore the perspective Heidegger's later work opens up for interpreting the voice of a kind of conscience that does not appear to involve other people at all – namely, *ecological* conscience. It will be suggested there that to be enjoined by ecological conscience is to be called upon by what I call an 'other-as-source' that is, in a certain sense, other than human.

Taylor's reading of the late Heidegger and Habermas's reading of the young Hegel pick up where Ricoeur leaves off. But the purpose of the preceding reflections has been to show how the hermeneutics of the self outlined in Ricoeur's *Oneself as Another* supplements and enriches Taylor's account of self-identity defended earlier in the chapter. Ricoeur's distinction between idem- and ipse-identity adds precision and complexity to our understanding of the contingency of selfhood as it emerged from our reconstruction of the debate between Taylor and Rorty. Building on the strong hermeneutic critique of the postmodernist self, Ricoeur puts the self-identity of an embodied, narratively temporalized, dialogically entangled existence on the other side of contingency, in a space that opens up radical choice without itself being subject to it.

3 Interpretation, practical reason and tradition

In chapter one strong hermeneutics was characterized as a 'realist' philosophy. Its realist character arises from its espousal of two basic principles: first, that horizons of significance open up a space which is habitable by non-instrumental *reason*; and second, that concerning strong evaluations there is a *truth* to the matter. It has already been noted that, like all types of hermeneutics, strong hermeneutics insists with normative force on the irreducible diversity of horizons of significance and frameworks of strong evaluation. The issue to be explored in this chapter is how strong hermeneutics attempts to make these two commitments – to realism and pluralism – compatible.

In current debates it is too quickly assumed that realism in any sense and a sincere commitment to pluralism are mutually exclusive. Indeed, critics of the two realist principles defined above regularly appeal to the fact of and aspiration to pluralism as decisive objections. Take the first principle, that horizons of significance, as background frameworks of strong value, are habitable by reason. There are, broadly speaking, three levels of scepticism to this view. According to the first, practical reason is extended beyond its legitimate scope when applied to conceptions of the good that give substance to a moral identity. Sceptics of this kind doubt that strong evaluations are subject to reason on account of their unsuitability for *universalization*: different people can, it seems, hold incompatible ideals with equally good reason. What are really so answerable, according to this view, are the norms that regulate social interaction, irrespective of particular strong values individuals or groups uphold. Such norms can be right or just but not, strictly speaking, good, so they need to be distinguished from the scope of application of strong evaluations. This kind of scepticism about the habitability of reason in horizons of significance, with its hard distinction between the cognitive domain of moral right and the contingent sphere of the good, is typical of deontological theories. At a second level, scepticism about the universalizability of the good is carried over into the domain of morality. Historicist sceptics are particularly suspicious of the idea that *practice* in general is arbitrable by reason: on the one hand, they hold that reason just is, as a matter of historical fact, what tradition substantiates; on the other, they reject the relationship between tradition and reason presupposed in the idea that concrete practice is accountable to independent theoretical abstraction at all. The suspicion of reason motivating the third level of scepticism is directed elsewhere. It maintains that the institutions and culture of modernity are *already* disfigured by the demands of abstract reason. The injuries inflicted by the principle of reason, these sceptics believe, include the cultural exclusion and marginalization of groups whose symbolic representation is associated with the concrete, the particular and the heterogeneous. These 'anti-realists' seek to circumvent or subvert the very reason through which, they believe, such marginalizing and excluding powers are exercised.

Just as this third kind of scepticism is characteristic of weak hermeneutics, so the first is crucial to the move beyond hermeneutics characteristic of discourse ethics. Both take the irreducible diversity of conceptions of the good to be explosive of the view that the horizons of significance they articulate might be within the provenance of practical reason. Hence both positions suppose hermeneutic realism to be incompatible with pluralism. Weak hermeneutics responds by weakening the claim to rationality to suit pluralism, discourse ethics by abstracting that claim from the sphere of strongly valued horizons. Moreover, both encourage the thought that the only position left for strong hermeneutics is the second just sketched – that practical reason is *exhausted* by tradition. And, to be sure, some of the main contributors to strong hermeneutics come perilously close to this view. For critics of strong hermeneutics, so long as reason is tied to tradition in this way, either one particular tradition is inflated as the privileged means of insight into the good (at the cost of pluralism), or particular traditions are protected from the rational criticism of others (at the cost of realism). It can then seem as if a *substantive* conception of practical reason – one that joins reason with matters of moral identity rather than deontologically abstracting from them – has nowhere to go but down the *contingency-negating* path of realist metaphysics or the *contingency-affirming* path of pluralist relativism.

Neither option has great appeal. This may be enough to persuade us to drop the substantiality condition of practical reason and take the deontological path of discourse ethics. But the position we reached at the end of our discussion of the Taylor/Rorty debate in the last chapter suggests a way of making inroads in a different direction, one that steers a path between metaphysics and relativism without sacrificing the kind of substantive orientation provided by strong evaluation. To frame the issue in the terms developed in the previous chapter, if we assume now the basic principle of Taylor's philosophical anthropology that it is a non-contingent fact about human beings that they are oriented against *some* background framework which confers moral significance on their identity, to what extent does it remain a contingent fact about any one particular framework, culture or tradition, that it commands allegiance? What, if anything, counts as a rational command here? And how would the acknowledgement or otherwise of contingency at this level affect the self-understanding of *critical* strong hermeneutic reflection?

In the next section, I shall briefly consider how, by appeal to a 'narrative' model of practical reason, strong hermeneutics might achieve the goal of making rational changes in frameworks of self-interpretation intelligible in a way that does justice to their substance, their criticizability and their historical facticity. Drawing partly on the work of Ricoeur, but more extensively, on this issue, on MacIntyre and Tugendhat, Taylor argues that changes in identity can be seen to constitute an epistemic gain once articulated in a narrative form.[1] Narratively structured practical reasoning is substantive rather than procedural in virtue of carrying the content of rich conceptions of human identity rather than rescinding from that content. But it is also substantive in that its conclusions are affirmed as admitting of and in some cases actually carrying truth. At this point, then, I turn to the second of the two key components of hermeneutic realism – the thesis that concerning strong evaluations there is a truth to the matter. The case for a realist reading of strong evaluative discourse is considered in the context of Crispin Wright's proposed recasting of realism vs anti-realism debates in analytical philosophy.[2] Finally, I consider the charge that any kind of moral realism is inappropriate as a basis for critical reflection in a plural context on account of its alleged privileging of one *predominant* tradition. This brings us back to the question of whether the entwinement of practical reason and the contingencies and parochialisms of history, tradition and embodiment robs reason of the critical powers proper to it. Is practical reason as conceived by strong hermeneutics sufficiently distanced from the givenness of horizons, cultures and traditions? The chapter concludes with some considerations aimed at relieving anxieties arising from the appearance of an excessive conservatism in strong hermeneutics. This is a goal I intend to pursue further in subsequent chapters, especially in chapters six and seven.

THE NARRATIVE FORM OF PRACTICAL REASON

Strong hermeneutics is impressed by the practical insights that only seem to be expressible in narrative form. In the previous chapter we considered the claim that the intelligibility of a human identity is inseparable from that of a moral identity, in the sense that a self-identity requires an orientation in moral space, a space mapped by a framework of qualitative contrasts. Yet, as postmodernism and weak hermeneutics insist, the orienting stand of one's identity may be entirely provisional, forever open to unmasking and change. This important point finds its way into strong hermeneutics through its claim that just as the self cannot but be oriented in moral space, so it is a non-contingent fact about a human identity that it moves in moral *time*. Tracing this movement is the task of narrative. Strong hermeneutics can then turn to narratively articulable changes in identity for dealing with the problem of practical reason.

The strong hermeneutic bond between narrative and practical reason is implicit in the philosophical anthropology already sketched. We saw that the non-contingency of the human orientation to the good is bound up with the inescapability of the question of identity. But since that question projects itself into the future and demands an answer at different times, it is bound to the further question of *becoming*.[3] In virtue of its temporal constitution, human agency is conditioned not only by an orientation towards the good, but also by the possibility of moral growth and decline. Faced with this possibility, the question of how to deliberate about the goods that give content to an identity arises. This is precisely the question which, according to strong hermeneutics, a theory of practical reason must answer. It must make sense of the possibility of a rational *transition* from one identity to another; it must give an account of the kind of move that constitutes practically significant epistemic gain.

Strong hermeneutics can point out considerable advantages to this approach to practical reason. First, by linking practical reason to changes in *identity*, it keeps the former well rooted in sources of human motivation. Second, by modelling practical deliberation on narrative rather than calculation, it does justice to the historicality and finitude of the self. These two points will be considered in detail in chapter six, where discourse ethics' problems with motivation and finitude are identified and discussed. Suffice it to say for the moment that in both these cases, strong hermeneutics acknowledges contingency at a level putatively transcended by Enlightenment rationalism. By contrast to Enlightenment rationalism and weak hermeneutics, the strong hermeneutic framing of the question of practical reason in terms of the transition between action-guiding orientations opens up a space between the denial of pure transcendence and the affirmation of pure contingency, between the weak hermeneutic forfeiture of *reason* and the Enlightenment rationalist forfeiture of *practice*.

On the strong hermeneutic view, the correctness of a particular practical deliberation is determined by the comparative superiority of the interpretive positions on either side of a move. To be favoured by reason is therefore not to be judged positively according to some fixed *criterion*, one that is applicable to *any* practical deliberation independent of context or horizon of self-interpretation.[4] As Taylor describes it, practical reasoning works well when it perspicuously displays epistemic gains or losses in particular concrete cases. Typical ways of achieving this goal are through identifying and resolving a contradiction in the original interpretation, pointing to a confusion that interpretation relied on, or by acknowledging the importance of some factor which it screened out. 'The nerve of the rational proof', Taylor writes, consists in showing that a particular transition is 'an error-reducing one. The argument turns on rival interpretations of possible transitions'.[5]

The logic of *practical* reasoning has a narrative form in the specific sense that it is how we account for *lived* changes in moral outlook. A change in moral outlook, understood as a change in self-interpretation, can be considered as constituting a change *of* the self. Accordingly, the argument that presents the challenge of practical reason has an *ad hominem* structure.[6] It is addressed from one particular locus of strong evaluation to another, and proceeds by way of contesting interpretations of the transition. The argument is trumped by the interpretation which, of those available, gives the most clairvoyant account of the error-reduction (or otherwise) of the transition lived through. The crucial point is that what *counts* as rationally defensible or a gain is not determinable independently and in advance of the actual transition. There is no appeal to neutral criteria which might be brought to bear *whatever* the transition is between. If such a standard were available *any* move would be justifiable in its terms. But because any move would therefore be in principle rationally determinable, the significance of the rationality of transitions themselves is lost.

The point bears repetition that failing the availability of such a neutral criterion, it can seem as if there is no scope for rational practical deliberation at all. But the strong hermeneutic non-criterial model for practical reasoning restores such scope by limiting it to the passage between rival practical alternatives. The error-reduction need not carry over to other interpretive positions. The validity of the transition is not transitive in the strict logical sense. This is simply a consequence of its *ad hominem* structure. And of course, since the validity of the interpretive position arrived at depends on its comparative superiority to the rival party to the transition, the new interpretation, and even the interpretation of the move to the new interpretation, is always vulnerable to succession by other, more perspicuous interpretations.

Defenders of strong hermeneutics are aware that the onus of argument is on them to show that the approach they favour to practical deliberation, with its appeal to narrative, interpretation and *ad hominem* structures of argument, does not short change on the force of reason as such. After all, by the standards of modern science, narrative and interpretation seem very much second best as vehicles of cognition and rationality. The case for strong hermeneutics would therefore be considerably strengthened if it could show how epistemic gains of the kind which practical reason displays also occur in the growth of scientific knowledge. The problem of the intelligibility of scientific progress has been highlighted, of course, by Kuhn and other post-empiricist philosophers of science.[7] Drawing heavily on MacIntyre's attempt to make the growth of scientific knowledge intelligible through the historically unfolding dialectic of rival traditions, Taylor proposes a way of joining the demands of explanation and practical reason that promises to disable a major obstacle to the acceptability of the narrative model of practical reason.

The strategy of this argument is to show a common structural core, captured in the idea of narrative, to the intelligibility of rational transitions in science and practical deliberation. The problem posed by Kuhn and taken up by MacIntyre and Taylor concerns the inability of the standard model of 'criteria' to perform this task. For in cases of radical, paradigmatic leaps in knowledge, where one theory is supplanted by an incommensurable other, there are no shared criteria by which to plot a progressive movement. A classical case of such a leap is the seventeenth-century revolution in Western science. For the pre-modern, Renaissance scientist, coming to an understanding of nature required reaching an attunement with the order of Ideas, conceived as the reality behind the changing flux of the apparent material world. Post-Galilean scientific practice, on the other hand, is a function of disengagement, and attunement is reinterpreted as a projection of human qualities onto a morally indifferent material world. Apparent flux is explained by a de-divinized or disenchanted underlying order of natural laws, according to concepts proper to the intelligibility of nature conceived as the realm of law as *opposed* to the realm of meaning. Hence we have two incompatible conceptions of scientific inquiry. They are also incommensurable because they incorporate rival norms for understanding physical reality. One cannot simultaneously aspire with success towards the attuned wisdom of the Renaissance magi and the disengaged objectivity of the modern scientist. Each is defined in contrast to the other. The reservoir of concepts and standards of explanation that make the universe intelligible as something with which the inquirer can be attuned are just what make them irrational according to the conceptual scheme proper to the intelligibility of nature as the realm of law. Which one, then, is the rationally superior, if the criteria for rational understanding differ?

Taylor and MacIntyre propose that rational superiority shows itself retrospectively in a narrative that follows the course of a tradition's capacity to resolve its crisis. In this particular case, the pre-modern paradigm of science is thrown into a crisis from which it will never recover by the multiplicity of unforeseeable practices the disengaged science makes possible. The massive technological spin-offs of modern science require a response from the pre-modern. Even though technological control is not criterial for that paradigm, the very emergence of Galilean science as a *rival*, the very fact that there is *crisis* at all, feeds back into the standards of rationality of the challenged tradition. The crisis raises questions the internal satisfactory answerability of which, in retrospect, can be seen to decide the fate of the tradition. In this instance, the question demanding an answer is how a move in the science which yields further and more far-reaching 'recipes for action' cannot be interpreted as constituting an epistemic gain, given that both pre-modern and modern science is the product of embodied beings active in the world. In such an explanation of the epistemic progress, no assumption is made about the 'criterial' status of technological control. But the efficiency of technological practices is something which, once established, must be accounted for by both rivals. And this accounting, of course, is only possible as a historical narrative.

The rationality or otherwise of the transition is displayed in the asymmetry of the best narratives the rivals are capable of producing to explain the transition as one of epistemic gain or loss, as a forward or backward movement in our understanding of the physical universe. The very intelligibility of such forward or backward movement is problematic, however, so long as our way of telling them is fixed by ahistorical criteria of rationality. For in the absence of such criteria – that is, in the presence of incommensurability – a sceptical wedge will always be ready for insertion in the space between traditions. Despite its historicist motivation, the sceptical model is essentially static. The narrative model, on the other hand, gives due recognition to the dynamics of conflict, crisis and crisis resolution that objectively shape the development of real traditions and cultures.

But if this is true of scientific traditions, it is even more so of the identities and values that give content to practical reason. If we take changes in practices of punishment as an example, the utilitarian, humanist case for reforms based on the overall minimization of pain, at the time it was commended, assumed a rational quality in virtue of the reliance of rival traditional practices on the objective existence of a cosmically instantiated moral order. With belief in the social hierarchy as a microcosm of the cosmic order firmly in place, criminal acts could merit punishments whose cruelty matched the cosmic significance of the transgression. But with the demise of belief in that larger order, the emergence of the utilitarian rival, and other factors, the old practices faced an ultimately irresolvable crisis in their legitimation. The change in punitive practice, assuming this to be a sound interpretation of it, thus merits a claim to rationality.[8]

In the biographical context, the case is simplified by there being only one person living through the transitions. As we have already noted, the preferred conclusion of a practical deliberation is shown *directly* in the perspicuity of the self-interpretation of the transition lived through. Practical deliberation is occasioned by problems that demand an answer by way of a rearticulation of self-defining beliefs and action-orienting ideals. But this process of seeing things more clearly, removing confusions and contradictions, including factors previously screened out, getting closer to what really matters, may well fail to determine an appropriate response to the challenge. In a sense, the resources of practical reason will at that point be exhausted. But if it is recalled that for strong hermeneutics practical reason also has an essential *dialogical* moment, a moment which is not under the narrating subject's own control, the potential for more than arbitrary self-reinterpretation in fact escapes the closure such an exhaustion would represent.

Strong hermeneutics claims not to find itself embarrassed by the cognitive advance made by modern natural science. On the contrary, I have suggested, the very intelligibility of cognitive advance in science points the way to a conception of practical reason that subverts the calculative, subsumptive model of Enlightenment fundamentalism. Yet irrespective of the *process* of that transition, its *outcome* still seems to pose an insurmountable difficulty for strong hermeneutics' realist thesis. For the operative epistemic gain in this case is achieved through the divorce of valid knowledge of nature from attunement with it. Doesn't this conclusion itself show that if there is no world with which humans can, in reason, be morally attuned, *any* conception of a moral reality is deluded, a mere projection of human attributes onto intrinsically meaningless substance?

STRONG EVALUATION AND MORAL REALISM

The argumentative strategy Taylor adopts for refuting the thesis that 'concerning strong evaluations, there is no truth of the matter', is to expose the absurdities accruing from a hard fact–value distinction.[9] According to Taylor's strategy, strong evaluative discourse will make the grade for realism if, under an anti-realist interpretation dependent on the metaphysical separability of facts and values, sense cannot be made of the distinctive characteristics of the discourse. A realistic interpretation will be warranted if it can be demonstrated that strong evaluative discourse is unintelligible as a discourse of values as *opposed* to facts. If strong evaluative discourse is one which is in some part true to the facts, then an anti-realist characterization of strong evaluatives is unwarranted.

The issue can be put another way. Taylor's primary concern is to attack the idea that the best way of understanding and explaining human reality – that is, of developing genuine human sciences – is to establish *a priori* demarcations between the domain of facts and the domain of values. So long as we think that the road to genuine human science *must* go through the fact–value distinction, we are bound to consider strong values as surplus to the facts, as ontologically superfluous. If we were to think that, it would follow that in order for the *human sciences* to be realistically construable, they would have to be purged of the language of strong evaluation. Conversely, it would follow that if the human sciences cannot be purged of that language, if they show ineliminable traces of strong evaluative discourse, they would fit an anti-realist construction. The thrust of Taylor's arguments is that the human sciences are *at once* realistically construable – there is a truth to the matter where they are concerned – and structured by the logic of strong evaluation. This means questioning the status given to the fact–value distinction in traditional anti-realist construals of the human sciences.

We have already seen that reasoning over strong evaluations is a matter of contesting interpretations. What grounds are there for thinking that the human sciences generally follow an interpretive logic? Why think that a constitutive task of the human sciences is to interpret texts or text-analogues? The answer lies in the extent to which the object of the human sciences has the following characteristics.[10] First, a sense, meaning or significance that can be more or less coherent, and so stand in need of interpretation. Second, if it can be more or less coherent, the sense of the object must be distinguishable from its expression – if more or less illuminating interpretations are possible, there must be an interpretable meaning which is more or less satisfactorily expressed. Meaning and expression cannot therefore be identical. Third, a hermeneutic science will be of a subject by whom or for whom there is meaning – though it is by no means obvious how to identify the subject correctly. The idea that the human sciences do have such an object is given prima facie support by the fact that we ordinarily describe and explain human action as if it possessed these three characteristics. Typically, we only speak of actions as needing explanation because, in the first instance, we cannot 'make sense' of them. Explanation proceeds by making sense of what otherwise seemed contra-dictory, arbitrary or confused, given assumptions about the purposes and situation of the agent. That is, the explanation involves a re-reading of the action in its situation. And it typically succeeds either by making explicit a meaning that was otherwise implicit and unacknowledged, or by bringing to light a significance that the previous 'reading' left in the dark. When ordinary explanations of action do take this form, they presuppose the applicability of the second condition for an object of interpretation – that meaning is not exhausted by a given expression. Since the meaning made explicit or the significance uncovered is that of the desires, feelings, beliefs, purposes and aspirations of a subject, and the way they relate to the subject's situation, the third condition is also satisfied.

On the hermeneutic view, the human sciences owe their cognitive power to the refinements they bring to our ordinary practices of description and explanation, rather than to any qualitative leap out of the structure of those practices. They begin with a difficulty – say, a contradiction, confusion or incoherence – facing the ordinary, pre-reflective 'reading' of a phenomenon. The problem puts the meaning of the phenomenon into question. A process of reflective re-articulation and reinterpretation begins that attempts to improve upon the naïve reading. The aim of the new interpretation is to give a more perspicuous, coherent, insightful account, but no clean break is achieved or sought from the initial understanding. For our ability to tell that something is an improved reading, or a better explanation, relies on intuitions concerning what 'making sense' consists in that also guided the initial reading or explanation. Someone who sincerely sees no sense at all in the initial reading – that is, someone who utterly fails to see what is explanatory about it – will be in no position to judge the merit of the new interpretation. On the other hand, it is only from the perspective opened up by the new interpretation that the intuitions of 'making sense' at work in the old one get properly applied. Interpretive cognition thus moves in a 'hermeneutic circle'. A good explanation is one that makes good sense of the phenomenon. But as Taylor neatly puts it, 'to appreciate a good explanation, one has to agree on what makes good sense; what makes good sense is a function of one's readings; and these in turn are based on the kinds of sense one understands'.[11] Of course, the circle is not static: the kinds of sense one understands and the readings through which one understands them are mutually transformed in the course of hermeneutic reflection. Furthermore, to the extent that the meanings interpreted are constitutive of the subject doing the reflecting – that is, to the extent that the meanings are also self-definitions – the subject *itself* is transformed through the re-reading. A hermeneutic science of politics, for instance, as much as a hermeneutic psychological science, seeks to improve our understanding of the human subject by offering re-readings of the self-interpretations that define subjectivity.

But is a hermeneutic human science really science? Or better, if we take modern natural science as our paradigm of a realistically construable discourse, is interpretive human science realistically construable too? Arguments against bestowing scientific status on interpretive human science – or more germanely, the status of a realistically construable discourse – typically turn on the verification procedure for contesting interpretations. We noted that a hermeneutic human science begins with 'given' readings of text-like phenomena – namely, the interpretations or 'proto-interpretations' that are pre-reflectively relied upon in ordinary practices of explanation and self-definition. Since interpretive science has this starting point, there is an unavoidable circularity to its method of verification. The persuasive power of its results will be limited to those who in some measure share the intuitions of sense and coherence belonging to the original interpretive language. The reasons for accepting the herme-neutic account will have no hold on someone who has no understanding whatsoever of the language. It follows that an interpretive human science cannot offer a testing procedure for its theories that will ensure universal consensus when one of its theories is true. This may be regarded as an intolerable feature of a discourse that claims to be scientific, or one that claims to be realistically construable. And it can be seen to arise from a failure to distinguish the facts of the matter – on which universal consensus can be achieved – from the interpretation of their meaning, which could guarantee universal agreement only if conducted according to fully formalizable, explicit and determinate rules of inference. On this view, a proper human science, one fit for a realist construal, rigidly separates the facts from their human significance. The data of such a science would record the facts in a way that obviated the need for interpretation; it would be data 'whose validity cannot be questioned by offering another interpretation or reading, data whose credibility cannot be founded or undermined by further reasoning'.[12] With the ideal of interpretation-free data goes the notion that the truth of a descriptive or interpretive expression resides in a relation of correspondence between the expression and the object interpreted or described. A statement in a genuinely scientific psychological vocabulary, for instance, would be true if it corresponded to independently, objectively existing sensations, feelings and desires, and false if it failed to correspond to them. In a different context, in political science, the proper procedure would be to gather the 'brute data', the objective and neutral facts that, beyond interpretive dispute, define social reality. Only after objective reality has been described does meaning enter the picture – namely, as the beliefs, attitudes and evaluations individuals have or make in relation to the social reality. By proceeding in this manner, by building a separation of facts and values into their epistemological and ontological foundation, the human sciences can claim the same standard of legitimacy – and the same warrant for realism – as the 'absolute account' modern science provides of physical nature.

However, a human science that goes through the fact–value distinction in either of these two forms will have serious shortcomings. First, there is the case of a scientific psychology that describes its objects in absolute terms – that is, in terms that separate out the objective facts from their significance for a subject. Such a discourse aspires to represent the facts as they exist independently of interpretations of their meaning. But it is hard to see how the truth of the matter concerning a wide range of psychological phenomena can fit this model. Many human feelings and emotions have an experiential content that is inseparable from a sense of their significance. That is to say, the way emotions such as shame, pride, attachment, loss, indignation and solidarity actually *feel* is a function of the language in which the situations that occasion them are read. In these cases, it is misleading to say that the interpretation comes after the fact. For the very quality or content of the feelings – the very factuality of the facts – depends on the interpretation given to them by the experiencing subject. To be sure, some feelings and sensations – of colours, for instance – are minimally interpretation-dependent. But then there are also feelings and emotions – like those assigned to early childhood experience – that in an important sense only come into being in the midst of a highly abstract theoretical vocabulary. Psychological phenomena comprise a spectrum of interpreta-tion-ladenness between these two extremes. Certainly, adopting new ways of identifying a feeling or emotion can coincide with an alteration in the experience of that feeling or emotion. But since the feeling or emotion just *is* the experience, true descriptions of the object cannot be said to be externally related to the object's significance for the subject. There is no heterogeneity here of interpretation and identity, of mechanism of representation and object represented, that is required by the correspon-dence view; for a change in interpretation changes the object identified. But nor are productive changes in modes of identification arbitrary – interpretations alone do not constitute the object, they fit or fail to fit the experience. In this sense we can speak of more or less felicitous identifications of the experience, of more or less true interpretations, without invoking some correspondence to the facts as they exist independently of their meaning for a subject. A psychology that ruled out this possibility in order to legitimate itself as a science, or in order to warrant the same kind of realistic construal as absolute accounts of nature, would be forced into either ignoring a whole dimension of the human psyche or reconstituting it beyond recognition.

A political science that allows its ontology to be determined by the distinction between objective, verifiable facts and subjective interpretive evaluation faces equally serious difficulties. In order to count as a genuine science or a realistically construable discourse, a science of politics can aspire to describe the political reality unencumbered by the meanings it has for subjects. Such a descriptive language would identify a class of objects and events – so-called 'political behaviour' – in a manner that defied interpretive dispute. In addition, it would identify the 'values' individual subjects place upon the facts – namely, their positive or negative beliefs about and attitudes towards them. In a sense, these values are facts too, but they are facts about the psychological properties of individuals, about their contingent subjective reactions to social reality, rather than the social reality itself. On this view, in other words, the ontology of meaning is exhausted by the subjective reality of psychological states. But just as the scientific psychology discussed above could not deal with the interpreted meanings that help make up psychic reality, so such a 'neutral' science of politics cannot deal with the intersubjective meanings that help make up social reality. Since it consigns meaning to a contingent feature of the mechanism of representation rather than acknowledging it as an intrinsic property of the object represented, the science cannot possibly identify or investigate the fate of constitutively communal meanings – that is, meanings that are not just convergences of individual attitudes and evaluations, but that are shared by subjects as part of a wider intersubjective reality. Political science, in order to make the grade for realism, strives for an absolute account of its domain by dividing the world into neutral facts on the one hand and individual psychological reactions to them on the other. But the pursuit of such realism exacts a high price. For it results either in a failure to give due representation to the whole dimension of political reality that possesses constitutively intersubjective significance or in a misrepresentation of that reality.[13]

However, even if it is accepted that interpretation has a vital, irreducible role in the human sciences, even if it is agreed that the object of the human sciences is a text or text-analogue, one might still want to divorce the logic of the human sciences from the logic of strong evaluation. For the option seems to remain open of extracting the descriptive component of the text or text-analogue from its evaluative component. At first sight, such an option might have appeal for an anthropologist faced with the task of understanding and explaining diverse and incommensurable cultures. Indeed, as we shall consider presently, the predicament of the anthropologist faced with a culture or 'text' very different to and incommensurable with her native one precipitates still another version of the fact–value distinction, and provides one of the key motivations for contemporary anti-realism concerning strong evaluation.

Just as living within a framework of strong evaluations is not an existential option for human beings, nor is it a methodological option for the anthropologist utterly to dispense with the horizon against which human beings understand themselves. Understanding other human beings involves being able to apply the strong evaluations the other applies in the way the other applies them.[14] But given the wide diversity of horizons of understanding, this act of interpretation seems bound, at least in some cases, to be accompanied by a withdrawal from the ontological commitments implied by a particular set of cultural beliefs. And this demand can be satisfied by separating the factual, ontological content of the belief from the evaluative, non-cognitive component. The latter may feature in the empirical anthropologist's *explanandum*, but ought not to determine the preferred *explananda* of agency. This requirement can then seem equivalent to the demand that the language of the explananda be culture-neutral. To be culture-neutral, this pattern of argument continues, is for those evaluative biases that distort the language's capacity to describe the world felicitously to be neutralized. These biases can then be analysed into non-truth-evaluable expressions of pro- or con- attitudes and reactions. Since they are non-truth-evaluable, they have no place in the explanatory language of the theory. The language can only be evaluatively neutral once it has identified the genuinely descriptive claims hidden in the object-language of self-understanding. The explanatory theory is then impelled to transpose the object-language of self-understanding into one that has purely descriptive criteria of correct application; correct, that is, independently of culturally specific evaluative conation.

We have already seen that for strong hermeneutics, the criteria for the correct application of key descriptive (or classificatory) terms in the language of human self-understanding are *inextricably* evaluative. Stripping the concepts that typically feature in strong evaluations of their evaluative force, far from 'purifying' their descriptive, truth-evaluable content, actually transforms that content.[15] This means that the transposition of the language of self-understanding into a neutral, value-free vocabulary cannot be achieved without a revision of the original vocabulary of self-understanding. The transposed language is a revision because the criteria for the correct application of its concepts are not equivalent to the criteria for the application of the concepts of the original object-language. But a grasp of the original criteria is a condition of the methodological requirement to *understand*. The requirement is thereby flouted because one cannot understand without appeal to the evaluative criteria filtered out in the neutral, purely descriptive vocabulary.

But this conclusion still leaves room for a further, more radical anti-realism. For release can be sought from the ontological commitments implicit in the object-discourse of strong evaluation not just by way of neutralizing the evaluative dimension of the particular discourse, but by burrowing beneath the ontological moment as such. Rather than finessing the value/ontological commitments of the language of self-interpretation, this position relativizes them to the form of life in which they have use. The recommendation here is to suspend judgement on the evaluative force *and* the ontological commitments accompanying the self-understanding of the agent. Suspension is urged because the form of life in which the strong evaluations are intelligible is not the kind of thing that can either be affirmed or denied. Since the theorist grasps the language of self-understanding of agents when he or she partakes in the form of life which the language expresses, and since forms of life are incorrigible, so also, according to this position, are the self-understandings of the agents.[16]

However, this conclusion now faces the arguments we have already given for the view that strong evaluative discourse is inhabited by reason. The force of those considerations as arguments for the second component of strong hermeneutics' realist thesis turns on a version of the 'best account principle'.[17] This principle holds for the human world as much as for the physical universe: in both cases, the favoured ontology is the one invoked by the most believable account. In the domain of human affairs – 'the domain where we deliberate about our future action, assess our own and others' character, feelings, reactions, comportments, and also attempt to understand and explain these' – a certain vocabulary will emerge as the most realistic as a result of the various means of rational discussion, deliberation and reflection.[18] If the defining terms of strong evaluative discourse – desirability – characterizations like 'authenticity', 'courage' and 'generosity' – are essential for understanding and explaining people's actions illuminatingly, as well as for deliberating effectively about future courses of action, then the characteristics picked out by these terms are real features of the world.

The real, then, is what is disclosed by the best account of any given domain. In this respect, there is continuity between the human and the natural sciences. But as their domains differ, so does the kind of vocabulary that features in the best account. The crucial point for Taylor's realist thesis is that the best account of human practical life cannot but incorporate a language of strong evaluation. In the previous chapter we considered Taylor's phenomenological–existential argument for the inescapability of frameworks of qualitative contrasts. We are now in a position to consider why such a *phenomenological* account must feature in the *best* account. Given the best account principle – that the best account determines our ontological commitments – the moral realism of strong hermeneutics can be understood as a doctrine of phenomenological ontology.

According to the orthodox view, the task of phenomenological ontology is to produce 'pure descriptions' of experience, and hence of the world as it appears from the point of view of an engaged inquirer. According to the standard objection to it, the exclusive focus on description rids it of explanatory power, and hence of any competence to determine ontological commitments. The best account principle disarms this objection, not by denying the relevance of explanations for phenomenological accounts, but by emphasizing the explanatory force of the language through which human beings make practical sense of their lives. Deprived of discourses of strong evaluation, reflection would be less perspicuous and deliberation less effective. But this means that explanations of practical matters that dispensed with these terms would also miss out on something fundamental to human agency that needs explaining. If strong evaluative discourse has an irreducible and ineliminable role to play in the best account of such matters, 'no epistemological or metaphysical considerations of a more general kind' can trump its ontological force.[19]

At this point a word of caution may be due.[20] The weight strong hermeneutics accords to phenomenological accounts of moral experience should be seen as a counterpoise to general epistemological and metaphysical considerations of the kind that issue in the modern fact–value distinction. The key consideration Taylor targets is the view that truth is attributable exclusively to propositions that feature in an absolute account of reality, one that abstracts from the meanings things have in the inhabited world. Corresponding to this commitment is the view that 'the terms of everyday life, those in which we go about living our lives, are to be relegated to the realm of mere appearance' and hence bereft of explanatory force.[21] As we have seen, this is a deep-seated premise of Enlightenment fundamentalism. According to that view, the only true account of reality is articulable in an absolute language of primary qualities. It follows, given this premise, that human affairs, like the physical universe, 'ought to be maximally described in external, non-culture-bound terms'.[22] But if the arguments given earlier were sound, there are significant dimensions of human reality – like interpretation-enriched emotions and intersubjective meanings – concerning which the best accounts cannot be 'absolute' ones. Although the reality disclosed by the strong value terms featuring in our best account is 'dependent on us', it is no less real, given human existence, than the reality disclosed in the absolute accounts of modern physics.

But it might still appear questionable that strong evaluative discourse thereby earns the right to realism. The framework for thinking about realism proposed by Crispin Wright may help to clarify why. In the most advanced formulation to date of the parameters of realism vs anti-realism debates in analytical philosophy, Wright rejects the usefulness of the paradigms of anti-realism that have traditionally motivated a realist response. Wright cites Ayer's emotivist expressivism and Mackie's 'error' theory as such unsuitable paradigms of anti-realism.[23] Both construe moral discourse anti-realistically, the former by analysing the evaluative component of moral judgements as a non-truth-evaluable expression of feeling, the latter by regarding the discourse as truth-evaluable but always false. We have seen that Taylor's hermeneutics does indeed define itself in opposition to both these anti-realist theories. But they are unsuitable as paradigms of anti-realism, Wright suggests, because they let realism in too quickly. According to these paradigms, discourses with well-formed declarative sentences properly taken at their face-value as truth-apt (without need of translation into genuine assertoric form) and with some true sentences amongst them, make the grade for a realistic interpretation. But so long as anti-realism is so defined, realism comes too cheaply. To show what might be at stake in the achievement of realism, Wright introduces the idea of 'minimal truth'.

Minimal truth is a metaphysically neutral, 'lightweight' conception of truth. It is a property of all discourses with the 'surface signs of discipline', like syntactically well-formed declarative sentences and terms whose application is governed by generally agreed standards of correctness.[24] Minimal truth is thus a merely formal notion: it has no intrinsic, substantive metaphysical import. Its demands are met rather by the satisfaction of platitudes like '"P" is true if and only if P', or '"P" corresponds to the facts'. Minimally truth-apt discourses also admit of pluralism: there is no convergence requirement for minimal truths. Because minimal truth is so metaphysically lightweight and plural, discourses characterized by it, including ordinary discourse about 'the delightful, the good and the valuable', should find 'no solecism in the description of contents concerning such matters as "true"'.[25]

So according to Wright's proposal, a discourse's possession of minimal truth is not enough to warrant a realist interpretation of it. How then is realism earned? What properties would a discourse show if it were to be the site of more than minimal truths? Most crucially, realistically construable discourses will show what Wright terms 'cognitive command'. In discourses where cognitive command obtains, 'any disagreement in the discourse involves something worth describing as a *cognitive shortcoming*'.[26] Cognitive shortcoming, for its part, is modelled on the failure of the capacity for representation. In discourses that exhibit cognitive command, a representative function is at play which, while in order, generates convergence of belief. More than minimal substantive truths thus issue from a properly functioning capacity to represent the facts. Conversely, 'cognitive shortcoming *always* has to be at work in the generation of conflicting views' within such a discourse.[27] For on this model, the function of realistically construable discourses is to represent, and 'if two devices each function to reproduce representations, then if conditions are suitable, and they function properly, they will produce divergent output only if presented with divergent input'.[28] Wright considers the test of cognitive command to be equivalent to the applicability of this model to processes of belief formation: it specializes the general model of neutral, objective representation 'to the case where the representational system is a thinking subject engaged in belief'.[29] Realism, so construed, is the view that 'the opinions to which we are moved in the prosecution of a favoured discourse are the products of (successful or unsuccessful) representational function'.[30]

Cognitive command is not a sufficient criterion for a realist discourse, though Wright suspects that 'all roads to realism have to go *through* cognitive command'.[31] If Wright's suspicion is correct, and the framework he proposes for thinking about realism is adopted, then strong evaluative discourse cannot be interpreted realistically. Seen through the perspective urged by Wright, the arguments we have been considering count towards a realist interpretation of natural science but not discourses of strong value. For only the former holds any prospect of satisfying the cognitive command test. To be sure, strong evaluative discourse is minimally truth-apt, but the truth it contains is metaphysically lightweight. And this is all, it might be thought, that has been shown by Taylor's hermeneutic arguments for moral realism. The point they establish, formulated in McDowell's terms, is that discourses exhibiting the intelligibility proper to meaning are apt for minimal truth, but they leave room for substantive truth on the part of discourses exhibiting the intelligibility proper to the disenchanted realm of law.

Should we adopt Wright's proposal for thinking about realism? It is not clear that we should. For the conception of the subject built into the cognitive command constraint is incompatible with many of the hermeneutic insights to which we have already adduced. On Wright's proposal, realist discourses articulate the beliefs of a thinking subject *qua* representational system. But to model the subject on a system of representation, one that produces divergent output only if presented with divergent input, is to short-circuit the interpretive process that is such a significant element, in a large number of cases, of belief-formation. But if this is so, then Wright is offering us a profoundly inappropriate model of the thinking subject engaged in belief *about itself*. The point here is *not* that the 'output' of the subject engaged in belief about itself should be construed *anti-realistically*. It is rather that if the subject is to be capable of producing a realistic discourse about itself at all, then it had better not aspire to cognitive command: aiming at cognitive command *diverts* discourse about the human subject from its proper course.

Evidence for this proposition is provided by the objections we made to absolute accounts in the human sciences. A psychological science or a political science that passed the cognitive command test would be forced into either excluding or distorting many psychic and sociopolitical phenomena that need explaining. It should be clear that a discourse that respected the ontological irreducibility of interpretation-enriched feelings and intersubjective meanings cannot meet the constraint of cognitive command: disagreement in these discourses is a normal part of their proper functioning and certainly cannot be ascribed *a priori* to cognitive shortcoming. On the hermeneutic view, there can be *genuine* – not pseudo – dispute here without the guarantee of consensus. By the preceding arguments, it is folly to aim for realism, in Wright's metaphysically heavyweight sense, in these cases. But nor is it clear what is gained by thinking of these discourses in *anti*-realist terms. For that would be to leave them with only minimal truth – that is, without any specific ontological significance. Since belief formation in the human sciences is in crucial respects a matter of interpretation, since it is through interpretations that the work of epistemic gain and loss is prosecuted, the framework proposed by Wright cannot but disable us from reflecting perspicuously on the ontological commitments brought by such beliefs. It would be most misleading to take the strong hermeneutic thesis that interpretations cannot be reduced to representations as definitive of its basic anti-realism, since all the interesting debate happens *within* the porous sphere of interpretation. In this respect the strong hermeneutic case against Enlightenment fundamentalism also holds against Wright's proposal: anti-realist readings of a discourse should not be favoured merely by the fact that the *subject-matter* is unsuitable for the kind of treatment required for cognitive command.

Strong hermeneutics does not burden moral discourse with the kind of metaphysical mortgage which, according to Wright's schema, would earn it the right to realism. The realism of strong hermeneutics is motivated against a prevailing *anti-realism concerning interpretation*. It calls itself a 'realism' to announce its acknowledgement of the cognitive power of interpretations and to declare its resistance to the representational paradigm of reason. Wright's motivation for positing a more than minimal concept of truth is to move beyond a 'bland perspective of a variety of assertoric "language games", each governed by its own internal standards of acceptability, each sustaining a metaphysically emasculated conception of truth'.[32] While strong hermeneutics sympathizes with this motive, it doubts that truth is preferably thought of by way of the model of cognitive command.[33]

PLURALISM AND CONSERVATISM

Thus, while strong hermeneutics affirms the truth-evaluability of strong evaluations and their immanent answerability to practical reason, it is a moral realism which need not cause alarm to those with a confidence in the cognitive powers of modern science and a modern scepticism about the existence of a cosmologically instantiated order of moral meaning. There is, however, a further ground for concern over its talk about moral truths. For though a substantive theory of practical reason need not be burdened by an insufferable metaphysical mortgage, it might still be supportive of excessive *conservatism* in practices of critical reflection. It may be recalled from chapter one that a charge like this may be prompted by the strong hermeneutic insistence on the immanence of reason. For the insistence on immanence may be taken to justify the imposition of limits on the accountability of actually existing cultural traditions. Does not the strong hermeneutic bonding of practical reason and horizons of ethical life rule out the possibility of a thoroughgoing critique of prevailing customs, traditions and institutions?

By way of a response, strong hermeneutics can invoke a number of distinctions that at least acquit it of blanket charges of conservatism. Firstly, as Taylor has noted, issues of ontology must be distinguished from so-called 'advocacy' issues.[34] Ontological issues concern one's most basic characterizations of being or the particular domain of being under consideration. There is an ontological issue at stake, for instance, between those who consider societies to be 'really' complex aggregates of atomic units, and those who consider social, intersubjective structures and institutions to be 'wholes' that are irreducible to their 'parts'. Atomists and holists are thus divided on the issue of social ontology. On the other hand, 'advocacy' issues pertain to one's moral stance or *policy* prescriptions. Collectivists and individualists, for instance, advocate different kinds of social policy, with one kind oriented primarily to the provision of collective interests, the other to the interests of discrete individuals. But one's stance on whether the needs and wishes of individuals or collectives should be given priority is not *entailed* by one's ontological position. Atomist and holist ontologies do not come *packaged* with a set of individualist and collectivist policy demands. To be sure, issues of ontology and advocacy are not completely independent of each other. For a moral or political stance is only formulable against the background of a particular ontology, and for that reason may be kept off the political agenda by a given ontological vocabulary. Ontologies are by no means policy-*neutral*. This point is of the utmost significance for thinking about practices of critical reflection. But for the time being, we just need to note that while an ontology may be necessary for the articulation and justification of a stance or policy, it is not thereby made a *sufficient* condition for advocacy.

But just such a conflation of the necessary and sufficient, I would suggest, helps fire the accusation of conservatism. This can be illustrated by considering some aspects of the role played by language in determining the ontology of strong hermeneutics. Language, on the strong hermeneutic view, helps constitute and give expression to modes of thought and forms of life. This constituting-expressive function is in some ways analogous to the sense in which social institutions help constitute and express a culture.[35] The family, civil society and the state, for example, might be considered as the 'objective' expression of the identity of those who participate in them ('objective spirit', as Hegel called them). Similarly, the objectivity of meaning consists in the publicly shareable rules which more or less rigidly determine the correct and incorrect application of concepts. Moral reality can thus be considered as the world disclosed by particular moral concepts, and access to this world is conditioned by competence in the use of those concepts. A moral reality can disclose itself, therefore, only to human beings who have been initiated into a language, which is to say to participants in a form of life that is expressed in and partly constituted by its language and other social institutions.

In brief, this 'expressive–constitutive' view of the ontological role of language arises by way of contrast to the 'instrumentalist–enframing' view, according to which language is a contingent, replaceable vehicle for the transmission of ontologically more primordial phenomena. Typical of the ontologically basic phenomena invoked on this view are 'mental states'. According to the instrumentalist–enframing account, words enframe a particular 'private' object or mental event and serve as an instrument for the transmission of subjective experiences. But on the hermeneutic view, language in all but its most primitive forms cannot be short-circuited in this manner. Rather than enframing independently subsisting objects or events, language is considered as the irreplaceable site of constitutively shared meanings. Now this account of language clearly has implications for one's social ontology. For it asserts that individuals become who they are only in an irreducibly intersubjective space. This conviction provides a point of departure from classical contract theories of society, for instance, that model the legitimacy of social institutions upon a rational agreement reached between sovereign, ontologically primordial individuals. From the hermeneutic perspective, such theories share with the instrumental–enframing conception of language a voluntarism that is intelligible only on the assumption of an atomist ontology. For voluntarism of this sort arises from considering language – and in general the common norms, institutions and customs that express a moral reality or *Sittlichkeit* – as an instrument of something ontologically more basic; namely, the will of the individual, self-defining subject. Supported by its expressive–constitutive conception of language, strong hermeneutics unambiguously rejects this ontology. In its place, it posits an embodied subject, embedded non-contingently in *some* language, encountering *some* moral reality.

Taylor describes this ontological condition as our 'defining situation'.[36] But simply as an ontological thesis, it does not advocate a particular policy or moral stance. Once the distinction between ontology and advocacy is in place, the worry that talk of a defining or transcendental situation 'naturalizes' historically and culturally variable norms – that it immunizes the norms and customs that constitute any given *Sittlichkeit* from criticism by 'ontologizing' them – should not arise. We might be further protected from the anxiety if we bear in mind another distinction. Drawing on Taylor's notion of a defining situation, Sabina Lovibond has distinguished between a benign 'transcendental' parochialism and a malignant 'empirical' parochialism.[37] Transcendental parochialism refers to the inescapability of the conceptual scheme to which we are related as self-interpreting and *embodied* beings. It is the parochialism of beings whose reality is mediated by language, but whose language is not *grounded* in rational choice or agreement. This much, that rational subjectivity arises out of a shared form of linguistic and biological life, cannot be changed. However, a parochialism of this transcendental kind is not in any way informative about where the limits of rationality lie for any *particular* belief, action or institution. Empirical parochialism, on the other hand, turns the acknowledgement of the immanence of rationality into a particular policy for conserving the actually existing *Sittlichkeit*. For whether a deviation from the prevailing *Sittlichkeit* is considered a challenge to its rationality depends not on transcendental limits, but on which of two contingent attitudes are taken up to 'moral anomalies'. The conservative *chooses* to adopt the attitude of an 'observer', whose objectifying gaze towards *'unsittlich'* practices transforms them into something to be 'managed', 'cured' or 'trained'. But a 'participant' attitude can just as well be adopted, according to which the practice is regarded as a *potential* act of rational subjectivity. The latter possibility is excluded *tout court* only by advocates of a wholly *static* moral organism. But the idea that any given *Sittlichkeit* is invulnerable to rational change is as alien to strong hermeneutics as the notion that all moral meanings can be overthrown and re-invented at will.

This image of *Sittlichkeit* as a monolithic, static entity, closed-off from all serious criticism and change, no doubt lies behind suspicions that it belongs to an intrinsically conservative outlook. But there is no reason whatsoever why strong hermeneutics is bound to project such an image. In the first place, it construes contexts of ethical life as normatively fulfilled when functioning as dynamic, self-reflexive sites of identity formation. Hence it considers the static, monolithic *Sittlichkeit* to be intrinsically at odds with itself. In the second place, the monolithic view gives a false impression of our actual historical situation. Even if the static model ever did have empirical application – that is, if there ever did exist a moral world that harboured no dissent or moral uncertainty – which is doubtful, modern societies are characterized by a plurality of more or less interweaving traditions and diverse modes of cultural identification. This is not to say, of course, that in modern societies *Sittlichkeit* reaches perfection, that it fully realizes its *telos*. On the contrary, on the strong hermeneutic view the public institutions of modern societies signally fail to embody satisfactory expressive relationships. But the resulting instability need not lead to collapse, strong hermeneutics can argue, because the *Sittlichkeit* also sustains itself by coercion, ideology and by the marginalization of potent but relatively untapped sources of normativity.

But even if we accept that strong hermeneutics sets up significant critical distance between itself and its surrounding cultural values, we can still ask whether that distance goes far enough. By setting its sights on *retrieval*, doesn't the hermeneutic approach look backwards to past achievements rather than forwards to unprecedented utopian possibilities? And by adopting a *comprehensive* critical approach – that is, by seeking to articulate the full range of goods which inform actual identities – doesn't hermeneutics sacrifice the *revisionary* thrust of rational critique?[38] Strong hermeneutics can answer that it depends on the *nature and standing of the goods themselves*. On the one hand, the task of retrieval involves not a return to the past but a *renewal* of lost or latent possibilities. Retrieval is required because goods have become covered up. But whatever their origin, the potency of these goods, and hence their reality, depends on their ability to convince and motivate in a *prospective* horizon. The hermeneutic approach neglects neither the historicity of the present nor its unprecedented futurity. On the other hand, even if the act of disclosure does not involve a process of ideological unmasking – though it may well do that – it might still have radically revisionary implications. Even the articulation of goods that are *implicit* in practices, rather than 'buried-over' in them, may countenance radical revisions to the status quo. To clarify this conjunction of comprehensive and revisionary approaches, Taylor distinguishes between 'internal goods' and 'transcendent goods'. Unlike internal goods, into which we are socialized as part of a *Sittlichkeit*, there are goods that 'transcend all our practices, such that we are capable of transforming or even repudiating some practices in the name of these goods'.[39] In other words, such goods cannot be affirmed without also challenging the validity of some constitutive practices of the prevailing culture.

If we keep in mind the distinctions between transcendent and internal goods, between issues of ontology and those of advocacy, and between transcendental and empirical parochialism; if we also acknowledge the revisionary potential of hermeneutic reflection and the radical implications of retrieving buried-over or suppressed goods, especially transcendent goods, what remains of the charge of conservatism? We can now say with some confidence that if anything does remain, it must apply very abstractly, and certainly not at the level of ruling out critique as such. The prima facie objection that hermeneutics has no revisionary or subversive moment simply does not stand up to reflection.[40]

But perhaps it is just the most abstract level of justification that continues to worry us. Like Habermas, we might detect a conservative remainder in the stubborn immanence of the hermeneutic situation itself. Habermas proposes various strategies for transcending this immanence, and thereby for *guaranteeing* protection against conservatism, at different stages in his intellectual career. In *Knowledge and Human Interests*, Habermas's strategy is governed by his suspicion that the language of hermeneutic reflection may be *systematically corrupt*. Habermas cannot discount the possibility that hermeneutic deliberation is prone to systematic distortion due to *extra*-linguistic pressures which themselves inflect the linguistic resources available to hermeneutic reflection. Indeed, for Habermas, systematic distortion is not just a possibility. He thinks it *must* be presumed to exist if certain practices of effective emancipatory reflection are to be made intelligible. Genuinely emancipatory reflection, on the 'deep hermeneutic' model Habermas develops here, manages to transcend the facticity of tradition – and with that the contingency of actual horizons of meaning – in a *qualitatively* more radical manner than 'strong hermeneutics'. We shall examine the nature and validity of this claim in the next chapter.

4 Deep hermeneutics, emancipation and fate

If it is believed that in the course of its enlightenment the human species learns that the order of nature is empty of moral signification, the following question can look compelling: how is moral identity to be grounded if not in the natural order of *things*? Aware of the threat that the objectivity of modern natural science posed to the identity of the reflective human subject – a reflexivity that is imposed historically with the collapse of the social fabric of religious tradition – Kant sought to bring the intelligibility of a moral identity to clarification in the rationality of free and responsible action. There may not be any ethical substance in the world that can be the object of cognition, but there is a moral law that can be tracked by a free subject acting on universalizable self-willed maxims. In the moral law, the human agent can be reassured that there are reasons for acting that have more than a merely optional, hypothetical, contingent status, since there is a class of actions that humans, *qua* rational beings, have an unconditional obligation to perform. The moral law, for Kant, puts constraints on matter of fact, empirically motivated action by opposing the universality of the rational, dutiful will to the particularity of sensuous inclination. Now as is well known, Hegel gives an extensive critique of Kant's way of making sense of moral identity. He argues that by abstracting the rational agent from the historically concrete intersubjective conditions of self-formation, and similarly by idealizing the source of the legitimacy of the moral law as *prior* to any institutionalized embodiment, the Kantian view disables itself from giving a plausible account of just what is threatened by the objectivating sciences and the fragmented social fabric of religion: a reflectively resilient, motivationally potent, sustainable moral identity. Such an account can only be given, in the view proposed by Hegel in his less well-known early writings, if instead of understanding the contingency-limiting moral order as the categorical determinations of law, we conceive it as an 'ethical totality' which exercises its compulsion upon acts that transgress it as a 'fate'.

Whereas strong hermeneutics sees itself as continuing a tradition set on its way by Hegel's critique of Kant, Habermas uses the young Hegel's model of a 'causality of fate' as a springboard for leaping *beyond* hermeneutics.

Habermas's early work is shaped by the conviction that since Hegel's alternative to Kant's account of moral identity formation implies a context-transcending moment of emancipatory insight, its deep truth is lost on hermeneutics. According to the view of *Knowledge and Human Interests*, it is Marx and Freud who come closest to discovering the secret behind the worldly operation of the causality of fate. For Marx, the revolutionary action of the universal class marks the moment of collective insight whereby the human species reappropriates its alienated powers and instantiates an ethical totality of mutual recognition between producers. Class society is not something given by law or nature, rather it is the historical fate of a 'dirempted' totality. Insight into this collective fate requires a special kind of theory-mediated self-reflection on the part of humanity as a whole. That is to say, since systematic self-delusion, or false consciousness, is one of the effects of diremption, the emancipatory act of collective self-recollection must be informed by a theory of history that gets behind misleading everyday appearances. It requires, to use Habermas's expression, 'deep hermeneutic' reflection.

But while Habermas's social theory is geared towards a retrieval of historical materialism, it is to Freud that Habermas turns when working out the complex logic of the causality of fate and its so-called depth-hermeneutic overcoming. For Habermas, the relationship between the analyst and analysand provides an exemplary instance of supra-hermeneutic reflection on Hegelian lines at work. That is to say, by interpreting the psychoanalytical situation as the site of a struggle for recognition, Habermas can read Freud as proposing a model of moral identity formation that mirrors Hegel's in its fundamental structure. According to Habermas, psychoanalytical reflection can help the subject regain identity by returning him or her to an 'ethical totality' the diremption of which had divided the subject, as a fate, from his or her own potential for self-realization. On this model, the symptoms of the analysand are manifestations of her alienation from herself. Since symptoms both testify to and disguise the effect of diremption, they must be interpreted as a special kind of text, one whose meaning is systematically distorted. Reconciliation to one's fate in this case requires a mode of self-interpretation which, in the course of a struggle for recognition with a projected other, recovers or reappropriates one's alienated forms of self-expression. It is by reflective insight into the 'fateful' causality of alienated meanings that the self regains its identity. This mode of reflection points beyond hermeneutics, Habermas believes, because of the *causal* efficacy it seems to have in emancipating the subject from the misery-inducing consequences of diremption.

Now although Habermas will later attempt, in his discourse ethics, to move beyond hermeneutics in a quite different fashion, he never explicitly renounces this Hegel-inspired model of moral identity as the emancipatory achievement of a struggle for recognition. On the contrary, in *The Philosophical Discourse of Modernity* he describes the goal of his theory of communicative action precisely as reconstructing 'Hegel's concept of the ethical context of life' in such a way that it 'disenchants the unfathomable causality of fate'.[1] The struggles for normativity that characterize the modern world, Habermas writes in the same text, can be brought to philosophical clarification in terms of a 'dirempted totality, which makes itself felt primarily in the avenging power of destroyed reciprocities and in the fateful causality of distorted communicative relationships'.[2] On the other hand, however, Habermas now considers the normative force of communicative relationships to be based not on 'deep'- or 'quasi'-anthropological interests, but on formal–pragmatic presuppositions of language use. I will examine the viability of Habermas's formalization of his alternative to hermeneutics in chapters five and six. In this chapter, I will consider whether his 'deep hermeneutic' model really does mark a significant departure from strong hermeneutics, and to the extent that it does, whether it marks an improvement upon it.

I shall begin my examination of the shape of depth hermeneutics by outlining how the notions of an ethical totality and causality of fate feature in the young Hegel's critique of the Kantian construal of moral order as the moral law. Against Kant, Hegel proposes a model of the self-formative process of the moral subject that appeals to the idea of a fatefully avenging ethical totality. I then discuss how the young Hegel's critique of Kant gets incorporated into Habermas's interpretation of the general pattern of disturbed and reconstituted identity formation in Freudian psychoanalysis. The issue taken up here concerns the *kind* of theory capable of articulating Hegel's insights. I then consider two general objections to Habermas's synthesis of Hegel and Freud: first, that in its neglect of the continuity between the human and the disenchanted world, it is insufficiently naturalistic; and second, that by taking for granted a mechanistic ontology of nature – and with it an epistemological short-circuiting of hermeneutic, self-transfigurative powers – it is in fact too naturalistic to serve its purpose. In view of problems the latter objection presents for Habermas, I conclude with a reassessment of his claim to have moved, via the young Hegel and Freud, beyond a hermeneutical conception of moral identity.

ETHICAL TOTALITY AND THE CAUSALITY OF FATE

Habermas's appropriation of the young Hegel's model of an ethical totality that avenges itself as a fate is decisive for his proposed resolution of the problem of the intelligibility of moral identity. However, we get only the roughest sketches from Habermas himself of the role played by Hegel's idea in shaping his theory. Even within the extensive critical literature on Habermas, its underlying significance has been slow to come to light.[3] I would now like to contribute to the growing awareness of the young Hegel's influence on Habermas by concentrating on the specific text by

Hegel to which Habermas most frequently and enthusiastically returns: *The Spirit of Christianity and its Fate*.[4]

In this remarkable essay, the young Hegel contrasts two ways of making sense of moral identity. According to one framework, which Hegel considers to structure both the Mosaic and the Kantian systems of ethics, morality has its source in law. That is to say, morality owes its binding, compelling character to the authority of law as such, to the 'universal' only. Within this framework, the moral demand – or 'the source of injunction', to use Ricoeur's apt expression – possesses a logic of universality as *opposed* to particularity; it originates in something external to particular human needs, it commands obedience for reasons that have no bearing on human fulfilment. When moral relations are disturbed – that is to say, when the law is broken – a punishment is inflicted on the perpetrator of the trespass, either 'internally' as bad conscience or externally through physical coercion. Something like the fear of penal justice, Hegel suggests, can therefore provide the motivational force behind the subject's obedience to the moral order. However, it cannot make the subject *identify* with morality. It is for this reason, Hegel believes, that the Kantian and Mosaic systems of ethics must eventually self-destruct. By contrast, the moral teachings of Jesus, as Hegel interprets them here, transfigure the division between particularity and universality. Within this framework, human nature and human need are not opposed to morality, nor do they enter it merely contingently. Hence the insoluble problem of *imposing* a form of identification with morality, of reconciling unbridgeable moments of particularity and universality, does not arise. It is precisely for the sake of elucidating the structure of this internal relation between subject and moral source that Hegel contrasts the 'fate' of the criminal with his punishment under penal law.

In the case where morality is grounded as law, the perpetrator of a moral transgression faces the following predicament. First, he faces a punishment that is a necessary and inescapable consequence of the criminal act. Punishment is *entailed* by the act of trespass. If the moral source is exhausted by law, and if punishment represents the avenging force of the moral source, then the 'must' of the punishment will be the imperative of law – namely, categorical. Since within this paradigm the requirements of morality are intelligible *solely* as the demands of law, the necessity of the punishment facing the criminal must reflect the imperative of the law. As the imperative of the moral law is necessarily and unconditionally – that is, categorically – applicable to the human being *qua* agent, so punishment is applicable unconditionally and necessarily to the agent *qua* criminal. This, as Hegel sees it, is the unbending demand of justice: 'so long as laws are supreme, so long as there is no escape from them, so long must the individual be sacrificed to the universal', that is, the law, in his punishment.[5] But it is only possible for the individual to be sacrificed to the universal in this manner, Hegel thinks, if the individual is *identified* with his standing with respect to the law. That is, with respect to the law, the criminal's identity is *nothing but* that of the perpetrator of crime. From the moral point of view, the point of view of the judge, he *is* a criminal, 'a sin existent, a trespass possessed of personality'.[6] Now the criminal would be *only* that, from the moral point of view, if the law felicitously represented the whole of the moral source. Yet it is an identity which an individual can acquire only by being abstracted from the concrete conditions of his life context. Since the moral source as law can avenge itself only upon an abstraction, it fails to impact on the concrete life of the individual human being. Furthermore, the moral source which exercises its avenging force as penal law is *external* to the identity of the criminal. The law stands outside and is unchanged by the transgressive act. The fear the criminal has of the universal is a fear of something that stands above and beyond him, as something alien, rather than as something arising from within.[7]

Such considerations lead Hegel to think that morality grounded as law leaves no room for reconciliation between the particular person who acts and the reactive force of the universal. First, the criminal faces the necessity of his punishment. Although contingencies can always intercede in the actual mechanisms of penal justice, say in the form of a judge's leniency or compassion, the 'contradiction between consciousness of oneself and the hoped-for difference in another's idea of one's self', as Hegel puts it, or the 'contradiction between desert in the eyes of the law and the actualization of the same',[8] is no basis for a *reconciliation* with the law. Second, given the abstraction of the criminal *qua* criminal from the point of view of the law, any erstwhile reconciliation with the law can only be what Hegel calls a 'conceptual reunion', involving 'man as a concept' rather than 'man as reality'. And third, so long as the act of transgression and the punitive reaction it occasions appear as the 'destruction or subjugation of something alien', of something external to and unchanged by the act, again the thought of reconciliation is absurd.

Hegel's conclusion is that within a framework structured by unmediated oppositions between 'universal' and 'particular', 'concept' and 'reality', punishment and law cannot be reconciled.[9] However, he wants to show that reconciliation is possible if these oppositions can be transcended. At this point, it may help to recall Bernard Williams's critique of morality as the 'institution of blame' introduced briefly in chapter two.[10] For Williams's description of the institution of blame that bears upon the transgressor of the 'system of morality' corresponds closely to Hegel's idea of the punishment through which morality as law avenges itself. Within the system of morality, the fundament of ethical life is construed as an unconditional obligation to act in accord with the moral law. The phenomenal appearance of an objective constraint on a subject's particular inclinations is then taken to represent an implicit recognition of the universality of the moral demand. The perception of bindingness is traced back to an intuited sense of one's overriding obligation to a moral law that is universal in virtue of being uncompromised by inclination.[11] This is the supposed achievement of the rational will. However, it is hard to see how the *experience* of the moral demand can be anything other than a confrontation with something that is part of one's inhabited world. As Williams points out, the force of the moral law is intelligible as something external to the individual rational will only when regarded as the law of a '*notional republic*' of ideal, autonomous citizens.[12] The law-like fundament of ethical life, in Hegel's terms, impinges on 'man as concept', and it does so by abstracting the demands of law from the concrete world in which 'man as reality' lives.

Moreover, the *stability* of the morality system requires a means of binding individuals which it is itself incapable of providing. The system of morality is inherently unstable, Williams suggests, because it does violence to the reality of the individual's life context. In order to be grounded as law, the system of morality needs its own peculiar sanction, and this it finds in a particular kind of punishment – in blame. As we observed in our discussion of the appeal of Rorty's model of the contingent self, allocations of blame tend to focus narrowly on an action or omission perpetrated by an isolated, ideally autonomous subject. It can then seem as if the agent who transgresses the system of morality always has a reason for acting otherwise – namely, to fulfil his moral obligation. This reason is then viewed as overridden by another reason upon which the transgressor chose to act, and for which he merits blame. The practice of blame thus presupposes that there is a common, basic reason for acting which all agents implicitly or explicitly recognize and to which the agent can voluntarily conform or dissent. But in line with strong hermeneutics, Williams argues that the entwined ideas of a basic reason and the ideally autonomous subject who chooses to act upon it are fictional. The practice of blame abstracts moral consciousness from the background context of self-formation and so from the surroundings in which the shape of the particular character blamed is forged. Williams suggests that the fictional foundation of the system of morality and its misrepresentation of the pull of the ethical as blame can be overlooked if one is convinced by the ideal that 'human existence can be ultimately just'; that luck in the process of character formation is adventitious to what is of fundamental value in life.[13] While Williams acknowledges that this aspiration towards 'purity' may have been of some beneficial practical consequence, the fiction underlying the practice of blame encourages people 'to misunderstand their own fear and resentment . . . as the voice of the Law'.[14] This misrepresentation can only be overcome, and the end of justice more felicitously served, Williams suggests, if the illusion of value completely void of luck is abandoned.

But where does the acknowledgement of contingency at this level leave us, and how might the opposition between particular and universal now be reconciled?[15] Let us return to Hegel's alternative to the Kantian system of morality. We have seen that for Hegel, the avenging force of law is experienced as something alien and abstract. Hegel contrasts punishment as a fate in the following ways. First, what avenges itself in the power of fate is not something external, but the 'defective life' of the agent *himself* in so far as this life is shared with the other members of his ethical community:

> When the trespasser feels the disruption of his own life (suffers punishment) or knows himself (in bad conscience), then the working of his fate commences, and this feeling of a life disrupted must become a longing for what has been lost. The deficiency is recognized as part of himself, as what was to have been in him and is not.[16]

It is most important to see that in this case, although the criminal suffers as a result of his act, he does not interpret his experience in terms of self-interest. The deficiency he experiences does not result from a sacrifice of his own particular interests to those of the universal moral law. The object destroyed by the trespass is neither the well-being of the individual self as opposed to others, nor the moral law as opposed to the self. Rather, it is the 'friendliness of life' which includes self and other. The longing for what has been lost is the longing for the friendly context of life which through his *own* act the criminal has disrupted, or distorted, into something alien. Hence the fear of the criminal is not directed towards an avenging force that pre-existed his act and remained external to it – as it is in the case where the moral source is identified with the law. Rather, the criminal's fear of punishment as fate is a 'fear of a separation, an awe of *one's self*';[17] he makes himself into his own enemy by separating himself from, and thereby making an enemy of, what was to have been but is not a friendly context or totality of life. For this reason, the moral significance of his act is not primarily the annulment of an external moral law but the *diremption* of a shared ethical totality.

In experiencing his punishment as a fate, the criminal longs for a return to an ethical totality, a friendly context of life, from which he has become 'split-off' as a result of his act. But since the friendly context of life is a *totality*, it follows that all other parties suffer the consequence. Not just the criminal and the victim, but all other members of the ethical community are implicated. The avenging force of punishment is thus also fateful in that it draws in all parties to the moral relation, even those who are innocent of any crime. In this sense, others also find themselves in a position of responsibility 'as an inescapable fate'. The necessity of fate, therefore, does not have the inevitability of the punishment that awaits the criminal seen from the point of view of the law. For the fate of the criminal is not just his. It is rather a collective fate for which there is collective responsibility. That is not to say, to return to the first of Hegel's contrasts, that justice is compromised by fate, since 'even in the hostility of fate a man has a sense of just punishment'.[18] The point is that this hostility is not *grounded* in the moral law. Rather, it owes its origin to a more primordial ethical totality presupposed in the experience of a dirempted life avenging itself as a fate. For Hegel, 'the law is later than life and outflanked by it', 'the law is only the lack of life, defective life appearing as a power'.[19]

In this manner, Hegel contrasts 'life' with 'law' as moral sources. Whereas law opposes the universality of the divine will and duty to the particularity of human need and inclination, in life these oppositions are reconciled. The issue of reconciliation cannot even be broached from within the law-based framework of morality. For the opposition between universal and particular, which is so decisive for the structure of morality as law, only arises from a forgetfulness or suppression of life as a moral source. For Hegel, 'only through a departure from that united life which is neither regulated by law nor at variance with law, only through the killing of life, is something alien produced'.[20] In other words, behind morality as an alien imposition of external rules and laws lies the occlusion of a vital force that joins the particularity of freedom with the universality of solidarity. Hegel refers to this force as self-moving 'life', 'faith' and 'love'.

Now Habermas has always acknowledged the force of the young Hegel's exposition of the weaknesses in the Kantian conception of the basis of morality. In particular, Habermas identifies those inadequacies that result from Kant's abstraction of moral action from the concrete inclinations that motivate it, and from his separation of the form of duty from the specific, context-dependent content of its application. Perhaps more importantly, Habermas is opposed to the abstraction of the self's autonomous will from the complex intersubjective nexus within which the self is formed. And it is precisely the emergence of moral identity out of a destroyed intersubjective nexus of mutual recognition that Habermas takes to be the central insight of Hegel's reflections. In the causality of fate, Habermas writes,

> the power of suppressed life is at work, which can only be reconciled, when, out of the experience of the negativity of a sundered life, the longing for that which has been lost arises and necessitates identifying one's own denied identity in the alien existence one fights against. Then both parties recognize the hardened positions taken against each other to be the result of a separation, the abstraction from the common interconnection of their lives – and within this, in the dialogic relationship of recognizing oneself in the other, they experience the common basis of their existence.[21]

In this passage, Habermas gives Hegel's view of moral identity a powerful re-articulation. For Hegel, morality and identity must be synthesized. The separation of the sense of self from the demands of morality corresponds to a diremption within a community (or 'ethical totality') of self and other. So long as morality is experienced as a system of impositions, the claims of others will impinge merely externally on the individual subject. But for others to impinge externally on the self is for them to be experienced as restrictions on the freedom of the self and hence to appear as hostile. Conversely, where morality is external to identity the punishment for breaking the moral law appears as the retribution of a wronged, generalized and alien other. However, it is just the feelings of loss and negativity that arise in face of this hostile fate that promise to redeem the self by reintegrating it with the other at a higher level. This way of synthesizing morality and identity does not involve a subsumption of the particular under the universal since the particular individual only 'comes to himself' – that is to say, only comes to enjoy recognition as such – by being reunited with a communal 'life'. All these points are here forcefully re-endorsed by Habermas.

But when Hegel refers to 'life', he is following the Romantics in positing a moral source. That is to say, life possesses unconditional worth; but it is also something which the self must be in contact with in order for it to realize its *own* worth. Life for the young Hegel is a constitutive good; it is what some, maybe all, good things owe their goodness to; it is that in virtue of which they are *affirmable*. But it also facilitates goodness: attunement with or love of life empowers authentic self-realization. Since life is a moral source, not to be in contact with it implies self-loss. Conversely, to be reunited with life is to achieve self-repossession. In his later work, Hegel distances himself from this early Romanticism by substituting for life a notion of rational Spirit (Geist). Now although Habermas is critical of the particular *conception* of reason Hegel deploys, *he too* will attempt to reformulate the normative content of 'life' in terms of the obligations of rational action.[22] For only in this way, Habermas believes, can the binding force of the moral demand be made both determinate and universal. But on the assumption that the cosmological paradigm of reason as the order of being is non-viable, Habermas maintains that reason can retain determinacy and universality only by becoming procedural. As we shall see in the next two chapters, it is by resort to such a procedural model of rationality that Habermas seeks to move beyond hermeneutics in his later work. It is worth noting at this point, however, that a procedural conception of reason looks far from suited for taking up the work done by the young Hegel's notion of 'life', since it is hard to see how reason, understood procedurally, can function as a moral source.

This is not a problem that obviously afflicts Habermas's earlier attempt at clarifying the intelligibility of moral identity by means of the young Hegel's idea of the causality of fate. For the insight to which deep hermeneutic reflection is supposed to lead actually puts the subject back in touch with a suppressed ethical totality. According to Habermas, the self-repossession that is the goal of an analysis can only occur once the subject learns to see its hostile, alien, unconscious other as the product of a diremption and identifies passionately with it. It is in this way that psychoanalytic reflection tracks the peculiar logic of the causality of fate and implicates its operation in actual self-formative processes.

HABERMAS, HEGEL AND FREUD

In the Freud chapters of *Knowledge and Human Interests* Habermas sets out the following argument. If Freud was *theoretically* correct in inferring a dynamic of inner conflict from phenomena of resistance within a subject's psyche to part of its own content, and if, by means of an act of communicated recollection on the part of the subject herself, he was *therapeutically* successful in undoing this resistance, then the dynamic of pathological inner conflict and emancipatory reconciliation, of illness and cure, must be articulable by the critical concepts of self-recognition and self-responsibility. But since self-recognition is possible only within an intersubjective context of shared linguistic rules, the private dynamic of inner conflict, resistance, pathological self-misrecognition and curative reflection will refer to a public dynamic of a distorted and reconstituted *grammar*. If so, Habermas argues, Freud was mistaken in presenting psychoanalysis as a science on a par with modern physics or biology. To think of psychoanalysis as such a science, to interpret the subject's predicament as determined by the law-like causality of the instincts, is to make the subject's misery comparable to what Hegel described as the suffering of the criminal before an alien, unbending penal law. For Habermas, on the other hand, the predicament facing the subject of analysis is that of a hostile fate. The common fate of Freud's analysand and Hegel's criminal, on Habermas's account, is the suffering of an excommunication, which means an alienation not from an external moral or libidinal law, but from an integrated, that is to say non-dirempted, course of life or 'ethical totality'.

With this overview in place, let us now try to unpack the key moves in Habermas's reading of Freud. 'The starting point of psychoanalytical theory', for Habermas's purposes, 'is the blocking force that stands in the way of free and public communication' of a class of psychic contents.[23] Restraint in communicating episodes in our psychic life is often voluntary; words can hurt, and aware of the social and moral pressures to avoid harm, we can choose not to express them. But in the situation of dialogue between analyst and analysand, customary restrictions on communication are bracketed. We have an 'experimental' situation in which the 'initial conditions' are designed to enable the analysand truthfully to communicate his or her mental history to the analyst. Psychoanalytical theory begins with experiences of resistance *here*. In the situation of dialogue between analyst and analysand, empirical data in the form of amnesias in the recounted mental history of the patient are interpreted as evidence of resistance within the patient to key episodes in that history. The twofold task of the psychoanalytical technique is first, to overcome this resistance, and second, to get 'behind the back' of apparent, manifest meanings by interpreting their hidden, latent content.

Overcoming resistance, on Habermas's view, involves neutralizing a blocking force to the communication of lost psychic contents. Given the initial conditions of the psychoanalytical situation – namely, the bracketing of habitual communicative restraints – the resistance encountered *between* the analyst and analysand in their cooperative effort at recollection can be seen as reflecting the unconscious resistance at work within the analysand to the same phenomenon. As is well known, Freud theorizes this resistance as repression. According to Habermas's interpretation of Freud, the class of psychic contents that is resistant to *free* and *public* communication in the analytical situation corresponds to that content of the mind that is resistant to *conscious* expression. Psychic content, on the Freudian model, is both affective and symbolic. It includes needs, desires, as well as cognitions. However, we can only talk about an affective content of the *mind*, Habermas thinks, to the extent that affects are attached to the specific *form* of mental operations. As the mind operates by way of symbols articulated in a language, so the affective content of the mind must be symbolically or linguistically mediated.

But if psychic contents are linguistic in constitution, and if, as Habermas maintains, language is constitutively a public practice of rule-governed communication, what bearing does this have on the 'repressed' content of the mind? In Habermas's view, it means that the repressed content of the mind corresponds to just those need dispositions which, in the course of the formation of the individual's psyche, are expelled from the public space of language. On this account, repressed content arises as the symbols through which needs are interpreted become 'split-off' from the public rules that form the grammar of 'the ongoing text of our everyday language games'.[24] Since we understand our *own* motives, actions and patterns of expression according to these rules, then those motives and actions the interpretations of which are excluded from the public space of language will appear incomprehensible even to ourselves. This, according to Habermas, is precisely the incomprehensibility of the unconscious. Hence the resistance that is the starting point of psychoanalytical theory – namely, the resistance to free and public communication of repressed psychic contents – corresponds to the resistance of the unconscious content of the mind to consciousness as such.

Comprehending the unconscious is of course the second task of the psychoanalytical technique. The task is manageable on the assumption that need dispositions expelled into the unconscious continue to leave their trace. 'Because the symbols that interpret suppressed needs are excluded from public communication', Habermas writes, '*the speaking and acting subject's communication with himself is interrupted*',[25] and this interruption in the communicatively mediated self-formative process has considerable repercussions upon the subject's identity. It is through the 'depth interpretation' of these repercussions that the lost content may be retrieved and the subject's communication with himself continued. In extreme cases, such as neuroses, the repercussions manifest themselves pathologically as 'symptoms'. Following Freud, Habermas theorizes the neurotic symptom as a defence mechanism of substitute gratification for early experiences of traumatically suppressed needs. But more distinctively Habermasian is the view that symptoms, such as compulsive repetitions, phobias and obsessional fixations, are distorted expressions of dispositions the interpretation of which has been expelled from the public space of meaning. The subject does not understand why she repetitively and compulsively acts in ways that defy her conscious preferences and beliefs. Nor does mere awareness of this discrepancy enable the subject to change her actions in accordance with her beliefs. Symptoms can therefore be understood as actions or texts that belie the subject's conscious motivations; they appear to impress themselves onto the subject, so to speak, from the outside.

The symptoms and conscious intentions of the subject belie the dispositions that motivate them in the sense that the latter are expressed in a disguised and distorted form. But if symptoms, as Habermas has claimed, are distortions arising from a splitting-off of the need disposition from everyday language, then the peculiar task of psychoanalytical interpretation is that of translating from the privatized or 'degrammatized' text of the symptom (or in normal cases, the dream) to a public language of linguistically statable intentions. The interpretive task involves 'translating symbols from a mode of expression deformed as a private language into the mode of expression of public communication', thus bringing 'to consciousness the person's own self-formative process'.[26] Translation is possible precisely because the distortions of the subject's text are not arbitrary. The distortions are meaningful as such in that they both resist conscious articulation – that is, expression according to shared linguistic rules – and reveal this resistance in disguise. This is one reason why psychoanalytical interpretation takes on a peculiar character. As Habermas puts it, 'the omissions and distortions' psychoanalytical interpretation rectifies 'have a systematic role and function. For the symbolic structures that psychoanalysis seeks to comprehend are corrupted by the impact of *internal* conditions'.[27] The meaning of such systematically distorted structures is opaque to the subject even though the subject is the author of them. And this gives rise to a second peculiarity of the psychoanalytic interpretation. For suppressed meanings can be made transparent, Habermas believes, only by way of an interpretation that simultaneously *explains the origin* of their opacity. The self-understanding generated in the analysis 'makes accessible the meaning of specifically incomprehensible forms of expression only to the extent to which it is possible to clarify the conditions for the emergence of non-sense in conjunction with the original scene'.[28]

But if the distortions are not accidental, what kind of 'necessity' is operative here? To answer this question we need to recall that the primary phenomenon Habermas wants to account for is the *externally* compelling character of the unconscious. Habermas invokes Freud's phrase 'internal foreign territory' to describe the phenomenon of symptoms.[29] They are foreign because they are not recognizable as the subject's own, they need translation into a language the subject understands. Yet they are internal because they are also an integral, though fragmented, expression of the subject. More generally, the compulsive force of the unconscious is experienced as external to the subject in that it manifests itself in actions and dispositions that are incomprehensible and threatening to the subject, even though these actions and dispositions are an undeniable part of that subject's identity. It is this externality of the compulsion that tempted Freud to think of the causality of the unconscious in terms of the naturalistic concept of instinct. To the extent that instinct determines behaviour, the subject's fate is ultimately in the hands of those mechanistic laws prevailing in disenchanted nature. Although, on Freud's view, scientific knowledge of the laws of nature might enable us to re-channel the flow of instinctual forces, the laws themselves are unalterable.

Habermas objects to Freud's naturalistic construal of the externality of the unconscious on the following counts. First, he claims that the concept of instinct is inapplicable to specifically *mental* contents. For Habermas, human experiences of all kinds – of love, aggression, even hunger – have some interpretive mediation, however minimal, rudimentary or diminished. Indeed, he suggests that it is only because human beings have such interpretively diminished experiences that the concept of instinct finds any application at all.[30] But whatever the applicability of the concept of instinct in general, Habermas regards it as unsuited for making sense of *human* experience because of the way it divorces mental content from its distinctive linguistic character. In this connection, Habermas opposes a pseudo-natural causality of instincts to a 'causality of fate' that 'prevails through the symbolic means of the mind'.[31]

If, in the present context, Habermas's idea of a causality of fate went no further than this, it would merely reiterate the familiar philosophical view that symbolic representations, considered as reasons, can be causes of actions without nomologically determining them. That is to say, the causality supposed to prevail through the symbolic medium of the mind would be distinct from the causality of nature simply in so far as reasons are not connected with the actions they cause in a law-like manner.

But the point of Habermas's claim that the connection between a symptom-action, original repressed desire and defensive reaction does not display the invariance of a natural law is rather different. For in this case, the 'causal' element relates to reasons that have become *split-off* from actions and dispositions in the course of the subject's self-formative process. For Habermas, we have seen, the unconscious corresponds to that content of the mind suppressed by being exiled from the public space of linguistic meanings. As the reactive force of excommunicated reasons for acting, symptom-behaviour appears necessary, law-like and external. In fact, however, the sequence of repressed desire, defensive reaction and symptom exhibits not the law-like regularity of natural events but 'the spontaneously generated invariance of life-history'.[32] This brings us to the crucial retort Habermas makes to the naturalistic, instinct model of the unconscious: the subject's power to change the course of her life-history by way of self-reflection in the analytical situation. If the causality of symptoms were that of disenchanted nature, Habermas argues, they would be treatable by way of a mechanical procedure that could in principle be repeated in all like cases to similar effect. But this is not the case with the therapeutic achievement. The psychoanalytic therapy requires an act of self-reflection by the analysand to be successful, and for this, as Habermas insists, there can be no technical substitute. On the contrary, the goal of the therapy, on Habermas's view, lies just in emancipating the subject from her apparent 'objectification'. The act of reflection brings about a *reconciliation* between the conscious self and those symbols and motives that have 'gone underground' and which appear as alien to the subject while belonging to him. Self-reflection 'transforms the pathological state of compulsion and self-deception into the state of superseded conflict and reconciliation with excommunicated language'.[33]

So for Habermas, the 'cure' of analytical reflective insight is intelligible only if the 'cause' is attributable not to instincts exercising their force externally to the subject but to a division or diremption within the subject itself. The subject is cured once reconciliation between the dirempted fragments is achieved. The therapy works by undoing the original process of splitting-off and thereby reconstituting a *'grammatical* connection between symbols'.[34] But what special property of this recollective act allows the reversal to come about? As Habermas reads Freud, the answer lies in the peculiar context of the reflection: the 'transference' situation. During the course of an analysis, the analysand can come to transfer his or her reaction to the symptom-forming occasion from the original traumatic scene to the artificially controlled analysis situation. Analytical self-reflection renders the latent meaning behind the apparently irrational and misery-inducing symptom comprehensible 'by reference to the unmutilated meaning of the original scene in infancy'.[35] This 'scenic understanding' is rendered possible under the presupposition that an *equivalence* is established between the everyday symptomatic scene, the transference scene, and the original scene. As we have noted, the suspension of customary normative constraints weakens the analysand's resistance to recollecting the original scene. But only with the help of the reconstructions suggested by the analyst, and only when 'confronted with the results of his action in transference', can the analysand come to recall the lost portion of his or her mental history.

It is crucial to the logic of this situation that the act of self-reflection, by virtue of which the analysand can emancipate himself from his illness, requires an encounter with an *other* through whom the analysand can recognize the split-off part of himself as his own. The analysand's achievement of self-consciousness – which is to say the undoing of the unconscious that has become lost to the self – is *constitutively* an achievement of mutual recognition made possible by communication in a shared, public language. Moreover, for successful therapy to be possible, for self-reflection to have its emancipating effect, it must have a real affective–motivational base in the analysand. At one level, there must be a passion for self-knowledge that is strong enough to overcome resistance. But more fundamentally, Habermas observes, there must be a 'passion for critique'. That is to say, in order to emancipate himself from his illness through self-reflection, the analysand must take *responsibility* for that which, like Hegel's criminal, 'was to be in him but which is not'.[36] And it is this adoption of 'moral responsibility for the content of the illness' demanded of the analysand which results, by way of that form of self-reflection called scenic understanding, in the shattering or disenchantment of the causality of fate.

> For the insight to which analysis is to lead is indeed only this: that the ego of the patient recognize itself in its other, represented by its illness, as in *its own* alienated self and identify with it. As in Hegel's dialectic of the moral life, the criminal recognizes in his victim his own annihilated essence; in this self-reflection the abstractly divorced parties recognize the destroyed moral totality as their common basis *and thereby* return to it.[37]

On Habermas's view, therefore, the scenic understanding reached in the dialogue between analyst and analysand moves beyond hermeneutics by tracking and disenchanting the causality of fate. But how plausible is Habermas's reconstruction of the logic of the analytical achievement? And how closely does it correspond to the dialectic of moral identity formation outlined by Hegel? On the one hand, it might be thought that Habermas's attempt to understand psychoanalysis by means of the Hegelian ideas of ethical totality, diremption and fateful reconciliation is misconceived from the start. It could be argued, for instance, that Habermas's Hegelian point of departure reinforces just those inflated metaphysical notions of human subjectivity and freedom which Freudian metapsychology implacably opposes. By emphasizing the role of reflection and recognition, it might seem, Habermas misleadingly understates the importance of *natural* forces in shaping the subject's self-formative process. On the other hand, it could also be argued that Habermas's reading of Freud does not lean on Hegel far enough; that it is *too* naturalistic to make sense of the self-productive and self-responsible activity of an analysis. This line of thought would also question whether the emancipatory effect of the scenic understanding really does amount to evidence of a transcendence of the hermeneutic situation. If we were to take this line, we might also wonder if Habermas's conviction that deep hermeneutic knowledge is constituted by a qualitatively distinct 'cognitive interest' does not lead him to exaggerate at a metatheoretical level the difference between the Freudian and young Hegelian accounts of disturbed and restored moral identity. In the next section I want to explore these two objections to Habermas's depth hermeneutic interpretation of psychoanalysis a little further.[38]

NORM, NATURE AND RECOGNITION

The first kind of criticism, that by reconstructing the normative achievement of therapy solely along the lines of a struggle for recognition Habermas intellectualizes and neutralizes nature, has been put by Russell Keat.[39] According to Keat, Habermas's approach is insufficiently naturalistic. By taking the domain of therapeutic understanding as the realm of a causality of fate, Keat claims, Habermas posits an incoherent alternative to the world of natural, causally determinate laws. This in turn blinds Habermas, Keat suggests, to therapeutic practices that rely for their success precisely on technologically exploitable knowledge of nature. Keat then imputes this blindness to a misleading conception of emancipation – the goal of therapy on Habermas's account. As Keat reads Habermas, emancipation is called for in face of 'the apparent objectivity of alienated, reified human *subjectivity*'.[40] According to Keat, this view commits Habermas from the start to an idea of emancipation rooted in a dualistic ontology of subjects and objects. The unconscious corresponds to alienated, reified subjectivity in so far as it takes up the stubborn appearance of an object following its own, external laws of behaviour. In Keat's opinion, Habermas traces the emancipatory effect of psycho-analytical reflection to an overcoming of the unconscious understood as this alien domain of law. Habermas construes the success of therapy, as Keat puts it, in terms of the subject's removal 'from the deterministic realm of causality'.[41] Keat presents the following passage as evidence of Habermas's commitment to this view.

> In technical control over nature we get nature to work for us through our knowledge of causal connections. Analytic insight, however, affects the causality of the unconscious as such. Psychoanalytical therapy is not based, like somatic medicine, which is 'causal' in the narrower sense, on making use of known causal connections. Rather it owes its efficacy to overcoming causal connections themselves.[42]

On Keat's interpretation, Habermas is thereby committed to the thesis that critical, emancipatory knowledge is directed towards the 'abolition of what only appear to be genuinely causal determinants'.[43] Against this view, Keat objects first that there are many manifestations of the unconscious, such as dreams and jokes, which cannot in any plausible sense be construed as 'pathological', as something to be 'cured'. Second, he rejects Habermas's identification of alienated, unfree subjectivity with causally determined action. For Keat, the causal determinations of human behaviour are, in principle, as susceptible to scientific investigation as any other part of nature. But this position does not entail, *pace* Habermas, the abolition of human freedom, since knowledge of causes can remove hindrances to purposive action. The domain of therapeutic reason is not pseudo-causality, on this view, but the competing causalities of different natural desires.

However, it seems to me that Keat's objections are misplaced. Regarding the first, Habermas explicitly accepts that the dream is 'the "normal model" of pathological conditions'.[44] His position is that dreams follow a pattern that has the same structure of 'pathologically distorted meaning' as symptoms – namely, the disguised manifestation of motives that have been excluded from the public space of language. So although dreams are the 'normal' case, they are nevertheless only possible given an infantile history of conflictual and traumatic will-formation.[45] Although dreams and symptoms show a functional convergence – they both compensate for repression – in the case of symptoms the compensatory mechanism issues in a *crisis of identity* that impels a certain *passion for critique*. Recall that the point of therapy on Habermas's account is not simply the *removal* of the symptomatic behaviour. It is rather to enable a *reconciliation* of the conscious agent with his unconscious or 'split-off' past.

The force of Keat's second objection turns on the meaning he gives to Habermas's reference to the 'overcoming' of causal connections in the passage cited above. But it is arguable that his interpretation conflates Habermas's point with the Kantian supposition that the category of causality is only applicable to the realm of phenomena as distinct from the noumenal realm of the transcendental will. Habermas does not maintain that the subject really inhabits a noumenal realm that only appears objectified under pathological conditions of alienation and reification. What Habermas *does* claim is that since the human self-formative process is mediated by language, peculiar constraints are imposed on the categories that can legitimately be used for comprehending its disturbance. The crucial point is that at the therapeutic level, 'overcoming' the disturbance renders articulate what was otherwise unfathomable. It is achieved 'dialogically', in a moment of reflection which simultaneously heightens self-consciousness and motivates altered behaviour through the affective content of what is brought to consciousness. The overcoming requires some responsibility on the part of the subject, who must act as if things could be otherwise if the therapy is to be efficacious. This is different to a patient acting as if, say, a cancer tumour is not going to develop, and it is a difference that is rightly registered at the metatheoretical level.

Keat also criticizes Habermas for simplifying the normative complexity and ambiguity of the therapeutic process by modelling it exclusively around the goal of subjective emancipation. After inviting us to consider cases where therapy emancipates the individual subject but only by encouraging him to oppress or exploit others, Keat concludes that 'achieving therapeutic autonomy is consistent with the adoption and practice by an "emancipated" patient of attitudes and values that are by no means unobjectionable'.[46] Consequently he finds it difficult to see 'how their acceptability or unacceptability can be determined without going well beyond the normative concepts illustrated by the model of psychoanalysis'.[47] But emancipation as it is understood according to Habermas's Hegelian reading of Freud is precisely not normatively naïve in the sense Keat alleges. For it involves recognition of the individual's immanence within a virtual ethical totality that is *itself* avenged in the individual's self-alienation prior to the therapy. This means, on the one hand, that the conscious self gains emancipation only by way of an acknowledgement of something other to it. On the other hand, it means that emancipation from unconscious dependencies represents only *one* moment of the normative structure that Habermas takes to be illustrated in the model of psychoanalysis. As Habermas puts it, 'the virtual totality that is sundered by splitting-off is represented by the model of pure communicative action'.[48] But alienated subjectivity is only one expression of this rupture. The key normative concept which Habermas takes to be illustrated by the model of psychoanalysis is intact or undamaged *intersubjectivity*, as represented by the concept of pure communicative action. The exploitative practices Keat suggests are consistent with the achievement of therapeutic success themselves transgress the normative model of an intact intersubjectivity to which Habermas appeals, as the analogy with the criminal who revokes the principle of ethical community makes clear. There are *other* ways, Habermas maintains, in which the diremption of a communicatively mediated ethical totality occasions disturbances in self-formative processes.[49]

While Keat's main objection is that Habermas's approach fails to address the fact that psychopathologies have natural causes, the depth hermeneutical reading of Freud can also be criticized for being *too* naturalistic. This is because for Habermas psychoanalytical self-reflection acquires its explanatory power by virtue of combining hermeneutic interpretation of apparently incomprehensible behaviour with empirical scientific insight into the causal origin of that incomprehensibility. To be sure, the imputed explanatory insight does not involve the covering of a particular event by a law-like generalization. Nor does therapy involve the technical manipulation of efficient causes. None the less, Habermas supposes both that there is a *determinable* split-off symbol and repressed motive which avenges itself in the fate of the analysand, and that this fate is disenchanted, to emancipatory effect, when it is 'recovered' in the analysis. Only on the supposition of a re-internalization of given excommunicated needs, Habermas believes, can the continuation of a disturbed self-formative process count as the criterion of validation for the theoretically constituted narrative of self-formation. These claims have been powerfully contested by Jay Bernstein. I would now like briefly to consider the arguments he marshals for questioning, on the one hand, the plausibility of the naturalistic assumption built into the former thesis (that the misery-inducing emotion has a determinable and recoverable identity), and on the other, its compatibility with the hermeneutic claim expressed in the latter (that the general psychoanalytical theory has validity as a practically productive self-interpretation).

Borrowing a formulation from Amelie Rorty, Bernstein maintains that the task of psychoanalysis is to identify 'the intentional component of the significant cause of the dispositional set that forms the intentional component of the (anomalous, intractable, misery-inducing) emotion'.[50] As the analysand may be aware, the intentional component of the neurotic feelings is not their apparent object. Rather, the object of the emotion refers back to a disturbance in the dispositional state of the subject, the particular nature of which the analysand is not aware. This is because the disturbance has a remote cause. But it is a significant cause in virtue of its intentional component: there are objects to the traumatic emotional conflict of the original childhood scene. As a result of this conflict, Habermas holds, the intentional object of the emotion becomes split-off from the emotion. The resultant disturbance in the dispositional set renders the actual meaning of the neurotic symptoms intractable. In the transference scene, according to Habermas, equivalence is established between the everyday expression of the disturbed need disposition in symptoms and the original significant cause of that disturbance.

But as Bernstein notes, Habermas's claim that equivalence can be established fits ill with the vague, under-determined nature of the intentional components of the misery-inducing emotions in question. Even if the criteria of correct identification were uncontroversial and determinate, the expectation of equivalence would be unreasonable given the remoteness of the phenomena to be retrieved. But no such criteria are available anyway: there is no neutral position outside the various psychoanalytical interpretive schema by which to specify the intentional component in question. This 'theory-ladenness' applies to the correct description of the latent intentional object of the currently disturbed need disposition as well as to the object of the remote significant cause of the disturbance. But in neither case can the identification simply be a matter of neutral, empirical discovery. Habermas's 'deep hermeneutic' construal of the scenic understanding is problematic because the criteria for determining equivalence are not independent of the interpretative schema through which intractable emotions and need-dispositions are identified. Moreover, Bernstein suggests, the intentional objects, and therefore the emotions and dispositions themselves, can hardly be said *to exist* independently of the schema. Different psychoanalytical theories are not, strictly speaking, *empirically* equivalent but incompatible. For 'what these reflective theories are about', Bernstein suggests, 'becomes different as the theories are accepted and so become true'.[51] But if there is a truth of the matter here, if psychoanalytical self-interpretations do admit of cognitive validity, and if the existence of the object-domain of psychoanalytic self-reflection 'is contingent upon the acceptance of the theory', in what can this validity consist, and in what sense can that domain be said to exist at all?

The validity, we have just seen, cannot reside in the re-representation of a split-off symbol; the conditions of acceptability of an analytical interpretation do not lie in an accurate representation of a determinable past. Rather, Bernstein observes, the truth of the self-reflection has a *practical*, productive character. It is fundamental to Habermas's view that analytical self-reflection is undertaken in the context of some pressing practical need. Therapeutic success presupposes a passion for critique, a resolve to settle accounts with certain aspects of one's life-history, with recurrent feelings, emotions and irrational behaviours. The conditions of acceptability for analytic insights must therefore have some affective basis. Success requires more than just correct beliefs about one's past; it requires passionately charged insight into the significance of dispositions as they are revealed to play a role in one's life as a whole. Since the 'as a whole' projects into future life, it orients the agent *to become* a certain kind of person. According to Habermas, deep hermeneutic self-critique seeks to dispel particular illusions within the totality of a course of life by way of a scientific explanation of their causal origin. But as Bernstein reminds us, the *practical* task of dispelling those particular self-deceptions is 'always already' oriented to the horizon of selfhood immanent to the interpretive framework of the theoretically mediated self-reflection. That is to say, the very identification of the cause of the disturbance in the self-formative process is *internally* related to the practical orientation provided by the theory. The criterion of emancipation is therefore not independent of the framework of interpretation within which the self regains its identity.

The refusal to posit a self that can be referred to as emancipated without further reference to frameworks of self-interpretation is of course a defining characteristic of strong hermeneutics. To the extent that Habermas's model of the scenic understanding presupposes the existence of pre-interpretively given and reproducible meanings, it veers from hermeneutics. Habermas's model also marks a departure from hermeneutics in so far as it presents the explanatory function of the self-transformative recollection on the one side, and the broader, normatively orienting function of horizons of self-understanding on the other, as fundamentally different *in kind*. But it is just these two properties of the 'depth' hermeneutic model – properties that allegedly transport psychoanalysis to the outer regions of hermeneutics if not quite beyond it – that seem so questionable.

In other respects though, Habermas's reading of Freud is profoundly hermeneutic. We have already noted Habermas's staunch opposition to biologism, his insistence on the interpretation-ladenness of motivationally potent, action-orienting instinctual drives, and his reading of the clinical context as a site of a hermeneutic praxis. Bernstein's reflections on Habermas show clearly that the scenic understanding enables the self-formative process to proceed anew – it enables the subject to continue her interrupted communication with herself – by providing a new framework of self-interpretation. But this is only possible if the analysand already has a will to change herself, it presupposes what Habermas calls a passion for critique. With hermeneutics and the young Hegel, Habermas insists that the identity of the self is internally related to this passion and so to its moral responsibility. The self is something that must interpret and be capable of reinterpreting its needs according to narratives that can retrospectively distinguish between a more or less fulfilled life. On the other hand, however, we should not let the constitutive, productive and transfigurative character of psychoanalytic reflection deflect attention from the real *limits to contingency* that are revealed by the original therapeutic need – that is to say, by the passion for critique itself. It is at precisely this juncture, incidentally, that Bernstein's own model of hermeneutic self-reflection is to be found wanting. For his well-motivated critique of the tacit objectivism and naturalism of Habermas's reading of Freud goes uncompensated for by a consideration of the *anthropological* basis of the need for recognition.[52] This is not to say that human nature is fixed and therefore a suitable object of empirical science. Nor is it to say that true theories of self-formative processes must converge into a single, unified account. Rather it is simply to take seriously the idea that pathologies *impose themselves* on the afflicted self-interpreting subject. If, following Bernstein, we assume that the plurality and indeterminacy of psychoanalytical self-interpretations undermine their claim to realism, we may be tempted to infer that the pathological effects of disturbed self-formative processes are also invented. But if realism itself is divorced from the naturalistic paradigm, as I suggested it should be in the last chapter, then discourses with a genuine realist claim need not be embarrassed by the absence of absolute, fully determinate criteria of validation. The crucial point for strong hermeneutics is that pathologies provide evidence of a real linkage between moral identity, mutual recognition and human need. It is in virtue of this connection that there exist limits to the contingency of self-formative processes. When the link is severed, the causality of fate begins.

What then is it for the causality of fate to be disenchanted? We can now distinguish two apparently competing answers Habermas offers to this question. Both appeal to the idea that the causality of fate appears 'behind the backs' of subjects and requires theoretical insight in order to be disenchanted. To the extent to which Habermas draws from the young Hegel, he claims that the insight into the common interconnection of lives – the cognition of the shared basis of human existence – when supported by a longing for what has been lost when this basis is revoked, *thereby* effects reconciliation with the ruptured ethical totality. This form of disenchantment is a matter of *hermeneutic* insight. On the other hand, however, Habermas appeals to a form of theoretical knowledge that disenchants by virtue of exposing pseudo-objectifications, by dispelling the illusion of nature-like necessity in the self-formative process. This kind of insight reconstructs distortions in the linguistic mediation of subjects within the framework of a theory of communicative competence. In the act of deep hermeneutic self-reflection, the two moments of the rational reconstruction of communicative competence and self-transfigurative, productive interpretation are supposed to be joined. But as we have seen, this synthesis creates tensions in Habermas's model of deep hermeneutics. In his later work, Habermas will separate out the supposedly autonomous moments of rational and hermeneutic reflection more radically. That is to say, he will attempt to resolve the ambiguities in his deep hermeneutic model by seeking out the contingency-transcending constitution of morality on the *other* side of hermeneutics.

5 Communication and the contingency of language

'The human interest in autonomy and responsibility is not mere fancy, for it can be apprehended a priori. What raises us out of nature is the only thing whose nature we can know: language. Through its nature autonomy and responsibility are posited for us'.[1] So runs Habermas's boldest and most frequently cited thesis. The human claim to a moral identity, Habermas is saying, does not rest on contingently occurring wants. The happening and satisfaction of wants, in humans or other animals, is intelligible as an event in disenchanted nature. However, if Habermas is right, the interest in autonomy and responsibility has a quite different kind of intelligibility. For language beings, autonomy and responsibility are posited irrespective of what nature holds for them. There is something about the structure of language as such, Habermas is claiming, that situates the beings who use it in moral space. It is as occupants of that space, as bearers of autonomy and responsibility, that humans are raised out of the realm of more or less efficiently satisfied contingently occurring interests. And it is a non-contingent fact *about* language that those who use it are so situated.

According to the deep hermeneutics of *Knowledge and Human Interests*, a pure communicative dialogue situation represents the site of a struggle for recognition whereby moral identity is regained through theoretically mediated self-reflection. Habermas's talk of a deep-rooted anthropological 'interest' in autonomy and responsibility registers that *passion* for critique that leads the subject out of its state of unfreedom and, in a sense, out of the pre-determined course of natural events. In subsequent writings, however, Habermas drops all reference to the emancipatory *interest* as such. He moves away from the project of showing how autonomy and responsibility are non-contingently posited as a matter of the philosophical anthropology of beings constituted by processes of recognition and misrecognition in language, in favour of one concerned to show how autonomy and responsibility can be reconstructed from the rational core of linguistically mediated interaction. Henceforth, Habermas aims to establish that language contains within itself a non-contingent basis for moral identity by way of demonstrating the rationality of the obligations implicitly or tacitly entered into whenever actions are coordinated by purely linguistic means.

According to Habermas's theory, communicative language use, or language used for the sake of reaching an understanding with someone about something in the world, presupposes the applicability of norms that provide the rational core of a moral identity. Habermas calls this kind of language use communicative action, and he terms the kind of rationality proper to it communicative rationality. But not all linguistically mediated interactions are *actually* of this kind, and not all rational uses of language are communicatively rational. Language can be used to coordinate actions independently of any aim to reach an understanding. As well as being communicatively rational, linguistic acts can have strategic rationality; the space they make for moral reasons can also be occupied by instrumental reason. Since it is undeniable that language users often do stand in a space fit for instrumental reason, Habermas feels compelled to show that they are *contingently* so situated *qua* language users. He does this by arguing that communicative interaction is in some sense 'originary' or intrinsic to language use, whereas strategic action is parasitic upon this original mode.

I begin the chapter with a discussion of Habermas's only explicit argument for showing that communicative action is the original mode of language use. I then examine two kinds of objection, which I call 'deconstructivist' and 'agonistic'. These objections, both of which are of weak hermeneutic provenance, find fault with the idea that reaching a consensus is in some sense primary or essential to language use. Although these criticisms do not always hit the mark, they do suggest that Habermas's thesis concerning the primacy of communicative action is in need of further support. I then reconstruct an argument based on Habermas's reading of Wittgenstein's remarks on rule-following that might provide it. According to Habermas, Wittgenstein helps us to see why certain pragmatic idealizations have application in all instances of communicative competence. For the very possibility of a sign having the *same* meaning in different uses, Wittgenstein allegedly shows, points to a formal relation of mutual recognition between speaking and acting subjects. As communication is only possible on the presumption of identical ascriptions of meaning, Habermas argues, so the intersubjectivity of mutual recognition on the basis of grounds is virtual to *sui generis* language use. Using Wittgenstein against this interpretation, I then question whether idealizations of the kind invoked by Habermas are really necessary for language to serve its communicative function. I suggest that to the extent to which Wittgenstein is an ally of strong hermeneutics, he invites us to question the primacy of intentional language *use* – whether consensual *or* agonistic in orientation – over the linguistic disclosure and articulation of significance.

COMMUNICATIVE AND STRATEGIC LANGUAGE USE

Habermas's concept of communicative action is designed to bring out the internal relations between three functions of language.[2] The first function is action-coordination. Language is required if any but the most rudimentary actions are to be coordinated. In processes of linguistic interaction, in the medium of which actions are coordinated in a society, human beings are also socialized and take on individual and collective identities. This is the second function: individuation through socialization. But language is also the medium in which understanding is reached between subjects on the basis of agreements concerning the validity of claims. That is to say, understanding the meanings conveyed by language, through which actions are coordinated and processes of individuation and socialization take place, involves the operation of a reason-giving capacity. The generation of objective meanings and valid claims corresponds to the third function of language. The fact that Habermas's theory of communicative action is at once a theory of action, a theory of society and a theory of meaning, reflects his belief that inseparable connections exist between these three basic linguistic functions.

Habermas's explicit argument for the primacy of communicative language use relates to the first functional aspect of language – action-coordination. By way of developing a theory of action, Habermas proposes that communicative action be distinguished on account of its 'attitude' or 'orientation'.[3] Whereas strategic action is oriented to 'success', communicative action is oriented to 'reaching understanding'. Under standard conditions, these distinct action orientations are identifiable by the actor. When an actor engages in strategic action, he seeks to *influence* an opponent. The purpose for which the action occurs is 'monological' in the sense that it is solely determined by the structure of subjectivity in confrontation with an external, 'objectivized' state of affairs. Habermas therefore classifies strategic action as a species of instrumental action, where another person is the means employed to realize a successful outcome. The rationality of this kind of action is determined solely by the efficiency of means–ends relations. The strategic actor achieves success by 'causally exerting an influence upon others' – that is, by exerting an 'empirical' force on others to act in accord with the strategic actor's goal. Strategic actions are typically mediated by threats and rewards.

Communicative action, on the other hand, is action with the attitude or orientation of reaching understanding. By 'reaching understanding', Habermas means agreement reached between at least two actors on the basis of the mutually acceptable validity of a claim. Communicative action, Habermas claims, is constitutively dialogical in that it is specifiable only in terms of an agreement made *with* another. It is also dialogical in the sense that the agreement is reached solely by virtue of that force which is peculiar to dialogue – the force of the better argument. A communicatively reached agreement is rationally based because it is grounded on the acceptability of a speech act. Each speech act, according to Habermas's model, raises a validity claim. One's partner in communicative action can reject or accept the validity claim raised by taking a 'yes' or 'no' position on it. Under genuine communicative conditions, a 'yes' will not be a mere *de facto* acceptance, and a 'no' will initiate argumentation, or in Habermas's technical sense 'discourse', for the sake of 'redeeming' the validity claim and reaching a communicatively achieved rational consensus. A communicatively reached agreement is distinguished from agreements 'causally induced by outside influence'.

Habermas recognizes that there are, 'without doubt',

> countless cases of indirect understanding, where one subject gives something to understand through signals, indirectly gets him to form a certain opinion or to adopt certain intentions... or where, on the basis of an already habitual communicative practice of everyday life, one subject inconspicuously harnesses another for his purposes, that is, induces him to behave in a desired way by manipulatively employing linguistic means and thereby instrumentalizes him for his own success.[4]

There are countless cases, then, of the strategic use of language in everyday life. Manipulation by linguistic means is a commonplace, as are matter of fact agreements or accords that facilitate action-coordination. But these habitual practices of empirically motivated linguistic instrumentalization, Habermas argues, are in some sense contingent upon the logic of communicatively rational practices. According to this argument, the strategic use of language, the use of language oriented to the successful manipulation and control of an opponent according to a monologically determined goal, is 'parasitic' upon the 'original' communicative use of language (oriented to reaching consensus). The claim that 'the use of language with an orientation to reaching understanding is the *original mode* of language use', as Habermas put it in the *Theory of Communicative Action*, 'upon which indirect understanding, giving something to understand or letting something be understood, and the instrumental use of language in general, are parasitic', can be redeemed by means of Austin's distinction between illocutions and perlocutions.[5]

According to Habermas's initial formulation of Austin's distinction, an illocutionary act refers to what is done in delivering an utterance. Under 'standard conditions' – that is, where everyday life contexts and conventions are not bracketed (as, say, in a play) – the illocutionary meaning can be traced to a literally significant performative; for example, an assertion, promise or avowal. The aim of the illocution is self-identifying in that it is manifest in the meaning of the performative verb. The illocutionary aim of 'please get me a glass of water', for instance, is self-identifying as a request. The addressee does not need to go 'behind' the speech act in order to find its meaning *qua illocution*. The meaning of the perlocution, on the other hand, is not transparent in this manner. A description of the perlocutionary act, according to Habermas's initial taxonomy, will include empirical consequences of the happening of the utterance that are only contingently related to the meaning of the performative verb. The perlocution will be successful if it manages to bring about an effect that is only contingently related to the illocutionary aim. In order to be able to talk of the perlocutionary effect as an 'aim', Habermas restricts it to the intention of the actor. The perlocutionary aim of 'please give me a glass of water', for instance, can then be formulated as what I want to get 'by' making the speech act. In this particular example, I may be seeking to get rid of the addressee, to show who's boss, or the like. In the circumstances, I may happen to succeed in bringing about such an end by means of the speech act. But, in contrast to the illocution, the perlocution stands to the end or aim of the speech act merely as a contingent instrument.

Habermas seems to be arguing here that if perlocutions are derivative upon illocutions, *eo ipso* strategic speech action is parasitic upon communicative action. As other commentators have observed, however, Habermas's argument would only work if the distinction between communicative and strategic action were either synonymous with or strictly analogous to the distinction between illocutionary and perlocutionary acts.[6] Prior to demonstrating synonymy or equivalence, the dependence of perlocutionary success on the conditions for successful illocution cannot ground strategic on communicative language use. But even our brief discussion so far suffices to suggest that the distinction between illocutions and perlocutions serves to *elaborate* the distinction between communicative and strategic action rather than to *justify* the priority of the former. As I indicated earlier, for Habermas the 'causality' of linguistically mediated interaction is one of reasons subject to 'external' distortion. The illocutionary force of a speech act is internally related to the meaning of the linguistic utterance, and achieves its coordinating effect between actors by virtue of this connection. Since, for Habermas, a speech actor understands the meaning of the claim raised in an utterance when she or he grasps the conditions of its validity, the causality of the illocutionary effect is validity- or reason-conditioned. The perlocutionary effect, however, owes its existence not to the intrinsic meaning of the speech act offer, not to its validity basis, but to causal powers independent of the (often implicit) warranty to justify the content of the utterance.

The virtual totality of the dialogue situation, then, refers to linguistic interaction in pursuit of exclusively illocutionary effects. Whereas perlocutionary effects 'are intended under the description of states of affairs brought about through intervention in the world', illocutionary results appear 'in the lifeworld to which the participants belong.... They cannot be intended under the description of causally induced effects'.[7] Rather, the illocutionary force of the speech act lies in the bond resulting from the warranty to justify the validity claim offered. This is conceptually independent of the empirically induced bonding of perlocutionary effects. The perlocutionary force of a speech act stands to its content as a *communicatively* 'irrational force' in that it is exerted independent of the redeemability of the validity of that content.

Even if the distinction between illocutions and perlocutions has an elaborative rather than a grounding function in the argument for the primacy of communication, it is far from clear that a substantive demarcation between illocutions and perlocutions can be established according to the criteria Habermas suggests. In Habermas's initial account of these criteria, much turns on an alleged difference in the expressibility of the illocutionary and perlocutionary aim. In this account, the open expression of the perlocutionary aim is self-defeating. Habermas argues that the difference between illocutionary and perlocutionary aims can be seen in the fact that,

> the predicates with which perlocutionary acts are described (to give a fright to, to cause to be upset, to plunge into doubt, to annoy, mislead, offend, infuriate, humiliate and so forth) cannot appear among those predicates used to carry out the illocutionary acts by means of which the corresponding perlocutionary effects can be produced.[8]

If such predicates as these were genuinely representative of perlocutionary effects, then indeed they would be best kept hidden for strategic purposes. But a much different picture emerges if rather than these antagonistic, non-cooperative perlocutionary effects, others such as 'to give relief to', 'to cause to be uplifted', 'to reassure', 'to boost confidence', 'to guide' were taken as exemplary. That they are not suggests that Habermas is *already* committed to the cooperative function of illocutions. Since he wants them distinct from perlocutions, he is blinded to the latter's cooperative potential. At least in his initial formulation, then, Habermas presupposes what he has to establish about the bonding, action-coordinative potential of illocutions as opposed to perlocutions.[9]

The distinction between illocutions and perlocutions really boils down to this: illocutions exploit the validity dimension of language that is irreducible to the causal dimension of language exploited by perlocutions. We should read Habermas's explicit argument for the priority of communication as a hasty attempt at elaborating the difference between communicative and strategic action, rather than as a justification of the priority of the former. Of course, this does not mean that the primacy of communicative action thesis is false. It just means that we have to look elsewhere for supporting arguments. One profitable place to look is Habermas's response to rival conceptions of the roles of consensual and strategic action in language use.

DECONSTRUCTIVE AND AGONISTIC OBJECTIONS TO THE PRIMACY OF COMMUNICATION

In this section, we consider Habermas's reply to two lines of criticism made of his understanding of the roles of consensus and strategy in language. The first takes issue with the very idea of an 'original' mode of language use, by way of highlighting the implicit bias involved in the distinction between 'normal' (consensus oriented) and 'abnormal' (non-consensus oriented) language. We can call this the 'deconstructivist objection'. The second goes by way of offering an alternative model of language that emphasizes and prioritizes precisely its strategic aspect. This view, put forward by Lyotard, I shall call the 'agonistic objection'. Although Lyotard draws upon certain Wittgensteinian themes, his position is quite alien to what can properly be called a Wittgensteinian one. But what can be so called is of no small importance to us. For as I shall go on to argue in the next section, further support for the thesis of the primacy of communication can be teased out of Habermas's interpretation of Wittgenstein's achievements in his remarks on rule-following. I will then return to a third set of objections directed against the adequacy of this interpretation and its implications for understanding the role of consensus in language.

The deconstructivist objection

When Habermas states that communicative action is originary, he is claiming that it must be taken as the normal case of linguistic interaction upon which other cases are parasitic or derivative. Habermas's analysis of communicative action appeals to a notion of a standard speech act that is uttered seriously and used as simply and literally as possible in normal everyday practice. Speech acts not specifiable in this way – such as jokes, playful fantasies, imaginative role-playing, puns and ironies – are thus derivative in that they necessarily presuppose the already established communicative competence of reaching understanding under standard conditions. The deconstructivist objection challenges the assumption of such standard conditions. For the deconstructivist, there is no innocent realm of ordinary language upon which other forms of discourse *can* be parasitic. According to this argument, that which counts as standard or normal reflects a pre-decided evaluative preference of the theorist; in Habermas's case a particular conception of truth, meaning and validity. Indeed the very term 'parasitic' seems to reveal Habermas's devaluation of the non-serious, the abnormal and the marginalized in language. From the deconstructivist's point of view, Habermas's distinction between communicative and strategic action betrays a metaphysical impulse 'to separate intrinsic from extrinsic or pure from corrupt and deem the latter irrelevant' or 'unworthy of separate consideration'.[10] Like all such impulses, it is best subject to a deconstruction that shows up the ever-receding interplay of the centre and the margin – and the arbitrary privileging of the former.

To counter this objection, Habermas can reply that the allegedly 'privileged' signifier in his account of linguistic interaction is by no means arbitrary. For if language is to play its role in the mediation of subjectivity, it must be able to coordinate the everyday interactions of subjects. And the coordination of actions that is a necessary condition of social life – and therefore of an individual's creative linguistic life – is itself conditioned by the presupposition of intersubjectively identical ascriptions of meaning in the content of speech acts. This shared consensus defines the literal meaning of the speech act, it constitutes the meaning exploited by illocutionary force and necessarily emerges under the constraints of rule-bounded action-coordination.

It is thus the *action-coordinative* property of ordinary language that, for Habermas, is at the root of the asymmetry between it and its poetic/fictive derivatives. These derivatives gain their power partly from the bracketing or withdrawal of the illocutionary force with which they are normally deployed for the sake of action-coordination in everyday life. Illocutionary forces can be bracketed where speech acts are relieved of the pressure of action-coordination. Even in contexts where the particular illocutionary force of an utterance is bracketed, as for instance with a quoted promise in a play, its meaning still depends on the existence of conventions that coordinate the actions of the actors *qua* actors, as speakers and hearers with a determinate kind of function that is mutually recognized. The effectiveness of the quoted or reported promise therefore presupposes 'the constraints under which illocutionary acts develop a force for coordinating action and have consequences relevant to action' in the realm of ordinary or 'normal' language.[11] It is just these 'consequences relevant for action' that circumscribe what Habermas means by 'standard' conditions.

Habermas is surely right to assert that the imaginative, creative linguistic inventions of irony, metaphor, and so forth, could not alone coordinate actions in the manner required for the social reproduction of life. In other words, they are incapable of performing that socially integrating operation that is the focus of Habermas's extra-hermeneutic theory of society. Non-serious contexts *are* irrelevant from the perspective of Habermas's social theory, but Habermas does not dismiss them as unworthy of *separate* consideration. Rather than having the validity of 'problem-solving' action-coordinative mechanisms, imaginative linguistic activity serves what Habermas calls a 'world-disclosive' function. Communicative actions gain their coordinative property by virtue of the bonding established by the warranty to justify the validity claim raised by the illocutionary speech act. To this extent, they meet problem-solving requirements that any society must satisfy. The world-disclosive function, on the other hand, releases the speech act from illocutionary obligations that arise in problem-solving contexts of everyday life. For Habermas, the deconstructivist focuses narrowly on world-disclosure, but world-disclosive capacities themselves only emerge in a language that already proves its worth in the problem-solving contexts of everyday interaction.

But what does it mean to say that a language must 'prove its worth'? The significance of this question can be drawn out of an objection Habermas makes of deconstructive practice in general. Any interpretive practice, Habermas rightly asserts, must make intelligible its own possibility of communication. An interpretive practice premised on the idea that 'every reading is also a misreading' fails this test, Habermas claims, in denying criteria for judging between interpretations and misinterpretations. While we can agree with this counter-objection to deconstruction, Habermas *then* goes on to claim that no matter how far removed interpretations are from the restraints of the everyday communicative situation, 'they can never be wholly absolved of the idea that wrong interpretations must in principle be criticizable in terms of a consensus to be aimed for ideally'.[12] The 'proving of worth' of ordinary language, by implication, resides not in its *de facto* meaningfulness; it is not by appeal to linguistic conventions that standard conditions are established. 'Rather', Habermas continues,

> language games only work because they presuppose idealizations that transcend any particular language game; as a necessary condition of possible understanding, these idealizations give rise to the perspective of an agreement that is open to criticism on the basis of validity claims.[13]

Language games are therefore in continual need of justification – they have 'to prove their worth' and are 'subject to ongoing test' – in a manner that points inexorably to an ideal consensus. The approximate satisfaction of the idealizations of pure communicative action in everyday practice can then be regarded as justifying the parasitism of non-coordinative, non-consensual strategic language use.

However, the deconstructive criticism about the vagueness of normal or standard conditions has not been fully met, since the deconstructivist can reply that the selection of *which* worth is proved of language only pushes back Habermas's theoretical bias. It is not, as the deconstructivist would claim, the theoretical bias *qua theory* that is effectively challenged by the criticism of partiality. The weakness in Habermas's account of the functional primacy of action-coordination over world-disclosure should not be diagnosed as a symptom of logocentrism. Rather, it is Habermas's attempt to move *beyond hermeneutics* that creates the problem. Habermas, it seems, does arbitrarily privilege a certain *context* in which world-disclosive language has to prove its worth; he assumes that the criteria of worth and validity have to be supplied *externally* to world-disclosive discourse. Now if the deconstructionist model of world-disclosure is adopted – according to which 'every interpretation is a misinterpretation' – this is not an unreasonable assumption to make. But on the strong hermeneutic model of world disclosure – according to which interpretations possess more or less validity *qua* interpretations – the assumption that world-disclosive discourse must be made externally accountable to count as valid or invalid at all, to count as proven or disproved in its worth, is quite unwarranted.[14]

The agonistic objection

The agonistic objection shares with the deconstructivist one a suspicion that the imaginative use of language is occluded or unduly marginalized in Habermas's emphasis on the consensus-building (or consensus-presupposing) function of language. But it proceeds not so much by stressing the interdependence of communicative and strategic linguistic interaction, as by prioritizing the strategic dimension of language as 'the first principle' of understanding the linguistic social bond.[15] Accordingly, for Lyotard, 'speech acts fall within the domain of a general agonistics', which is to say within the domain of strategic interactions of adversaries.[16] This is of aesthetic significance not only because one of the chief adversaries is the accepted language, but also because it is strategically effective to create new moves rather than relying on reactional countermoves, which Lyotard suggests are 'no more than programmed effects in the opponent's strategy'.[17] According to Lyotard, speech acts are best accounted for as moves made between opponent players of language games in the medium of which social bonds are forged.

The social bond is considered by Lyotard to be, at the very least, a function of language 'effects'. These effects position the sender, addressee and referent of speech acts, as nodal points within the perpetually shifting local networks of strategic relationships that constitute the social world. The diversity of language effects supports flexible modes of utterance in everyday discourse. But this flexibility becomes ossified by institutional constraints that privilege particular kinds of language game: 'orders in the army, prayer in the church, denotation in the schools, narration in families, questions in philosophy, performativity in business'.[18] Yet the tendency towards the bureaucratization of the social bond, Lyotard suggests, is simultaneously threatened by the possibility that such institutionally imposed limits on potential language moves be themselves taken as 'the stakes and provisional results of language strategies'.

For Lyotard, then, the best way to approach speech acts is as moves in language games made between adversaries according to strategies with the power to subvert established meanings. This approach, he thinks, shows greater sensitivity to the diversity of language games that people play, games that have no metalanguage to commensurate them. But to accept this incommensurability is to reject the consensus model of linguistic interaction, since it is to deny the assumption that 'it is possible for all speakers to come to agreement on which rules or metaprescriptions are universally valid for language games, when it is clear that language games are heteromorphous, subject to heterogeneous sets of rules'.[19] Consensus cannot be the goal of dialogue, Lyotard insists, because there is no possibility of a metalanguage into which the diversity of language games could be translated and in terms of which agreement could be formulated. And worse, consensus reinforces that tendency towards bureaucratization – towards the ossification of language and hence of the social bond – by imposing the very conformity that is resisted by the strategic tapping of the heterogeneous potential of language games.

One can say then that from Lyotard's agonistic perspective, the distinction between 'manipulatory speech' and 'free expression and dialogue' is to be rejected on three counts. First, because all utterances have effects that are of significance in the forging of social bonds. Second, the distinction overlooks the diversity of effects specific to utterances within different language games, of which Lyotard mentions 'denotatives', 'prescriptives', 'evaluatives', and 'performatives'. And third, because 'free expression' can itself be considered as creative manipulatory intervention oriented towards the dissolution of consensus.

Habermas has not replied directly to Lyotard's criticisms, but we can reconstruct a response as follows. Regarding the first point, although it may be true that utterances are constantly placing and displacing sender, addressee and referent in such a way as to make and break social bonds, we can nevertheless distinguish between those bonds that are forged on the basis of the validity of the utterance, and those that are otherwise motivated. Habermas may exaggerate the degree to which the bonding between individuals in modern societies is ascribable to rationally motivated agreement, but Lyotard's agonistic approach makes the very idea of a rationally achieved consensus hard even to conceive. This relates to the second point, since the coordinating effect of the rationally motivated agreement depends upon the recognition of the distinct *validity-claims* raised in the utterance. So the 'effect' of a denotative will differ from that of a prescriptive for no other reason than that for which the effects of a communicatively and strategically oriented denotative utterance differ, except in so far as different resources of the lifeworld are at stake in the communication. As Peter Dews has observed, since these resources correspond to different kinds of validity-claim, Lyotard's objection seems to involve a confusion between language-games and validity-claims.[20] Denotatives do indeed differ from prescriptions, but *qua* denotatives and prescriptions, they differ not in their 'effects' (which depends on the context of the speech act), but on the validity-claim (in these cases truth and normative legitimacy) that they *thematize*.

It follows that the charge against Habermas's alleged assumption of a metalanguage in virtue of which all different language games are commensurable is misplaced. Validity claims are already either implicit or explicit in the diversity of language uses, in such a way that no further commensurating metalanguage need be invoked to account for consensus about them. What is perhaps more worrying about Habermas's position, however, is that it does seem to require that all claims to validity are differentiable into truth, normative legitimacy or rightness, and sincerity or authenticity. We have already seen that strong hermeneutics regards world-disclosive discourses as potential carriers of validity, even though they do not fit into Habermas's taxonomy of speech acts and validity claims. And our discussion of the realism of strong evaluations suggests that this kind of discourse too fits awkwardly, if at all, into Habermas's theory, since strong evaluations raise claims to validity the truth-evaluability of which is inseparable from their action-orienting legitimacy. In the next chapter I will argue that even within Habermas's theory, there is a key class of critical concepts that follows the same disruptive logic as strong evaluations – namely, 'clinical intuitions'.

Turning to the third aspect of the agonistic objection, is language oriented to consensus disposed to 'bureaucratization' in the manner Lyotard suggests? The *de facto* agreements concerning obeisance to military orders, rote learning in school and efficiency in business have no bearing on the issue, of course, because the kind of consensus proposed by Habermas is an ideal one, the conditions of which are not met where institutional constraints are normatively ascribed rather than communicatively established. Habermas can reply here that the objection rests upon an equivocation concerning the concept of 'strategy'. To be sure, the institutional ossification alluded to by Lyotard can be strategically subverted by invention, but this is just to say that a condition of communicative action is the setting loose of all three validity claims. Indeed, the scenario depicted by Lyotard represents on the one hand systemic constraints upon communication, and on the other hand, a one-sided rationalization of lifeworld institutions. The tendency towards bureaucratization, therefore, is just as well explained internally to Habermas's position. And it could further be argued that the strategy of subversion is better explained within it, since it gives a point to the subversive critique beyond the strategy of sheer subversiveness – namely, the establishment of communicative interaction *in its full scope*.

Now I want to move onto an alternative argument to support Habermas's thesis that strategic linguistic interaction is in principle derivative from linguistic interaction oriented towards consensus.

WITTGENSTEIN, IDEALIZATIONS AND HERMENEUTICS

When considering the deconstructivist objection to the primacy of reaching consensual understanding, I mentioned Habermas's view that communication is possible only under the presupposition of intersubjectively identical ascriptions of meaning. The possibility of perlocutionary success presupposes the prior possibility of reaching understanding in that the utterance employed strategically, to be effective at all, must first be intelligible to the opponent. In order for the manipulation of meanings to be possible, there must first be meanings to manipulate, there must be something to be used as a means to an end. But if meaning is itself not something that can be strategically decided upon then the strategic use of language cannot be originary.

Habermas recognizes this point, and interprets Wittgenstein's remarks on rule-following – which are pertinent for Habermas's purposes in helping to explain that which makes for the 'sameness' of the various applications of a concept – in a way that indirectly supports his own thesis that the communicative use of language is the original mode. But it is just at this point that Wittgensteinian counter-objections can be wedged. For although Wittgenstein gives reasons for thinking that some form of consensus is a necessary condition of meaningful utterance, it is questionable whether the consensus that must be presupposed in acts of communication is of the *kind* proposed by Habermas and at the *level* he takes it to be operative.[21] And it is just the kind of consensus and the level at which communication presupposes it that are the crucial features of Habermas's normative model of intact intersubjectivity in so far as it is derived from the concept of pure communicative action.

For Habermas's purposes, the import of Wittgenstein's remarks on rule-following rests in establishing an analytical connection between 'identical meanings and intersubjective validity'.[22] Rule-following is the *sine qua non* of propositionally differentiated language use since through it the more or less diffuse criteria of correct application of a concept are determined. Of course, if there were no such thing as the correct application of a concept, there would also be no such thing as an incorrect application, and if this were the case there would be no concept to be applied or misapplied at all. This, in essence, is the objection Habermas puts to the deconstructivist. If the meaning of a concept is to be the same in the ongoing applications of it, it must be by virtue of a rule that determines what counts as the 'same' meaning. Habermas rightly points out that this 'sameness of meaning' is not something that can be inductively inferred from empirical regularities in the application of the rule, since the rule itself is needed to determine what counts *as* a particular instance of an empirical regularity. For this reason, what counts as 'going on in the same way' in the application of a rule cannot be determined by appeal to something external to the rule and its application.

The ability to follow a rule is the ability to apply the rule in the same way in different particular cases. But that which counts as the same way is not reducible to any empirical or non-normative phenomenon. Habermas rightly takes this to imply that a condition of sameness of meaning is intersubjective validity in the application of concepts. Given that identity of meaning is conceptually tied to intersubjective validity, it follows, according to Habermas, that the violation of a rule by a particular subject must be criticizable by another subject who has grasped the rule. Further, this will be by way of a 'critique which is in principle open to consensus'.[23] 'Without this possibility of reciprocal criticism and mutual instruction leading to agreement', Habermas continues, 'the identity of rules cannot be secured. A rule has to possess validity for at least two subjects if one subject is to be able to follow the rule'. This is a consequence of Wittgenstein's argument against the possibility of a subject following a rule 'privately'. The intersubjective validity of rules is a validity that must obtain between at least two subjects where both 'must have a competence for rule governed behaviour as well as critically judging such behaviour'. A single isolated subject, who either could not act in accord with the rule or critically judge rule violations, 'could no more form the concept of a rule than he could use symbols with identically the same meaning'.

For Habermas, then, sameness of meaning, being bound to the intersubjective validity of rules, implies the ability to take a 'critical yes/no position' on the correctness of a particular application of a rule. But such a concept of rule-competence refers, *inter alia*, 'to the ability to produce symbolic expressions with communicative intent and to understand them'.[24] So at the most fundamental level, linguistic competence presupposes the grasping of rules the validity of which is in principle open to a consensus on the basis of reciprocal critique and mutual instruction. The qualifiers 'reciprocal' and 'mutual' are crucial here since they circumscribe the critique and instruction presupposed in the very foundation of language use exclusively within the *illocutionary* realm. And implicitly, the kind of consensus to which the intersubjective validity of rules is accountable is one divorced from causally induced effects. Since any actual consensus is always conditioned by some empirical motivation, there is an *ideal* consensus presupposed in the original use of language. Although an idealization, it is nevertheless an assumption which the possibility of identical ascriptions of meaning demands. Virtual to linguistic competence, then, is the consensus of an ideal communication community, which is to say the consensus of subjects in a dialogue situation pursuing solely illocutionary aims – or in other words, pure communicative action.

Of course, by this point Habermas recognizes his radical deviation from Wittgenstein's views. As in his reply to the deconstructivist objection, Habermas insists *against* Wittgenstein that it 'is not habitual practice that determines just what meaning is attributed to a text or an utterance', rather 'language games only work because they presuppose idealizations that transcend any particular language game'. Habermas's reading of Wittgenstein follows Apel in construing communicative discourse as presupposing an entwinement between 'a real communication community' into which the participant has become socialized, and 'an ideal communication community' in which arguments would be properly understood and judged.[25] As the previously quoted remark suggests, the idea of an ideal communication community is invoked to save rationality from the inertia of custom and tradition.

But can Wittgenstein be turned around so as to show the primacy of communicative action and the immanence of the ideal communication community?[26] Is linguistic interaction oriented to reaching an intersubjectively valid consensus shown to be presupposed by (or analytically connected to) the possibility of identical ascriptions of meaning? As I indicated, the problem lies in the kind of agreement that is presupposed in communication and the level at which this agreement is operative. On the first point, Wittgenstein is emphatic that the kind of agreement that valid argumentation presupposes is not one of opinions, but *practices* or 'forms of life'. The consensus here is not one of the 'yes' or 'no' of the interpreter of a rule. It is not itself an interpretation, but the background against which interpretations are made. As Baker and Hacker have argued, for Wittgenstein following a rule is founded on agreement, but agreement over the background framework of action 'within which the concept of following a rule has intelligible employment', not over 'the explanation of what "following a rule" means'.[27] So not only is the kind of agreement at issue here one of practices rather than opinions, but the level at which it operates is that of the *pre-conditions* of correct or incorrect opinions. To paraphrase a remark of Wittgenstein's to make it directly applicable to Habermas's view, 'the agreement of validations is the pre-condition of our language game, it is not affirmed in it'.[28]

Habermas's fear is that this seems to abolish argument.[29] Argument – the raising, criticizing and redeeming of validity claims – seems to be reduced to matter of fact habitual practices. But for Wittgenstein, neither actual nor ideal agreement is that by virtue of which an application is in accord with a rule. *No* agreement is necessary to mediate between a rule and the correct application of it, since rule and application are, as Habermas recognizes, internally related.

To be sure, there are elements in Habermas's doctrine of the lifeworld that come closer to Wittgenstein's view. The following passage, in which Wittgenstein sums up the role of agreement in his rule-following considerations, highlights this proximity nicely:

> It is of the greatest importance that a dispute hardly ever arises between people about whether the colour of this object is the same as the colour of that, the length of this rod the same as that, etc. This peaceful agreement is the characteristic surrounding the use of the word 'same'.
>
> And one must say something analogous about proceeding according to a rule. No dispute breaks out over the question whether a proceeding was according to a rule or not. It doesn't come to blows, for example.
>
> This belongs to the framework, out of which our language works (for example, gives a description).[30]

Giving reasons requires an acknowledgement of a standard for reason giving, just as the practice of measuring requires a background agreement upon the standards of measurement. In exceptional conditions, there may be reason to doubt such standards, but there will come a point at which the questionableness of them *threatens the possibility of communication*. It follows that, contrary to Habermas's view, the use of language oriented towards a 'communicatively reached agreement' which 'must be based *in the end* on reasons' cannot be the original use of language.[31] For the rationally motivated agreement of communicative action presupposes a prior agreement about the standards of reason giving. A reason cannot be given for the justification of these standards, since they determine what is to count as the justified and unjustified use of words at all. To put it another way, Habermas's view is that linguistic interaction oriented to a validity conditioned agreement falls foul of Wittgenstein's point that not all propositions can be *problem-solving hypotheses*, since the very possibility of judgement presupposes commonly agreed standards or norms of judgement. If communicative action were originary, then it would be possible that all propositionally differentiated speech acts were hypothetical in form.

On the face of it, Habermas's reply would seem straightforward: these Wittgensteinian objections neglect the complementary roles of the concept of communicative action and the concept of the lifeworld. For the lifeworld, according to Habermas, is just that tacitly accepted and mutually agreed upon background framework of taken-for-granted assumptions and meanings against the horizon of which validity claims are criticizable. The problem remains, however, that the agreement to which 'reaching understanding' is oriented must be of a *different order* to the background agreement in action that constitutes the lifeworld. In this sense, the concept of the lifeworld actually serves more to undermine than to complement the concept of communicative action, at least in so far as the latter is understood as the original mode of language interaction.

Consider again Wittgenstein's remark that 'agreement of ratifications is the pre-condition of our language game, it is not affirmed in it'. Now the agreement to which communicative action is oriented, unlike the lifeworld agreement in action, is precisely such an affirmation. Habermas brings together these radically different senses of consensus in his concept of communicative action, enabling him to shift from the original validity *conditioning* lifeworld agreement to the validity *conditioned* communicative agreement, and then to assert the latter as the originary form of agreement or consensus that all linguistic interaction presupposes. Further, the level at which the fundamental agreement operates is not one that transcends the internal relationship between the rule and its correct application. Such an idealization is not necessary to *explain* intersubjectively identical ascriptions of meaning, but it is just upon this presupposition that the primacy of communicative action thesis rests.

But although we can now say that communicative action is not the originary form of linguistic interaction, we are also committed to saying that *strategic* interaction is not fundamental either. Background lifeworld agreement is not a 'giving something to understand' nor an inconspicuous harnessing or manipulation of another person's intentions for one's own purposes. Both strategic and communicative action as defined by Habermas imply a voluntarism that the coherence of lifeworld agreement will not tolerate. We can see a way out of this incoherence only by returning to the question initially posed by Habermas and taken up by his critics. It asks for an original mode of language use and proposes communicative and strategic action as alternative answers. That neither is adequate suggests there may be something misleading in the formulation of the question itself. Is the idea of an 'original use' of language really intelligible at all? Within Habermas's argument, 'use' stands for intentional action and he considers two different kinds of action-orientation as possibly originary. But the concepts in relation to which action is oriented cannot themselves be decided upon intentionally, *whatever* the orientation of the action. Both communicative and strategic action presuppose the possession of concepts that are prior to any intentional use of language. This thought points to the presence of world-disclosive capacities in language that are not appropriable by language users of whatever orientation. McDowell's formulation is hard to better: 'the language into which a human being is first initiated stands over against her as a prior embodiment of mindedness; of the possibility of an orientation to the world'.[32]

To judge from his response to Taylor's account of language, Habermas has two basic objections to this strong hermeneutic view.[33] On the one hand, he supposes hermeneutic approaches to language like Taylor's to fall victim to 'epistemological relativism';[34] and on the other, he thinks that they wrongly allow the problem-solving capacity of language to 'disappear' behind its capacity for world-disclosure.[35] But in light of the arguments laid out earlier in the book neither objection looks very convincing. We saw in chapter one that as a defender of strong rather than weak hermeneutics, Taylor emphatically rejects the subsumption of ontology to epistemology that stands behind 'perspectivism'. For Taylor, the world-disclosive powers of language do undermine foundationalism, but the philosophical significance of this is to preserve the intelligibility of actual interpretive practices, not to expose the groundlessness of our best knowledge-claims. Nor can Taylor's view rightly be accused of ignoring the problem-solving capacity of language. In chapter three, we saw that Taylor appeals to the technical, problem-solving success of modern science as something that needs to be accounted for both by advocates of the rationality of modern science and defenders of pre-modern cognitive practices. But Taylor does this not in order to posit inner-worldly problem-solving as a criterion of the rationality of world-disclosive languages. Rather the aim is to show how the intertwining of world-disclosive and problem-solving capacities *can* form the basis of judgements of validity.

In this chapter I have considered Habermas's arguments for the primacy of the communicative use of language drawn first from his theory of action

– where the argument is explicit – and then from his theory of meaning.[36] While, as the former asserts, communicative action may be conceptually prior to strategic action in the sense that language is a mechanism for the coordination of intentional actions, Habermas has not demonstrated that this is something that can be established on the basis of the intelligibility of the domain of meaning as such. For Habermas, the domain of meaning is opened up by the pragmatic presuppositions of communication, by the possibility of identical ascriptions of meaning and therefore, on Habermas's account, a formal intersubjective structure of mutually and reciprocally recognizing subjects. In this manner, Habermas proposes that a source of normativity is always already present – there is a 'virtual ethical totality' at play – whenever speakers and hearers meet.[37] There are good Wittgensteinian reasons, I have suggested, for being sceptical about this claim. But Habermas argues implicitly for the primacy of communicative action in his social theory too. Although I will not be able to deal with Habermas's social theory in any detail, I shall say something about its articulation of the primacy of communication thesis, and the status of this articulation in relation to hermeneutics, in the next chapter.

6   Strong hermeneutics and discourse ethics

In *Legitimation Crisis*, Habermas raises a series of questions which effectively launches his discourse ethical investigations. 'If world views', Habermas asks, 'have foundered on the separation of cognitive from socially integrative components', if such world views 'today belong irretrievably to the past', what else can fulfil 'the moral–practical task of constituting ego- and group-identity?' How can a morality without roots in 'cognitive interpretations of nature', as Habermas puts it, still 'secure the identities of individuals and collectives?'[1] To be sure, in their original context, these are primarily sociological questions. Habermas's main concern there is to explore the empirical hypothesis that the separation of cognitive from socially integrative components of the lifeworld precipitates legitimation crises in late capitalist societies by unleashing the forces of instrumental reason.[2] But in his more recent work the same questions reappear in a more philosophical light. Habermas's various programmatic elaborations of a discourse ethics are attempts at a *justification* of the rationality of the moral point of view understood as both independent of cognitive interpretations of nature and as compatible with the diverse and decentred individual and group identities of the modern lifeworld.

Discourse ethics follows Kant in assuming that the rationality of the moral point of view is its moment of unconditionality. The normative demands to issue from the moral point of view have a *sui generis* binding force; the moral legitimacy of a norm, according to discourse ethics, is conditional on nothing other than the force of practical reason itself. As the questions above indicate, discourse ethics starts from the assumption that if there is to be any objective content to moral beliefs, it cannot be by virtue of them accurately representing a pre-given natural order of things. Cognitive interpretations of nature cannot lend support to moral belief because, to follow McDowell's formulation, such interpretations are couched in concepts fit for the realm of law rather than meaning. Disenchanted nature is a realm of utter contingency from the moral point of view. Given a universe with the intelligibility of the laws of physics, it is hard to see how the natural order can secure sense and legitimacy to moral belief. The idea of a normatively instructive natural order also fits ill with the incommensurability of cultural values. What kind of plausibility, for instance, can be given to explanations of the diversity of moral beliefs as so many failed attempts at mirroring?[3] If it is assumed, as discourse ethics does, that historical and cultural differences in standards of proper conduct do not reflect cognitive shortcomings, and if it is also assumed that some measure of right *is* applicable to human conduct, then that measure, according to discourse ethics, must hold independently of any particular cultural tradition. It has to be a standard which in some sense stands outside the contingencies of history and culture.

In face of the plurality of cultural values, it can seem forlorn even to consider locating the pull of practical reason in the content of substantive conceptions of the good life. Moreover, a society characterized by value-pluralism faces the problem of resolving potential *conflict* situations arising precisely out of value-differences. We are well on the road to discourse ethics if we find ourselves asking what it means for such differences to be decided by 'right' rather than 'might'. Like other deontological theories, discourse ethics answers this question by separating the right from the good; by according priority to the right over the good; and by construing the intelligibility of right in terms of a procedural conception of practical reasoning. Discourse ethics seeks to save the intelligibility of the moral demand in the face of the contingencies of history and nature by separating the moral domain from the domain of the good. Its peculiarity as a deontological theory arises from its *dialogical* specification of the normative demands to issue from practical reason.[4]

The discourse ethical project of grounding the intelligibility of the moral demand independently of history marks a clear point of departure from hermeneutics. But discourse ethics comes into dispute with hermeneutics in a variety of ways, which I want to explore in this chapter. I shall begin by commenting on how Habermas envisages the status and objectives of discourse ethics. In general, Habermas sees philosophy working on two fronts.[5] On the one hand, it 'stands-in' for strong empirical theories that seek to reconstruct the conditions of rational speech and action. On the other, supplementing the narrowly circumscribed endeavour of rational reconstruction, philosophy, like art and criticism, mediates and interprets on behalf of the lifeworld. Discourse ethics undertakes the former kind of activity: it seeks to make the rationality of claims to normative rightness intelligible. In the first section of the chapter, I briefly rehearse the major steps in the discourse ethical designation and reconstruction of the moral point of view. In the next section, I bring strong hermeneutic considerations critically to bear on the idea that a 'moral' domain is really suitable for rational reconstruction. I argue that there are, moreover, good reasons for thinking that the very idea of an autonomous moral domain in the discourse ethical sense is misguided. Note that the hermeneutic case I present here is not so much that the procedural criteria of practical reasoning reconstructed by discourse ethics need 'compensating for' by substantive standards available to other forms of interpretive and mediating reflection. Habermas acknowledges that much himself.[6] It is rather that the very division of philosophical labour proposed by Habermas is inappropriate for making sense of moral identity and the contingencies confronting it. From the vantage point gained by our hermeneutic reflections, a new perspective opens up on the debate between Habermas and so-called 'neo-Aristotelianism'. The chapter concludes with some comments on the prospects for a critique of procedural reason from a strong hermeneutic point of view. First, though, let us look a bit more closely at the motivations behind Habermas's move to a discourse ethics.

DISCOURSE ETHICS AND THE MORAL POINT OF VIEW

Soon after completing *Knowledge and Human Interests*, Habermas conceded that the deep hermeneutic paradigm of reflection conflated the distinct tasks of 'rational reconstruction' and 'methodically carried out self-critique'.[7] Rational reconstructions, the business of reconstructive science, serve to raise the intuitive know-how presupposed in the varieties of communicative competence to the level of theoretical self-awareness. Communicative competence, as displayed in the raising and redeeming of validity claims, is modelled on the intuitive mastery of rule-systems. The command of these procedures is presupposed in the ability to produce such things as grammatically correct sentences, sound judgements and good arguments. Philosophical disciplines like epistemology, philosophy of language, and moral philosophy, are considered by Habermas as 'stand-ins' for scientific theories which, in their reconstruction of the rule-systems implicitly mastered in rational speech and action, help make up a general theory of rationality. Rational reconstruction is a 'post-metaphysical' mode of reflection in that it eschews *a priori* status and embraces fallibilism. On the other hand, however, the reconstructions reached have a claim to *universality*. Rational reconstructions are not proposed as hermeneutic interpretations of patterns of thought and behaviour judged rational in one tradition but irrational in another. For the reconstructive sciences as Habermas considers them, the force of sound judgements, good arguments and rational actions transcends local boundaries. For Habermas, the universalistic but fallibilist theories of the reconstructive sciences are the most appropriate way of making sense of the demands of reason, given the demise – from a cognitive point of view – of religious–metaphysical world views and the diversification of cultural values. Rational reconstructions seek to make the demands of reason intelligible not by way of ontology, but in terms of the formal, context-transcending moment of validity-redeeming procedures.[8]

Accordingly, Habermas assigns moral philosophy the task of explicating, by means of rational reconstructions, the conditions that make validity claims to *normative rightness* intelligible. In Habermas's view, to do this is simultaneously to explicate the universality of such claims and to construct a theory of practical reasoning. His arguments turn on identifying the procedural constraints that must be presupposed by participants in rational discourse. These constraints include an equal and reciprocated opportunity on the part of each participant to raise and criticize claims without fear of coercion, authentic openness to the potential validity of the claims of others, and truthfulness in the articulation of one's own claims. The validity of claims to normative rightness can then be rendered intelligible in terms of the consensus reached between participants in discourse over the norms that commonly affect them. According to Habermas, the participants in practical discourse can have different, incommensurable, rationally undecidable conceptions of the good, but the norms that regulate their collective life remain amenable to rational consensus. It is these norms that constitute the moral domain. Concerning it, then, we have claims that are valid or invalid, claims to normative rightness that, in admitting of a rational consensus, have an intelligibility analogous to that of truth claims. But unlike truth, normative rightness does not come tied to empirical cognition concerning the domain of facts.[9]

In this way discourse ethics seeks to reconstruct the rational basis of the strong (because universal) but minimal (because formal) constitution of an autonomous moral point of view. The moral point of view means the impartial perspective of participants engaged in practical discourse. In his first programmatic writings on discourse ethics, Habermas identifies practical discourse with a formal procedure of argumentation through which participants seek to arrive at a rationally motivated consensus over the legitimacy of a norm. Discourse ethics then attempts to derive the universality of the moral point of view from the pragmatic presuppositions of moral argumentation. The thread of Habermas's argument is as follows. The point of engaging in moral argumentation would be lost if it were not for the possibility of reaching a valid consensus. But the condition of reaching a valid rather than *de facto* consensus is that each participant has an equal right to raise criticizable validity claims that is reciprocated amongst all the participants. From these procedural normative constraints on participating in practical discourse, a moral principle that is universally binding on communicative actors is derivable, namely: 'For a norm to be valid, the consequences and side-effects of its general observance for the satisfaction of each person's particular interests must be acceptable to all'.[10]

The substance of valid norms can only be determined by participants in actual practical discourses. But to count as just, their content must pass this formal test of universalizability. Only those norms that pass this test are valid in the strict moral sense. Nor is moral validity, the kind of validity that is displayed in the moral domain, contingent upon a particular cultural tradition or form of life. According to the basic pattern of discourse ethical argument, the normative force of the pragmatic presuppositions of argumentation as such operates universally, it extends to all situations of language use irrespective of the substantive values any particular language discloses. Thus although the object of rational reconstruction is the 'post-conventional' moral consciousness of modern cultures, the discourse ethical principle of universalizability itself has a claim to rationality that applies not just internally to particular traditions or forms of life but *between* them. The main theoretical burden of discourse ethics is to demonstrate how the sceptic's attempt to deny the context-transcending rationality of the moral point of view must always involve her in a performative contradiction.[11]

As a consequence of its status as a stand-in for reconstructive science, discourse ethics eschews all substantive consideration of what constitutes the good life. This is inevitable, Habermas thinks, as soon as the scope of the moral domain is determined by that of the applicability of the principle of universalization. This principle 'makes razor-sharp cuts between evaluative statements and strictly normative ones, between the good and the just'.[12] Further, the separation between the good and the just conditions the cognitive advance achieved through the exercise of practical reason. Since under conditions of cultural diversity only the norms that regulate collective life can be debated with the prospect of consensus, Habermas considers the separation that issues in an autonomous moral domain – and the 'transformation of questions of the good into problems of justice' – to register a gain in rationality.[13] Unlike questions of morality, which arise in a field of conflict *between* individual and group identities, evaluative questions, or questions of what constitutes the good life, 'are accessible to rational discussion only *within* the unproblematic horizon of a concrete historical form of life or the conduct of an individual life'.[14] Questions of the good life, Habermas continues, 'have the advantage of being answerable within the horizon of lifeworld certainties'.[15] Those cultural values that make up a conception of the good life can be 'candidates' for legitimate norms. At least according to Habermas's first formulations of the principles of discourse ethics, conceptions of the good become objects of practical rationality, and potentially legitimate norms of action, as soon as a 'hypothetical attitude' is taken towards them by participants in moral argumentation. Upon taking this attitude, the norms and institutions that were taken for granted suddenly appear as problematic. Particular norms can be tested as hypothetical legitimacy claims under the moralizing gaze of the problem-solving participants in practical discourse. As such, the moral point of view stands *outside* the provincialism of any lifeworld.

The guiding intuition of Habermas's thought here is that the concrete institutions of any particular *Sittlichkeit* are accountable to an independently standing rational principle of *Moralität*. For Habermas, if the conviction is to be upheld that the norms and institutions of a prevailing *Sittlichkeit* are answerable to reason, if sense is to be made at all of a criticizable normative *validity* claim, and if incommensurable but mutually impacting identity-shaping traditions are taken as given, the source of accountability of those traditions, institutions and norms inevitably assumes a highly abstract form. Getting oneself into a position to see things from the moral point of view requires an effort of abstraction from the contingencies shaping one's particular concrete identity. But as soon as the moral point of view is adopted those contingencies reappear as criticizable in terms of an abstract justice they do not yet embody.

Habermas has always acknowledged that limiting the domain of moral philosophy to the refutation of moral scepticism and the reconstruction of the universality of the moral point of view has its price. The separations of the right from the good, of normative questions concerning just principles of social interaction from evaluative questions regarding the proper ends of life, and of an abstract moral domain from the more existentially resonant sphere of the ethical, remind us of those Kantian 'diremptions' that motivated Hegel's critique. Now Habermas is very much aware of the extent to which the viability of discourse ethics turns on the ability of its predominantly Kantian framework to incorporate Hegel's insights. But while this has been a requirement for discourse ethics from its inception, Habermas's later formulations show a greater sensitivity to problems arising from the inflexibility of the Kantian schema. For instance, the earlier emphasis on defending the rational basis of a narrowly circumscribed domain of morality resulted in conceptions of the good sometimes appearing as unfit for rational assessment *at all*. The restriction of practical reason in the essays of *Moral Consciousness and Communicative Action* to the realm of universalizable norms is emphatically rejected in *Justification and Application*. In the latter work, Habermas distinguishes between the different *uses* of practical reason – the pragmatic, the ethical and the moral – in which different kinds of question regarding what one ought to do are addressed. Again, as Habermas has come to acknowledge, the earlier programmatic writings on discourse ethics failed to deal adequately with the issue of how to return from the rarefied perception of missing abstract right to the instantiation of concrete justice. The abstractions of the moral point of view, as Habermas put it in an early formulation, 'risk all the assets of the existing ethical substance'.[16] Consequently, there arises the problem of 'how to make up for this loss of concrete ethical substance, which is initially accepted because of the cognitive advantages attending it'.[17] The lifeworld must be such as to allow for the application of the norms that are abstractly justified and to motivate action based upon them. By way of dealing with this problem of *mediating* morality with ethical life, Habermas now stresses that the effort of abstraction required for the sake of *justifying* norms needs to be supplemented by an independent *rational* act of suitable *application* of norms in a context-sensitive manner.

But do these concessions to so-called 'neo-Hegelian' and 'neo-Aristotelian' thought go far enough? And to the extent that they do, what remains of the claim that discourse ethics marks a move *beyond* hermeneutics? In the next section, I shall address these questions by exploring how discourse ethics deals with difficulties concerning first, the status and rationality of evaluative statements; second, the circumscription of the moral domain; and third, Habermas's proposals for mediating the differentiated spheres morality and ethical life. In the course of these reflections it will become apparent why, even on Habermas's own terms, a rethink is called for on the relation between the reconstructive and hermeneutic moments of critical moral and ethical reflection.

MORALITY AND ETHICAL LIFE

(1) Habermas's first reconstructions of the procedural competencies of practical reasoning leave the status of 'evaluatives' – statements expressing values which shape the identities of groups and individuals – in a curious limbo. In these early programmatic remarks, he fluctuates between proposing that evaluatives do not admit of rational intelligibility at all because they do not admit of general consensus, and, more typically, asserting that argument over evaluatives is possible but not, strictly speaking, as practical discourse.[18] Discourse over evaluatives has more 'lenient' criteria of rationality in that, unlike discourse concerning moral norms, no requirement is built into its procedure for generating universalizable validity claims. Given Habermas's communication-theoretic assumptions, this lack of consensual foundation can only compromise their claim to rationality. In so far as evaluative statements, as opposed to moral norms, have a claim to reason at all, Habermas suggests, it is of the same weak kind as possessed by the judgements made in 'aesthetic' and 'therapeutic' discourse.[19]

The difficulties facing Habermas's proposal appear as soon as we try joining it to his notion of the differentially thematizable validity claims truth, rightness and authenticity. Recall that for Habermas, 'gains in rationality' characteristically arise from the differentiation of the three validity claims, and from the differentiation and specialization of discourses thematizing them. Hence, and paradigmatically on this view, modern science owes its rationality to the way in which it thematizes 'truth' in differentiation from 'rightness', 'authentic' self-expression and 'beauty'.[20] By approaching its object-domain as if it were completely uninformative about questions of right, science satisfies a claim to reason. Similarly, according to this model, the demands of justice acquire a more rational content in virtue of being thematized in discourses separated off from those dealing with issues of aesthetic interest. The process of determining whether a norm is just, in other words, becomes more rational once the validity basis of social norms and institutions is sharply differentiated from that of artistic expression and scientific research.

But how do 'gains in rationality' concerning evaluatives fit into this schema? Is it due to their thematization in 'aesthetic discourse'? Of course, even if evaluative judgements – conceptions of the good life that help define the self – are comparable to aesthetic judgements in not commanding universal consensus, it does not follow that they raise the same kind of validity claim. Even if we accept, for the moment, that aesthetic discourse gains in rationality for being differentiated from moral and scientific discourses and in thematizing authentic self-expression, evaluatives do not on the face of it concern *just* authenticity, or authenticity as *opposed* to truth or normative rightness. In any case, it would certainly be absurd to suggest that evaluatives gain in their rationality as a result of being thematized in a differentiated discourse of art and criticism. So do evaluatives owe their gain in rationality for being thematized in a differentiated 'therapeutic discourse'? On Habermas's account, therapeutic discourses do not thematize a validity claim, but they do presuppose a criterion of judgement; namely, 'health'. We shall return later to the impasse this idea represents for Habermas's theory. Suffice it for the moment to observe that while Habermas uses the expression 'health' to signify something like 'the good', the awkwardness of Habermas's locution suggests an underlying artificiality in the differentiation of 'evaluatives' into an autonomous quasi-discursive domain.

As we noted before, in his reformulation of discourse ethics Habermas turns away from a theory of differentiated 'practical', 'aesthetic' and 'therapeutic' discourses, proposing instead an account of the 'pragmatic', 'ethical' and 'moral' uses of practical reason. Habermas now draws on Taylor's notion of strong evaluation to capture the idea of value-preferences that are 'not merely contingent dispositions and inclinations' but 'inextricably interwoven with each individual's identity'.[21] Strong evaluations, Habermas accepts, 'both admit and stand in need of justification'.[22] Such justification, he continues, comes through 'hermeneutic self-clarification', whereby one's life history and process of self-development becomes 'appropriated'. Habermas interprets this appropriation, or 'striving for self-realization', in terms of the '*resoluteness* of an individual who has committed himself to an authentic life'. He describes it as 'the capacity for existential decisions or radical choice of self' which 'always operates within the horizon of a life-history, in whose traces the individual can discern who he is and who he would like to become'.[23] Hence, the 'ethical' employment of practical reason aims at justified evaluatives, and is addressed to 'the resoluteness of the authentic, self-realizing subject'.[24] In the idiosyncratic vocabulary used by Habermas, the ethical employment of practical reason supports or undermines 'the clinical intuitions' of the subject. In other words, it does the job previously assigned to 'therapeutic discourse'.

According to this position, the rationality of evaluative statements is discernible by way of hermeneutic self-clarification. But it is far from clear how this insight can simply be *added on* to a theory of rationality fundamentally modelled on the rational reconstruction of differentiated discursive competencies. For instance, take the distinction Habermas invokes between who one is and who one would like to become. Each corresponds to two components that are interwoven, according to Habermas, in all evaluatives: the descriptive and the normative. In this case, they correspond to 'the descriptive component of the ontogenesis of the ego and the normative component of the ego-ideal'.[25] While Habermas asserts that 'hermeneutically generated self-*description*' (my emphasis) does not issue in 'value-neutral self-understanding' – and hence that the descriptive and the normative components of the evaluation are *inseparable* – he is also committed to the view, proposed in defence of the method of rational reconstruction, that the descriptive component of the ontogenesis of the ego is the prerogative of strong *empirical* theories, *independent* of the normative context of processes of development. In this case, therefore, rational hermeneutic and rational reconstructive reflection are not supplementary at all: they run in quite opposite and incompatible directions. If the very intelligibility of hermeneutic reflection is problematized by the differentiation of normative and descriptive components, then a 'gain in rationality' from the point of view of rational reconstruction will constitute a *loss* of reason for the purposes of self-realization.

If the description of who one is is inseparable from its normative context, then it will admit of a truth value that has an inseparable normative force. That implies that the validity claim raised, and in some cases redeemed, by evaluations is truth. It seems to me that Habermas can respond to this anomaly for his theory in one of two ways.[26] On the one hand, he can accept the implication, but insist that evaluatives are *combinations* of truth, rightness and authenticity claims. The problem with this response, however, is that nothing *distinctive* is thereby said about evaluatives, since on Habermas's account *every* speech act forms a syndrome of the three validity claims. On the other hand, Habermas could insist that the validity claim raised in so-called 'clinical advice' is authenticity, not truth. But this cannot be correct either, since it is what the self stands in an authentic relation *to* that is operative here, something which is independent of, or contingent to, the will to realize it. That is precisely why *resoluteness* becomes an issue: the normative force of the description exercises a pull that transcends my matter of fact capacity to live up to it. Habermas's voluntarist construction of the logic of strong evaluation, incidentally, is reflected in his reading of Heidegger's idea that *Dasein* is a being whose own being is at issue, which we considered briefly in chapter two. For rather than interpreting this thought in strong hermeneutic fashion as a general ontological structure of self-interpreting animals, Habermas construes it as evidence of Heidegger's *existentialism*.[27] Given that Habermas associates strong evaluation so closely with the existentialist ethic of radical choice, it is not surprising that he considers it the site of claims to authenticity rather than truth claims.

(2) What about the discourse ethical circumscription of the moral domain? Where practical reasoning is taken to be the subject of a rational

reconstruction of procedural competencies, it makes sense to talk of conceptions of the good as embryonic justice claims. The idea here is that conceptions of justice *emerge* out of the horizon of concrete historical traditions and institutions he calls at various points the lifeworld and the context of ethical life (*Sittlichkeit*). Lifeworld claims to rationality, however, and therefore their right to the moral domain, depend on their successful passage through the procedure of practical discourse. Given that this procedure defines practical rationality, and that the moral domain is the one covered by norms that are rational in virtue of passing the procedural test, lifeworld conceptions of the good are of 'moral' significance, strictly speaking, only in so far as they are candidates for institutionalization as just norms.

That this way of talking shunts from view the dimension of goods clustered around the so-called 'self-regarding' virtues of dignity and integrity will be obvious and Habermas has been quick to correct it.[28] Nevertheless, it might be instructive to conject why Habermas should have made this oversight in his initial characterization of the moral domain. On the account I would offer, it occurs as a result of combining a conception of morality oriented primarily around the demands of social integration with a model of social evolution based on a rationally reconstructible logic of development. Consider the following passage from Habermas:

> All moralities coincide in one respect: the same medium, linguistically mediated interaction, is both the reason for the vulnerability of socialized individuals and the key resource they possess to compensate for that vulnerability. Every morality revolves around equality of respect, solidarity, and the common good. Fundamental ideas like these can be reduced to the relations of symmetry and reciprocity presupposed in communicative action. In other words, the common core of all kinds of morality can be traced back to the reciprocal imputations and shared presuppositions actors make when they seek understanding in everyday situations.[29]

The strong link between morality and social integration is obvious here, but there is also an implicit model of the structure of social development at work which creates tensions in Habermas's understanding of the 'moral' as a domain of communicatively rationalized norms. To bring this out, I would like to invoke a distinction Taylor makes between 'cultural' and 'acultural' theories of modernity.[30] 'Cultural' theories account for the transition to modernity in terms of the intrinsic appeal of the normative content of a specific cultural form. Taylor himself adopts this kind of approach in his explication of the modern identity as shaped by ideals of inwardness, freedom and the affirmation of ordinary life.[31] 'Acultural theories', on the other hand, explain the transition in terms of the actualization of some universal but dormant capacity for thought and action, or by way of the performance of some social operation which is definable independently of culture. On this model, *all* cultures could, under suitable conditions, undergo the transition to modernity; any culture could in principle serve as 'input' for the chosen 'culture-neutral' explanatory procedure. Functionalism has been an influential theory of the 'acultural' kind, but theories which construe the transition to modernity as a rationalization process also tend to take this form.

I would like to suggest that Habermas's skewed account of the moral domain arises from prior 'acultural' theoretical commitments. Without involving ourselves in the details of Habermas's social theory, we can gather from the passage cited above that it assumes that linguistically mediated interaction functions as the 'culture-neutral' mechanism by which, to use Habermas's own terminology, societies reproduce their 'symbolic resources'. The symbolic resources of a society are made up of inherited stocks of implicit knowledge, mechanisms of communal bonding and patterns of individualization. All sustainable societies must be successful at reproducing these resources. In modern societies, however, the *rational* mode of linguistic interaction – namely, communicative action – becomes the predominant vehicle of reproduction. Symbolic resources are reproduced rationally when their conviction-carrying power feeds off the illocutionary warrant to justify validity claims when challenged. This, for Habermas, is the crux of the 'internal relation' between modernity and rationality: modernity has a claim to rationality in so far as it can 'generate its normativity out of itself',[32] which is to say out of the *procedural* mechanism for *reproducing* its symbolic resources, rather than from the contingent substance of those resources themselves. The affinity between the 'acultural' character of Habermas's theory of modernity and its reliance on the method of rational reconstruction should now be evident. For the whole direction of Habermas's approach is set by the assumption of 'internally reconstructible sequences in stages of competence' in the reproduction of symbolic resources, where the reproduction of symbolic resources constitutes a culture-neutral operation, definable independently of their substantive cultural production.

With such a theory of social development as background, Habermas can give a plausible account of how the rational core of moral intuitions of equality and formal respect can be clarified by way of a reconstruction of the symmetry and reciprocity conditions of communicative action-coordination. But it is far from evident how intuitions concerning the significance of the self-regarding virtues – indeed, of the whole range of strongly valued characteristics not obviously bound to the requirements of social integration – can be clarified in that manner. This point connects back to problems we noted in the previous section concerning Habermas's theorization of evaluatives. For Habermas faces the difficulty of explaining how interpretations of self-regarding virtue are capable of carrying *conviction*. Let us assume that such interpretations help constitute notions of self-realization. Then since Habermas conceives the evolution of modern societies as a process of rationalization, and since he includes a conception of self-realization in the normative content of modernity, he must also accept that *transitions* in conceptions of self-regarding virtues are subject to rational assessment. On the other hand, however, it is hard to see how the source of such convictions can be reduced to the procedural presupposi-tions of communicative action. That is to say, it is far from clear how transitions between such beliefs can derive their *cognitive* moment just from the idealizing presuppositions of the mechanism for reproducing symbolic resources.

Habermas wants his theory of practical reason to meet two seemingly incompatible objectives. On the one hand, his model of rationality is designed to account for the transition to modernity as a process of rationalization reconstructible by a culture-neutral theory. In order to do this, it must incorporate the differentiation of validity claims and the discourses thematizing them. On the other hand, his theory must also account for how context-specific developments of ethical life are accountable to reason, as well as culture-specific changes in conceptions of self-realization. Both tasks require the mediation of differentiations. The first Habermas attempts to fulfil by way of a distinction between justificatory discourses and discourses of application. He tries to achieve the second by resort to 'clinical intuitions' concerning the 'sickness' and 'health' of a form of life as a whole. I turn now to the adequacy of these gestures at mediation.[33]

(3) According to the discourse ethical model, participants in practical discourse abstract the values which emerge on the horizon of the lifeworld and put them to the universalizability test. This is the process of justification. In discourses of justification, participants stand back from the lifeworld and adopt a hypothetical attitude to particular normative aspects of it. But they must then concretize these abstractly justified norms, they must recontextualize them as appropriate moral judgements in the here and now of the lifeworld. The job of concretizing abstractly justified norms in a context-sensitive manner is the business of discourses of application. Drawing on the work of Klaus Günther, Habermas has now elaborated this distinction in some detail.[34] But it seems to me that despite these refinements, the whole enterprise of mediating logically distinct discourses of justification and application faces two basic difficulties.[35] First, there is the general problem that the very meaning of a norm is hardly separable from its appropriate application. It is not just, as Habermas acknowledges, that 'moral justifications are pointless unless the decontex-tualization of the general norms used in justification is compensated for in the process of application'. Rather, it is not clear how norms gain significance unless *there is* some point built into them from the outset. From a hermeneutic perspective, the error here lies in thinking that the application of a rule is somehow a second step made after and contingently

to its justification. To the degree to which Habermas's afterthoughts converge on this point of correction, the line between discourse ethics and hermeneutics fades away.

This leads to a different kind of objection to the discourse ethical distinction between justification and application, one that Habermas refers to as the Hegelian charge of 'rigorism'. By focusing exclusively on the abstract universalism of morally justified judgement, Hegel argued, the Kantian approach neglects the affective dimension of moral competence and maturity. Habermas's reply is to acknowledge the constitutive role of emotional dispositions and attitudes in the characterization of moral maturity, but only when integrated with the universalizing cognitive operation of the participants in practical discourse. Any adequate description of 'the highest stage of morality', he writes, must integrate an ethics of love with an ethics of law and justice. The target for the charge of moral rigorism, as Habermas sees it, is really 'an impairment of the faculty of judgement'.[36] But it is not clear how this highest stage of morality can be articulated through the model of communicative action. Drawing on the work of Carol Gilligan, Benhabib has argued forcefully and famously that action motivated out of an ethics of love may be oriented around the particular rather than the general neediness of an other.[37] The other may appear in need of sympathy, encouragement, affection, support. But this could well be in conflict with the requirements of communicative action: not only may the raising and redeeming of the validity claims of truth, justice and sincerity simply lack relevance from the point of view of the concretely appearing other, but more radically, the appearance of neediness requires an orientation that can only fit into Habermas's typology of action as *strategic* in kind.

Let us now turn to the second of Habermas's compensating mediations. This has to do with the possibility of rational reflection concerning conceptions of the good, or the value of forms of life as a whole. As Habermas insists, it is impossible to adopt a hypothetical attitude to forms of life as a whole. Nor, he thinks, do conceptions of the good admit of rational consensus. But he also recognizes that notions of ethical life 'transcend de facto behaviour', he observes that through them 'subjects can distinguish the good life from the reproduction of mere life'.[38] As things stood in his early formulations of discourse ethics, where the boundaries imposed by the method of rational reconstruction were at their most inflexible, this recognition sat extremely uneasily with the claims about practical rationality and the moral domain. For if conceptions of the good are capable of transcending *de facto* behaviour, it follows that they are capable of motivating *rational* behaviour. As we have already noted, Habermas later defuses this objection by distinguishing between the pragmatic, ethical and moral employments of practical reason. But the following difficulty remains. If, by means of conceptions of the good, subjects can distinguish the good life from the mere reproduction of life, such value orientations (the horizon of ethical life) must be distinguished from the 'always already' naïvely accepted lifeworld. Habermas does affirm that value orientations towards the good congeal into historical and biographical syndromes which are subject to hermeneutic justification. But remarkably little – considering their importance – has been forthcoming on how such justification happens.

On the occasions when Habermas does affirm the accountability to reason of forms of individual or collective life as a whole, he calls upon a notion of 'clinical intuitions' that deploy a standard of 'health'. But Habermas's attempts at justifying his use of this idea are characterized by uneasiness. For instance, when asked in an interview about the appropriateness of a standard of sickness and health as a basis for critique, Habermas replied revealingly that for intuitions concerning the value of a form of life as a whole, 'we apply yardsticks which are valid in the first instance in the context of our culture or plausible in the context of our tradition. . . . So far I have no idea of how the universal core of those merely clinical intuitions – if indeed they have one at all – can be theoretically grasped.'[39] The problem Habermas faces here reflects the dilemma posed just earlier about the conflicting objectives of his theory of rationality. First, Habermas is committed to the view that normative universality is only graspable from a position of impartiality. Second, he claims that impartiality requires a transcendence of the culture in the context of which validity is provided in the first instance. He thus needs to show how the universal core of clinical intuitions can be theoretically grasped *independent* of particular cultural 'yardsticks'. But this is an impossible task, since clinical intuitions can never have application outside of particular cultural contexts. Habermas speaks of a criterion of sickness and health that is universal in virtue of its impartiality between cultures, in the same way as the criterion of justice is. But sickness and health (in the present context), Habermas also claims, are inseparable from need-interpretation, and not reducible to medical or biological invariables. That Habermas requires a yardstick that has a universal core in virtue of being culture-neutral betrays his commitment to rational reconstructions beyond hermeneutics, yet the conceptual resources of his reconstructive theory are unable to yield just what needs to be theoretically grasped. In order to be rendered intelligible, the claim to *universality* of clinical intuitions would need to be conceptualized non-criterially: their validity would have to be construed in a way that is bound to particular cultural contents, but not merely in the *first* instance. As we have seen, Habermas has since turned to the appropriative understanding of hermeneutically generated self-clarification for a model for how changes in clinical intuitions are rationally justifiable. In so far as they are rationally justifiable, they have some claim to universality. This accords with the hermeneutic model of epistemic gain considered in chapters three and four.[40]

To sum up these objections, in discourse ethics the claim to reason of ethical life is at once claimed and denied. On the one hand, discourse ethics states that conceptions of the good can motivate rational behaviour, it acknowledges the normative assertoric force and rationality potential of strong evaluation. On the other, communicative competence differentiates between truth value and normative value, it *opposes* rationally motivated agreement to empirically motivated assent. Ethical life and the discourse appropriate to it oscillates erratically in and out of the space of reasons. If we find this way of thinking unsatisfactory, we should think again about the claim of rational reconstruction to move beyond hermeneutics.

HABERMAS AND NEO-ARISTOTELIANISM

In fact, Habermas has always acknowledged that the rational reconstruction of the moral point of view along discourse ethical lines is not without unhappy consequence. By separating the right from the good, and by construing the former as the basic moral phenomenon, it abstracts the agent from the requisite motivations to act morally. By privileging the moral competence that manifests itself at the level of the justification of maxims of action by reference to a principle of universalizability, it abstracts the agent from the particular lived situations in which norms are applied and competence tested. And by according priority to general principles of morality over particular contexts of ethical life, it lends itself to atomistic and contractarian conceptions of the person and society. But by way of reply, Habermas insists that there can be no simple cancelling out of the dilemma between form and content. 'The neo-Aristotelian way out of this dilemma', he writes,

> is to argue that practical reason should foreswear its universalistic intent in favour of a more contextual faculty of judgement. Since judgement always moves within the ambit of a more or less accepted form of life, it finds support in an evaluative context that engenders *continuity* among questions of motivation, empirical issues, evaluative issues, and normative issues.[41]

Against this, discourse ethics refuses to go back prior to Kantian thought, insisting that the idea of impartial application is preferable to the idea of prudential judgement as a conception of practical reasoning. Habermas gives a twofold reason for its preferability. First, the neo-Aristotelian approach is said to be encumbered with 'metaphysical premises' incompatible with the evolution of the learning process thought to characterize the transition to modernity.[42] Second, once this metaphysical basis for critique is renounced, Habermas supposes that neo-Aristotelianism assumes a relativistic and thereby essentially *conservative* character. It seems to offer no rationally forceful protection against prejudice and parochialism.[43]

The metaphysical premise of the neo-Aristotelian approach, it seems, lies in its presumption of continuity between motivational, empirical and normative issues. For the neo-Aristotelian, as depicted here by Habermas, how the objective world is (an empirical, quasi-motivational issue) sets the standard for how to act (a normative, quasi-motivational issue), and this provides the basis of the objectivity of a moral order. As a neo-Kantian, Habermas insists that an objective moral order can be grounded only on the basis of universalizable norms of action discontinuous with 'empirical issues', since the empirical issue of how the objective world is can offer no reason for moral action. Only the neo-Kantian position, he thinks, is consistent with the evolution of learning processes in modernity – that is, the actualization of the formal capacity to differentiate and thematize truth, rightness and authenticity aspects of validity claims. But recall now the status of the 'clinical intuitions'. The coherence of Habermas's concept of clinical intuitions, I argued, depends upon them being construed firstly as premonitions of the good life, and secondly as truth-evaluable *in their action-orienting aspect*.[44] But this is just the 'metaphysical premise' of the neo-Aristotelian. So far as the ethical employment of practical reason goes, then, Habermas is *already one step down* the neo-Aristotelian path, since the presuppositions of that use of practical reason are *no less metaphysical* than those proposed by the neo-Aristotelian, thus far defined.

This conclusion is corroborated by an objection Habermas puts to Bernard Williams, whom he places in the neo-Aristotelian camp. 'How truthfulness to an existing self or society is to be combined with reflection, self-understanding, and criticism', Habermas cites Williams as asserting, 'has to be answered through reflective *living*'.[45] He then objects that 'Williams is compelled to attribute to practical reason a form of rationality which goes beyond sheer common sense but whose difference from scientific rationality remains to be determined'.[46] But here again, driven by the need to defend his neo-Kantian rational reconstructions, Habermas neglects the third path which he himself has opened up in his conception of theory-mediated, autobiographically informed reflective living, which has a claim to rationality *neither* reducible to common sense *nor* to scientific rationality. What is true of deep hermeneutic reflection also holds for the claim to therapeutic rationality of justified clinical intuitions. This alternative to common sense and scientism, in Habermas's reformulated and less cumbersome jargon, is precisely excellence in the ethical employment of practical reason.[47]

If Habermas already has one foot on the 'neo-Aristotelian' path, perhaps the reason he does not take it lies with the second of his objections, that neo-Aristotelianism displays a conservative bias. Habermas does indeed suspect it of being inappropriate as a philosophical basis for critical reflection. 'In modern societies', he writes,

> we encounter a pluralism of individual life-styles and collective forms of life and a corresponding multiplicity of ideas of the good life. As a

consequence we must give up one of two things: the claim of classical philosophy to be able to place competing ways of life in a hierarchy and establish at its acme one privileged way of life over against all others; or the modern principle of tolerance according to which one view of life is as good as any other, or at least has equal right to exist and be recognized.[48]

And he continues,

if we wish to remain faithful to the Aristotelian conviction that moral judgement is bound to the ethos of a particular place, we must be prepared to renounce the emancipatory potential of moral universalism and deny so much as the possibility of subjecting the violence inherent in social conditions characterized by latent exploitation and repression to an unstinting moral critique. For only the post-traditional level of moral judgement liberates us from the structural constraints of familiar discourses and established practices.[49]

Certainly, if the neo-Aristotelian position entails that competing ways of life be dogmatically placed in a hierarchy with one particular way of life unassailably imposed at its highest point, if it really does rule out the very possibility an unstinting moral critique of latent exploitation and repression, it is unfit as a philosophical basis for critical reflection. But the alternatives presented in these passages by no means exhaust the possibilities for critical reflection, even on Habermas's own terms. For a start, the critique of 'the violence inherent in social conditions characterized by latent exploitation and repression', is on Habermas's account the job not of discourse ethical moral philosophy but deep hermeneutics. Under pressure to defend his neo-Kantianism, we witness Habermas ushering from view just the means for countering conservatism opened up by deep hermeneutics and the so-called clinical intuitions of therapeutic reason. Secondly, Habermas's theory can itself be seen as presuming the ethical superiority of a particular form of life. Habermas concedes as much when, in reply to objections that the psychoanalytical model of critique presumes a privileged epistemic and evaluative standard on the part of the theorist, he states that the emancipatory psychoanalytical narrative does not define how the life of the individual must continue, only that it return the subject to the dignity of *homo sapiens*.[50] But of course the idea of human dignity helps constitute a strong evaluative framework. It follows that Habermas cannot but be prepared to privilege *at least one* way of life over others.

Something like this thought stands behind Taylor's critique of Habermas's metaethic.[51] According to Taylor, Habermas's moral theory is best seen as an elaboration of a particular vision of the good: the life of rational cooperation and mutual understanding between autonomous individuals. Far from abstracting from considerations of the good, discourse ethics has this 'constitutive good' built into it. Although

Habermas himself has not responded in detail to Taylor's objection, William Rehg makes it the decisive issue of his systematic reconstruction and defence of discourse ethics.[52] Rehg sees that Taylor's point threatens the viability of Habermas's theory, at least in so far as discourse ethics claims to reconstruct the universal basis of morality independently of contingently occurring, local and substantive conceptions of the good. Rehg's strategy for defending Habermas is to argue that, to the extent to which discourse ethics does depend on a constitutive good, the good in question is a *unique* one to which there is *no alternative*. So long as the good of rational cooperation enjoys this special status, Rehg argues, discourse ethics' dependence on it compromises neither its claim to universality nor its exclusion of a broader ontology of the human. I shall now examine whether this strategy succeeds in vindicating the claim of discourse ethics to move beyond hermeneutics.

Rehg's strategy follows three stages. In the first, he refers to Habermas's reply to an objection put by Agnes Heller that his theory does nothing to convince any particular individual why, in any given context, he or she should follow communicative rather than strategic–instrumental rationality.[53] For Habermas, the criticism is unfounded because such an individual, the 'moral sceptic', implicitly relies on communicatively structured networks of interaction for the formation and maintenance of his own identity. To withdraw completely from communicative contexts of interaction, to isolate oneself in an enclosed, monological sphere of self-interest, is to put one's sanity at risk. Habermas here invokes the 'causality of fate' theme that played such a crucial role in his model of depth hermeneutics: the suppression of an ethical totality of mutual recognition avenges itself in crises of individual and collective identity. As we saw, for Habermas communicative contexts of interaction are an essential condition for processes of non-pathological identity-formation. With this assumption, Habermas can argue that the sceptic gets involved in a kind of performative contradiction. Since his very identity is supported by communicative structures that he simultaneously denies, the sceptic would not be in a position to perform his speech act if his claim were true.

It is for this reason that rational communicative interaction occupies a 'special position' in the lexicon of constitutive goods. But so far Habermas's argument is not incompatible with hermeneutics. On the contrary, a defining characteristic of hermeneutics is its insistence that language provides an emphatically intersubjective space in which subjectivity both emerges and is sustained. Hermeneutics is at one with Habermas in its belief in the irreplaceable role of language in processes of self-formation and self-expression. The strategic actor who renounces this space also renounces himself. On the hermeneutic view, self and other co-constitute an 'ethical totality'; hence neither can survive a splitting-off from the other. However, this will only furnish the sceptic with a reason for behaving 'morally' to the extent that he actually *identifies himself* with an ethical totality. The hermeneutic argument then proceeds by making clear and explicit various ways in which the sceptic's sense of self does indeed rely implicitly, confusedly and unacknowledgedly, on such an identification. It involves bringing out hidden, but motivationally potent, commitments from his background horizon of self-interpretation. This means that, for hermeneutics, the sceptic can only be 'refuted' from *within* a shared cultural horizon. Discourse ethics, on the other hand, wants to move beyond hermeneutics by way of universalizing the validity of its anti-sceptical claim. As Rehg sees, Habermas attempts to do this by showing that 'the imperative towards rational cooperation extends without alternatives not only to all those sharing in a form of life but also across different cultures and language groups'.[54]

According to the second stage of Rehg's reconstruction, Habermas can only demonstrate this if he supplements the 'no alternative thesis' with a 'moral formalism thesis'. The formalism thesis asserts that the good of rational cooperation is built into formal structures of language in general, irrespective of the substantive goods that a particular language may help constitute or disclose. It maintains that communicative actors of whatever linguistic and cultural background cannot in reflective lucidity renounce the normative validity of rational cooperation, since rational cooperation is 'a good given with the rational potential of speech itself, in particular, with the power of validity claims to transcend local boundaries and submit themselves to a potentially universal testing'.[55] With the support of the formalist thesis, discourse ethics abstracts from the world-disclosive powers of any particular language, finding its basis in 'a telos shared by all languages'. While substantive goods must be disclosed by particular languages, while their realization is specific to a concrete form of life, the good of mutual understanding 'resides in the validity orientation of language as such'. If this thesis is sound, the anti-sceptical foundation of discourse ethics is distanced from the self-interpretive resources of any local language, and therefore from any substantive conception of the good or particular historical development. Any culture should at some point be able to reconstruct the discourse ethical insight into the unavoidability of rational cooperation since all cultures are mediated to a greater or lesser extent by communicative action. Although different cultures, with their varying languages of self-interpretation, will disagree in reason about substantive goods, the existence of formal structures of language allows all to agree on the validity of the good of rational cooperation.

For discourse ethics, then, the good of rational cooperation is unique in that it is written into formal structures of language. But it is also unique in that it provides the only acceptable basis for conflict resolution in pluralist societies. In the third stage of his reconstruction, Rehg considers the unavoidability of the discourse ethical constitutive good for social stability. This leads him to formulate a much weaker version of the 'no alternative thesis', that in pluralist contexts rational cooperation is unavoidable as a mechanism of conflict resolution 'on the whole and in certain domains'.[56] Here again, hermeneutics need not disagree. However, of more conse-quence for our current concern is the fact that the imperative of conflict resolution is used by discourse ethics to justify a conception of practical reasoning that *does* seem to be at odds with the hermeneutic view. Discourse ethics derives the normative force of practical reason from the formal, pragmatically structured intersubjective basis of language. And it is just this reliance on the formalism thesis that in Rehg's opinion, gives discourse ethics the edge over hermeneutics. For Rehg, the decisive point in favour of discourse ethics is its *intersubjective* notion of practical insight. For whereas *others* supposedly enter the hermeneutic model of practical reason only as an accidental spin-off of considerations of self-interest or group-value, Rehg suggests, through its formalism thesis discourse ethics incorporates the voice of the other into the very constitution of practical reason. For discourse ethics, 'what ultimately generates one's concern for the welfare of the other, what requires participants to undertake a cooperative search for moral values around which a rational cooperation amongst autonomous individuals can develop, are the cognitive pressures that arise from language itself'.[57]

Does the formalism thesis rescue discourse ethics from Taylor's criticism? There are a number of difficulties with Rehg's proposal. Recall that in Taylor's view, discourse ethics presupposes the 'constitutive good' of rational cooperation among autonomous individuals. Rehg correctly sees this as a threat to Habermas's theory, in so far as discourse ethics allegedly moves beyond hermeneutics by abstracting from all reliance on contingently occurring substantive conceptions of the good. However, the discourse ethical project can be redeemed if it can be shown that there is no alternative to the good of rational cooperation, which is also unique in residing in the formal, intersubjective structure of language as such. We have already noted that the 'no alternative' thesis, at least as formulated by Habermas in response to Heller, serves only to reinforce Taylor's initial suspicion that the theory of communicative action incorporates a conception of the good. For according to the 'no alternative' argument, there is no alternative to communicative action in precisely the same sense that a philosophical anthropology of the kind favoured by Taylor requires of *all* goods that are constitutive of human agency. The success of Rehg's strategy therefore turns on the validity of the 'formalism' thesis. But it is not at all clear how formalism answers the specific hermeneutic complaint raised by Taylor. In the first place, formalism adds nothing to the way in which the 'no alternative' thesis answers the problem of moral motivation. Even if rational cooperation is built into universal structures of language, why should that move anyone to act in a rationally cooperative manner? Habermas replies to this objection by insisting that moral theory is in the business of justifying moral motivations and practices rather than generating them. Whether or not one is motivated to follow communicatively grounded norms has no bearing, on discourse ethical premises, on whether or not norms are communicatively – that is, rationally – grounded. But it is just at this deeper level of assumptions about the function of moral theory and the nature of practical reasoning that hermeneutics wedges its fundamental objections. In construing the demands of practical reason independently of the motivational resources available for actualizing them, discourse ethics perpetrates a *rationalist reduction* of practical reason. The decisive point for hermeneutics is that the issue of moral sources is not an *additional consideration* for a theory of practical reasoning: *the nature and availability of moral sources is not contingent to the demands of practical reason as such*. From the hermeneutic point of view, the question of what reason there is for recognizing the objective claims of *Moralität* cannot be decided in advance of considerations concerning the availability of *moral sources* to empower morally motivated action.

Discourse ethics forecloses consideration of moral sources for two main reasons. First, because it allegedly lies outside the realm of philosophy. Second, because such considerations introduce contingencies that deflect attention from the essential feature of the moral demand; its unconditionality. On the first point, Habermas insists that it cannot be the business of philosophical reflection to undertake a hermeneutic of moral sources because philosophy is 'too belated' to sensitize us to morality and is 'overtaxed' by the goal of orienting the subject to the good.[58] It is overtaxed given the legitimate pluralism of conceptions of the good in relation to which subjects are oriented. It is too belated because an agent's moral motivations come from socialization processes not philosophical reflection: 'We learn what moral, and in particular immoral, action involves *prior* to all philosophizing.... The inarticulate, socially integrating experiences of considerateness, solidarity, and fairness shape our intuitions and provide us with better instruction about morality than arguments ever could'.[59] Accordingly, Habermas thinks, philosophy can only reconstruct the rational core of moral demands, it cannot *produce* their force. This is why he believes that an articulation of moral sources of the kind proposed by Taylor cannot hope to meet its goals. But in making this objection, Habermas fails to appreciate that the validity of the hermeneutic approach requires only that the force of the moral demand is not *fully* given by socialization processes. Hermeneutics only claims to enable retrieval, renewal, recovery. It starts from the premise that the force of ethical life can be close or distant, potent or dormant. Articulation can reawaken a sense of ethical life to some degree, it can bring it closer, just as radical changes in self-interpretation can help constitute or produce self-transfigurations. But a hermeneutic approach to ethics does not, as Habermas's objection implies, attempt to create a motivational set *ex nihilo*. In so far as the sceptic stands in a hypothetical position completely outside moral space, hermeneutics has nothing to say to him. It refuses to take up the hypothetical sceptic's gauntlet precisely because it is aware that practical reasoning can only get going on the basis of some shared horizon of moral conviction. In fact, if any moral theory implies the need for a complete overhaul of existing motivational structures, it is the Kantian one, both in so far as it attempts to meet sceptical objections which stand outside any horizon of moral commitment, and to the extent that it requires the demands of morality to be satisfied *whatever* the actual dispositional set of those affected by them.

What about the second objection, that concerning unconditionality? The specific virtue Rehg claims for discourse ethics in contrast to hermeneutics is its ability to demonstrate the 'equiprimordiality' of rational insight and universal intersubjective solidarity. Again, this is supposed to be a consequence of the formalist thesis. So long as moral insight is conditioned by the world-disclosive semantic powers of a particular language, defenders of discourse ethics fear, the bonds of solidarity are restricted to groups, traditions or lifeworlds. But this view imports a monolithic view of horizons of linguistic disclosure that is quite alien to hermeneutics. For Gadamer and Taylor, there is no doubt that two languages can impinge on each other in a rationally progressive manner. It is just that they do not *explain* this phenomenon by reference to universal linguistic structures that allow for abstraction from particular world-disclosive contents. Rather, they point to how 'fusions of horizon' open up unprecedented points of comparison in the light of which practical insights can be made. Such a notion of insight is neither less cognitive nor more monological for having little to do with formal pragmatic structures of linguistic intersubjectivity.

Hermeneutics is thus far from resting content with the constitutive power of any given particular language. But it is only on the assumption that it does that a formal thesis needs to be invoked to account for the rational resolution of conflicts between languages of self-interpretation. Indeed, discourse ethics considers the truth of an internal relation between the validity of moral claims and their acceptability to others as *equivalent* to the truth of formalism.[60] But it is better to think of the difference between discourse ethics and hermeneutics as turning not on *whether* they make the constitutive connection between self and other but on *how* they make it. By appealing to what all languages share in their pragmatic structure, discourse ethics links validity with acceptability to a 'generalized' other. By appealing to the comparable content of horizons of world-disclosure, hermeneutics links practical reason with a 'concrete' other. So the crucial difference between discourse ethics and hermeneutics lies not in whether they accept the dialogical nature of reaching understanding as such. Rather it resides in the particular conception of intersubjectivity or 'dialogicality' they do uphold. Nor should discourse ethics be distinguished from hermeneutics on account of its commitment to the universal *reach* of moral respect. Hermeneutics does not propose that people only have basic moral rights and entitlements if they belong to a particular group or community. It certainly is not of the opinion that rational conflict resolution is a matter of self-interest or the dictates of a group's world view. Again, the real difference between discourse ethics and hermeneutics concerns their understanding of the *basis* of the respect that is owed to others, irrespective of the group to which they belong or the world view they share. Whereas the formalism thesis bases this respect on cognitive pressures built into the pragmatics of language, for hermeneutics it is grounded in the evolution of ideals of democratic citizenship, self-determination, the rule of law, and the like. Hermeneutics does not substitute partiality for unconditionality, it just theorizes the normative force of unconditionality by drawing on the more or less explicit content of substantive ethical ideals, rather than by resorting to a formalist thesis.

So what conclusions can we make about Rehg's strategy for rescuing discourse ethics? If the arguments just outlined are broadly sound, the 'no alternative' thesis is systematically ambiguous. On the one hand, it contains a claim about the role played by communicative action in constituting forms of self-realization. There is no alternative to communicative action, in this sense of the claim, because of its replacement by other forms of action-coordination issues in individual and social pathologies. To suppose there to be 'no alternative' in this sense is to suppose a non-contingent fact about the constitution of self-interpreting animals. The force of the claim arises from the hypothesis that there are anthropological limits to the contingency of self-formative processes. Unless a deep-seated anthropological interest in communicative mediation is satisfied, the claim runs, no other worthwhile interests will be. This view is clearly consistent with the philosophical outlook of strong hermeneutics. On the other hand, there is 'no alternative' to the constitutive good of communicative action because linguistic acts unavoidably presuppose procedural normative constraints. The unavoidability here is logical and formal rather than substantive and anthropological. Its limits to contingency are derived as a transcendental structure of *linguistic action* rather than as a transcendental structure of *language beings*.[61] The 'formal thesis' – which allegedly transforms unavoidability into uniqueness – relies on the former kind of unavoidability only. As such, formalism is not, as Rehg's argument requires, a development of the first sense of the no alternative thesis. Rehg introduces the formalist thesis because, like Habermas, he believes that without it, rational cooperation between autonomous individuals becomes just one constitutive good amongst others.[62] However, I have argued that this way of thinking about the unavoidability of communicative action only causes alarm because discourse ethics misrepresents the consequences of upholding the hermeneutic position. Hermeneutics does not exclude the other from processes of practical reason; it does not relativize normative validity to monolithic linguistic traditions; and it does not impose artificial restrictions on the reach of moral predicates. Rather, it includes the other at a concrete rather than a generalized level; it links processes of practical reason with productive transformations in the content of interpretive horizons; and it defends the unlimited reach of basic moral entitlements in terms of unrenounceable constituents of modern identity. Once hermeneutics is seen aright, discourse ethics looks strangely unmotivated. Hence the argument that discourse ethics presupposes a unique constitutive good does not undermine the conclusion we reached at the end of the previous section, that the claim of discourse ethics to advance beyond hermeneutics has not been satisfactorily established.

CONCLUSION: TOWARDS A CRITIQUE OF PROCEDURAL REASON

My argument has not just been that, in key respects, Habermas's move away from hermeneutics lacks motivation. I have also urged the stronger thesis that the shift from hermeneutics is self-defeating given the overall ambition of the theory of communicative action. As we have noted, the ultimate goal of Habermas's theory is to clarify the normative grounds for the critique of instrumental reason. As an object of 'critique', the deficiencies and deformations of instrumental reason must be demonstrated from within reason's purview. With the assumption steadfastly in place that 'the disenchantment of religious–metaphysical world views robs rationality, along with the contents of tradition, of all substantive connotations', Habermas naturally concludes that critical, communicative reason must have a 'purely procedural character'.[63] But it is hard to see how the critique of instrumental reason can effectively be prosecuted on a procedural normative basis. That is not to say – as defenders of strong hermeneutics, including Taylor, sometimes do argue – that the critique of instrumental reason *must at the same time* be a critique of procedural reason. Proceduralism does not coincide with instrumentalism, nor *need* it reinforce an objectifying or reifying point of view. But a procedural conception of reason cannot suffice for diagnosing and correcting reification. In my concluding remarks to this chapter, I will briefly consider the extent to which Taylor's hermeneutic critique of procedural reason applies to Habermas's theory.

There are two quite different contexts in which Taylor examines the nature and shortcomings of a procedural conception of reason. In the first, he associates proceduralism with the ideal of rational disengagement found in Descartes but only fully developed in Locke's conception of a 'punctual self'. The punctual self identifies itself 'with the power to objectify and remake'.[64] Procedural reason, according to this model, is the mechanism by which the self exercises control over its own pre-objective experience. In order to render experiential content maximally transparent to – and therefore controllable by – itself, the punctual subject analyses experience into self-evident, 'given' atomic constituents, such as 'ideas', 'impressions' or 'sense data'. Given the disenchantment of nature, rational experience – the experience of the rational subject – thereby loses any normative character. Now while a critique of procedural reason so conceived clearly overlaps, if not coincides, with a critique of instrumental reason, it is hardly applicable to communicative reason. On the contrary, Taylor's depiction of procedural reason in this context is almost identical to Habermas's portrayal of 'subject-centred reason', precisely the conception of reason in opposition to which he offers his communicative model.[65] To appreciate the difference between Habermas and Taylor on the relation between procedural and instrumental reason, we therefore need to turn to the second context in which Taylor attacks proceduralism: his discussions of procedural ethics.

Taylor's attacks on procedural ethics in general – those that take on classical utilitarianism and traditional liberal contract theories – focus on its alleged refusal to acknowledge qualitative evaluative contrasts. Since Taylor's main thesis is that it only makes sense to talk of procedures as *ethical* in so far as they contribute to some substantive conception of the good life, he has to demonstrate that there are unacknowledged notions of the good implicitly at work in proceduralist theories. The two mainsprings of proceduralism Taylor identifies are the goods of freedom and benevolence. For Taylor, validity in ethics can only seem intelligible solely in terms of procedures because substantive goods like freedom and benevolence are implicitly assumed to have unconditional validity. *Given* the goods of freedom and the alleviation or minimization of suffering, it makes sense to argue about procedures necessary for non-violent conflict-resolution. But a theory that dismisses qualitative contrasts of the kind that make goods like freedom and benevolence intelligible in the first place will be inarticulate about its normative foundation. Any proceduralist ethic cannot avoid this performative contradiction, so Taylor argues.

Clearly, despite the tensions in Habermas's account of evaluative discourses and the relationship between morality and ethical life, he does not deny the validity of qualitative distinctions. Habermas's theory is not nearly as unrefined as the versions of proceduralism Taylor generally attacks. Nevertheless, Taylor can make the same basic objection to discourse ethics as he does to procedural ethics in general. Procedures are only of moral or ethical significance, Taylor insists, if agents believe it good to follow them. So the first – or last – thing a proceduralist theory must seek to establish are reasons to support that belief. Communicative ethics can provide such reasons by showing 'the way in which human identity is formed through dialogue and recognition', but not by formal arguments purporting to demonstrate 'the pragmatic contradiction involved in the violation of certain norms'.[66] Habermas's theory will succeed to the extent that it establishes on the one hand, the superiority of the 'constitutive good' of rational cooperation and mutual understanding between autonomous individuals over others, and on the other, certain essential conditions for the realization of this good. Its ability to convince therefore depends on it dropping its claim to stand independently of any notion of the good. For only once the constitutive good built into the theory is fully acknowledged does the *significance* of the procedures reconstructed by the theory come to light.

In the last section, I argued that Rehg's attempt to save Habermas's proceduralism from this objection by incorporating the good of rational cooperation into discourse ethics via the 'formalist' thesis fails. I argued further that the strategy of incorporating Taylor's point via the 'no alternative' thesis only confirms, rather than confounds, the hermeneutic–ontological status of the theory of communicative action. We are now in a position to see how strong hermeneutic presuppositions also come inescapably into play in the critique of instrumental reason and reification. As we have observed, the wider aim of the theory of communicative action is to establish just what Taylor thinks is required of an ethics properly – that is to say, substantively – conceived: that the mediation of individuals and collectives by instrumental reason issues in individual and collective pathology. The ambition of Habermas's theory as a whole, in other words, is to show that a reified form of life offends deeply ingrained *clinical* intuitions. Now although Habermas refuses to posit any criteria of validity for 'health' – indeed he maintains that health cannot be judged against rational criteria at all – the critique of reification undertaken and grounded by the theory of communicative action implicitly relies on the *holistic* value of a balanced, integrated and meaningful life. Rather than ascribing a validity claim to judgements of health, Habermas appeals to a holistic conception of *aesthetic* truth that harmoniously mediates the differentiated moments of validity in a manner analogous to Kant's notion of reflective judgement.[67] As David Ingram observes, Habermas relies implicitly on Kant's account of aesthetic judgement for solving the problem of how to bring to account imbalanced or disharmonious *relations* between incommensurable dimensions of rationality.[68] For Habermas, aesthetic judgement involves a moment of 'seeing as' whose rationality is indirect, pre-discursive and metaphorical. Since it is not tied to any particular aspect of validity, it can be used for making sense of criticizable relations between differentiated and reified validity complexes that characteristically deform modern forms of life. In this manner Habermas's aesthetic runs against his proceduralism. And as Ingram observes, it performs an analogous role to Taylor's notion of an 'epiphanic experience' in grounding the critique of social reification.[69]

But there is a crucial difference between Taylor's notion and Habermas's suggestions about the critical function of art. According to Taylor's view, modern art achieves excellence in the disclosure of goods that are constituted by something *other* than human needs or capacities. If that is the case, then even the incipient move away from proceduralism marked by Habermas's appeal to the mediation of judgement is an insufficiently radical departure from subject-centred or instrumental reason. So far as the critique of subject-centred reason goes, the significance of art – on Habermas's view – lies primarily in its potential as a surrogate for religion understood as a 'unifying power'.[70] Against Habermas's focus on the demise of religion as a medium of sociation – that is to say, the 'public consequences' of instrumental reason – Taylor foregrounds the way in which modern art addresses itself to the 'experiential' consequences of the instrumentalized culture of modernity.[71] For Taylor, the critique of social reification by way of epiphanic experience is exemplary because it addresses the key issue of *moral sources*. The epiphanic dimension of modernist art, on Taylor's account, issues from the 'search for moral sources *outside* the subject through languages which resonate *within* him or her'.[72] As Taylor points out, the modernist exploration of a moral order through a language of personal resonance is unintelligible within Habermas's schema of validity claims, with its differentiation of objective truth, normative rightness and subjective authenticity. But even if, as Ingram suggests, Habermas's references to judgement mitigate against the rigidity of this formal framework, *it still prevents us from asking the question of the meaning of moral sources residing outside the subject*. And arguably it is only with this question that we genuinely break out of the paradigm of subject-centred reason and open the way for an effective critique of instrumental reason.

7 The ecological politics of strong hermeneutics

According to the argument of chapter one, Enlightenment fundamentalism proves itself unable to sustain a satisfactory articulation of the relation between contingency and moral identity. This *theoretical* weakness motivates a variety of hermeneutic responses. But as a reconstruction of the appeal of hermeneutics, my account has been rather one-sided. For it has not taken into consideration reasons for a profoundly *practical* dissatisfaction with the Enlightenment stance. It has neglected, in other words, the extent to which the decline of Enlightenment fundamentalism has been precipitated by perceptions of its disastrous practical *effects*. Foremost amongst these, of course, have been perceptions of environmental devastation. Critics of Enlightenment fundamentalism often regard it as providing ideological support for untrammelled technological interventions in finely balanced natural processes. They regard it as *politically* suspect. By implication, a *critique* of these practices must have different philosophical resources to draw upon. It is only to be expected, therefore, that critics of the technological domination of nature should be drawn to hermeneutic thought. But which of the hermeneutic orientations outlined so far provides the most suitable framework for this kind of critique?

I shall address the issue of the applicability of hermeneutics to environmental politics by way of examining the philosophical resources needed to make sense of ecological responsibility. First, let us briefly remind ourselves of how the ideals of the Enlightenment might be thought to license ecologically irresponsible action. The Enlightenment invites us to celebrate the immanent arrival of cognitively mature, self-determining humanity. Cognitive maturity, according to the Enlightenment picture, is reached when the tendency to project meaning onto nature is overcome and the bare disenchanted truth of things is squarely confronted. Self-determining humanity, cognizant of the lack of purpose in nature, sees the contingencies of nature for what they are and sets about transforming them into effective instruments of its own will. To be sure, contemporary defenders of Enlightenment ideals rarely advocate such an unqualified instrumental stance. The problem for them is not just the empirical point that the instrumental orientation correlates with environmental carelessness of potentially disastrous consequence for humans. They are also troubled by the philosophical idea that an exclusively prudential conception of reason may be incapable of grounding well-oriented interactions with nature. For the instrumental understanding of the natural environment jars with deep intuitions about responsibility to and for the *other side* of the human/nature relationship: the voice of 'ecological conscience', if I may use this term to describe such persistent intuitions, seems to resist translation into the vocabulary of enlightened self-interest.[1]

But if defenders of the Enlightenment ideals of cognitive maturity and self-determination sway under the pull of ecological conscience, they stand their ground as soon as cosmologically rooted orders of moral meaning are invoked to ground its claims. There can be no return, they insist, to normatively instructive metaphysical world views. No backward step to stages prior to the maturation of human cognitive capacities is permissible. Likewise, the defenders of Enlightenment are anxious to see that the ideal of self-determination does not go under in the salving of ecological conscience. In particular, they are suspicious of the anti-human sentiment betrayed in some of the more radical expressions of environmental protest. In the place of counter-Enlightenment, anti-humanist rhetoric, they foreground the rights and peculiar dignity of the human subject, they point to the unfulfilled emancipatory promise of sensitively applied technology, and they warn us of the dangers of subordinating humanist conscience to ecological conscience.

At issue, then, is a post-metaphysical way of thinking about responsibility that refuses to *finesse* the enduring voice of ecological conscience.[2] How is a more than prudentially compelling responsibility to nature *intelligible* under conditions of cognitive maturity? In this chapter I shall defend a strong hermeneutic answer to this question. In the first section, I set the stage a little more fully by introducing a notion of 'subject-centred responsibility'. Subject-centred responsibility is the kind of responsibility that is apt for a subject as conceived in the subject–object paradigm of philosophy. It aspires to cognitive maturity and self-determination but is heedless to the voice of ecological conscience. I then turn, in the second section, to one attempt at rethinking responsibility by comprehending it independently of the axioms of subject-centred reason. In his book *Political Theory and Postmodernism*, Stephen K. White gives an account of how a paradigm shift in our thinking from subjectivity to language can make sense of that moment of responsibility suppressed in modern, Enlightenment thought.[3] Following in the steps of Habermas's linguistic turn, White distinguishes two basic functions of language: action-coordination and world-disclosure. But turning then to postmodernist insights about language – particularly those of Foucault, Derrida and Heidegger – he invokes a corresponding division of basic and irreducible dimensions of responsibility. He calls these the 'responsibility to act' and 'responsibility to otherness', corresponding to the action-coordinative and world-disclosive capacities of language respectively. White's postmodernist understanding of responsibility is of interest to us because it promises to make sense of a more than prudential responsibility to nature by non-metaphysical means. I then argue that while this promise cannot in the end be delivered, there are instructive reasons for its failure. I maintain that there are grounds for having serious misgivings about postmodernist representations of the world-disclosive capacity of language and its ability to function as the basis of an intelligible sense of responsibility. My claim is that postmodernism, in so far as it opens a space for thinking about 'responsibility to otherness' at all, does so *in spite of* its account of world-disclosure. This is not to say that world-disclosure is irrelevant for a renewed understanding of responsibility. Quite the opposite. But for nature as an 'other' to feature meaningfully in the field of responsibility, I argue, it has to be understood in *hermeneutic* terms as a contingently distant moral source. In section four, I turn briefly to an alternative understanding of the phenomenon of world-disclosure which, truer to the spirit of hermeneutics, might make better sense of the intelligibility of ecological conscience. However, for reasons outlined in the concluding section, we should also be careful not to exaggerate the political dividend of the strong hermeneutic approach.

ECOLOGY AND THE SUBJECT OF RESPONSIBILITY

In deploying the term 'subject-centred responsibility', I mean to evoke a conception of responsibility with features both of what Habermas calls 'subject-centred reason' and what Charles Taylor calls, borrowing in turn a phrase from Husserl, 'self-responsible reason'.[4] These features include a subject–object ontology, a conception of reason as the power of subjectivity to represent, reorder and control, and a conception of subjectivity as self-determining, reflexively retrievable, and potentially transparent to itself as pure self-consciousness. I want to unpack this familiar idea of the sovereign rational subject in just enough detail to show how it co-emerges with a conception of responsibility.

First, subject-centred responsibility finds its ontological location in the subject confronting an object and reflecting upon itself. There are negative and positive reasons for this. Negatively, in the world as it appears from the disengaged point of view of the rational subject, in a universe that shows itself fit for scientific representation and technological control, it seems as if there is *nowhere else* for responsibility to reside but the subject's own generative powers. In this sense, responsibility assumes intelligible form as a structure of subjectivity by default. Technology marks the rupture of meaning and cognition, of norm and nature, accelerating – so to speak – the ontological migration of responsibility from the world to its source of representation. For the subject reflecting on the questions 'what kind of being is it possible to be responsible to?' and 'what kind of entity is it possible to be responsible for?', there is only one intelligible answer: itself, its own powers of generativity. But if the subject assumes responsibility to and for itself merely by default, the coherence of the very idea of responsibility is at risk. For as an object of its own reflection, it is subject to the same empirical, nomic determinations as any other in the disenchanted world. A more positive ground for its responsibility is thus called for. This is gained from the idea that the technologically controlled and scientifically represented world of objects is an *achievement* of rational subjectivity. In a twofold movement, the subject first disengages itself from the spontaneous flow of experience and events, then reorders experience and events according to some canonical set of rules. In doing so, the knowing subject takes responsibility. It finds itself, in its capacity as the site of objective representations, to be the guardian of truth; and in its capacity as the site of actions rather than events, as a will with the power to determine itself in transcendence of all contingency, it finds itself in the position of a supreme legislator.

On the one hand, then, the subject of subject-centred reason, to borrow Habermas's phrase, *has to* generate its normativity out of itself.[5] There is nowhere else for it to be generated from. So long as responsibility is understood in terms of the self-generating powers of subjectivity, there is nothing but itself to be furthered *in* the subject's responsibility. But far from diminishing the demands of responsibility, this process of subjectivication transforms and radically aggravates them. For the Enlightened subject is now to be the shaper of his own destiny rather than the product of a destiny shaped for him by environment, instinct and tradition. The reflexive retrievability of the subject in its knowledge of itself is paradoxically an expression both of its freedom and its imprisonment to its own objectifying powers. Subject-centred responsibility is initially posited as the only kind of intelligibility responsibility can have in a disenchanted cosmos and a de-traditionalized form of life. Yet, as part of nature, the subject can have its objectifying gaze turned on itself, and as part of society, it can be subsumed to larger demands of systemic self-preservation. In both cases, the same structure which grounds subject-centred responsibility undermines the very conditions of subjectivity, leaving the subject fluctuating between the space of intelligibility of free, unconditioned sovereignty, and that of the inert object, void of significance, manipulable in principle like any other.

The theoretical instability and normative deficits of the subject–object relation are well known enough and there is no need to rehearse them in any more detail here.[6] The fault-lines in our understanding of responsibility are bound to remain, however, unless there is a shift in our thinking towards an alternative paradigm. Moreover, it may be that our tendency to think of responsibility within an implicit subject-centred paradigm runs deeper than our readiness to reject that paradigm on explicitly articulated grounds. For instance, when pushed on the question of what differentiates humans from the rest of nature, what grounds the privileged status of humans as objects of moral concern, it is easy to fall back on characteristics like self-consciousness, the possession of a 'point of view' or self-determining action. Might not such ready-made answers merely be the reflexes of subject-centred reason? And might not this taken-for-grantedness of the axioms of the subject-centred paradigm also be at play in the tendency to regard environmental problems as essentially highly complex technological ones?

POSTMODERNISM, POLITICAL THEORY AND RESPONSIBILITY TO OTHERNESS

At any rate, my presumption is that the question of how to rethink responsibility independently of the axioms of subject-centred reason needs answering. As for the right way of going about the task, recent philosophy points firmly to the 'paradigm shift to language'. This is the approach, as I suggested above, followed by White. According to White's argument there are two fundamental dimensions to responsibility. As the starting point of philosophical reflection, one of these is at home in the modern tradition of political theory, the other is wholly foreign to it. Neither dimension, however, properly comes to light within the subject-centred paradigm. Responsibility becomes intelligible in both its dimensions, White maintains, only on the other side of the paradigm shift, where attention is focused on the generative and normative structures of language and intersubjectivity rather than those of subjectivity and consciousness.

The first, more familiar kind of responsibility, is the 'responsibility to act in the world in a justifiable way', or, as White himself abbreviates it, simply 'responsibility to act'.[7] The responsibility to act is typically represented as 'a moral–prudential obligation to acquire reliable knowledge and to achieve practical ends in a defensible manner'.[8] It refers to the responsibility incumbent upon the human *agent* – a being with no option but to respond in more or less justified ways to innerworldly cognitive and practical demands. This dimension of responsibility has been interpreted and grounded in various ways in a tradition of thought stretching from Hobbes to Habermas, though only with the latter's communicative ethics is a decisive break made with subject-centredness.

Postmodernism, on the other hand, marks a more radical point of departure: *pace* Habermas, it does not merely put the responsibility to act thematized in the modern tradition on a sounder intersubjective basis, it opens up a further dimension of responsibility suppressed and concealed in the modern tradition. According to White, the importance of postmodern political thought – as represented in the work of Heidegger and post-structuralists like Derrida, Lyotard and Foucault – lies in the sensitivity it shows to this other dimension of responsibility. It opens up unprecedented strategies for the exploration, and perhaps even retrieval, of otherness as an axis of responsibility. It is because, in pursuing these strategies, postmodern thinkers are not responsible in the *traditional* way, White suggests, that they are vulnerable to the charge of intellectual irresponsibility. For White, this objection carries with it a kind of metonymic fallacy. For while irresponsible from the point of view of the responsibility to act, the intellectual conduct of postmodern thinkers is born out of a strong sense of 'responsibility to otherness'. Whereas ideals of harmony, unity and clarity are suitable for showing how the responsibility to act is best fulfilled, they are of necessity inappropriate for articulating the claims of 'otherness'. For the other just is what is excluded and devalued 'in the infinite search for a more tractable and ordered world'.[9] Hence the accusation of irresponsibility arises from confounding the two different and incommensurable dimensions of responsibility. For this reason, the charge can be reciprocated: from the postmodern perspective of responsibility to otherness, there is a will to mastery (of situations) and closure (to alternative possibilities) always and to some ineliminable degree already at play in assuming the responsibility to act, where mastery and closure are paradigmatic of unfulfilled responsibility to otherness.

To get a clearer picture of what White means by the term 'responsibility to otherness', it helps to ask why just *these* two dimensions of responsibility? White's answer is that they mirror the two fundamental and irreducible dimensions of language. In its action-coordinative dimension, language is a medium of social interaction. Language, in this capacity, is a suitable object for a theory of pragmatics. As we saw in the last chapter, such a theory can reconstruct immanently applicable normative constraints on those engaged in such linguistic activity.[10] White takes on board the idea that there is a responsibility to act in accordance with these 'speech-act immanent obligations' that is, so to speak, written into the *telos* of language understood in its action-coordinating capacity.[11] By reconstructing the normative presuppositions of language oriented to rational action-coordination, Habermas thematizes the responsibility to act without reference to the axioms of subject-centred responsibility.

But while Habermas's distinction between the two modes of language enables him to put the responsibility to act on a sound footing, he remains insensitive to that dimension of responsibility which corresponds to the world-disclosive moment of language. In a move that will prove significant later, White begins by proposing that the meaning of this world-disclosive dimension of language – at least in so far as it is the correlate of responsibility to otherness – can be gleaned from a consideration of Habermas's main differences with Derrida. For Habermas, participants in communicative action make unavoidable idealizations about the meaning and context of their speech acts. These idealizations are considered to be pragmatically inescapable. For Derrida, on the other hand, idealizations of the kind imputed by Habermas unavoidably impose closure: they constitutively issue from a recognition of the structural possibility of the negative (in this case non-serious, abnormal, non-literal language use) that is at the same time excluded as accidental.[12] It is precisely such closure that language, in its world-disclosive capacity, always already undoes. In this way, postmodern thinkers like Derrida alert us to the 'fictional' character of the foundations of the responsibility to act, an insight they join with 'a concerted deployment of new fictions against whatever fictions are socially in force'. 'Both of these tasks', White continues,

> require a deep affirmation of the world-disclosing capacity of language, since it is the use of that capacity that can loosen our world's hold upon us by confronting us with the ways in which it is structured by unrecognized or forgotten fictions. And as this hold is loosened, we become far more sensitized to the otherness that is engendered by those structures.[13]

Postmodernism, then, affirms the world-disclosive capacity of language *in* its very scepticism about foundations and in its tactics for loosening the hold of our so-called 'truths'. But, by way of intervening in rather than just recasting the debate between modern and postmodern political theorists, White maintains that acknowledging the world-disclosive capacity of language need not entail neglect of action-coordination. Nor does it require a denial of the demands of the responsibility to act in rationally warranted ways. Rather, White counsels against the prioritization of either dimension of language: he wants to confront them on equal terms and to bring their advocates into fruitful debate.

It is not clear, given this framework, how the other of Nietzschean or deconstructivist scepticism can do anything but undermine the claims of the responsibility to act. This is one reason why ultimately White considers neither Derrida nor Nietzsche but Heidegger to be the best postmodern advocate of responsibility to otherness. It is Heidegger who has done most to draw out the implications of the potential for world-disclosure and its concomitant responsibility: 'Heidegger's work is the best source to turn to in order to deepen the analysis of both of the distinctions. . . . There the side emphasized by post-structuralists and other postmodernists receives its most careful elaboration'.[14] Heidegger demonstrates, more than anyone, why responsibility to otherness cannot be subsumed under the responsibility to act. The argument White gives for this claim runs as follows. The first stage purports to identify a certain blindness in the architectonic of Habermas's knowledge-constitutive interests.[15] Prior to his investigations into communicative pragmatics, Habermas advanced a philosophical anthropology according to which there are three fundamental cognitive interests – mastery of nature, reaching understanding and emancipation – corresponding to three spheres of human knowledge – the objectivating sciences, the human sciences and 'depth hermeneutics' as illustrated by psychoanalysis and ideology critique. But within this conceptual grid, White argues, responsibility to otherness as such remains *unintelligible*: 'all of the three interests he delineated fall within the sway of the responsibility to act; they refer to moments of that responsibility'.[16] What, then, is this missing moment of intelligibility? White's answer is 'mortality': 'within Habermas's framework we are creatures who seek to manipulate things in the world, to understand one another, and to get out from under domination, but we are not creatures who die'.[17] Habermas's schema forgets finitude, 'and to do that is in effect to essentialize human being under the sway of the responsibility to act'. White continues,

> To confront our finitude is to confront a closure beyond our will. And to confront that is to begin to feel the precariousness of all our willed closures. Those willed closures thereby start to lose that sense of potential for infinite mastery that they take on when we are under the exclusive sway of the responsibility to act. And it is only as that certainty begins to ebb that we really become open to hearing one another.[18]

It is at this point that Heidegger is introduced as a salutary corrective to the hegemony of the responsibility to act. For White, the culmination of Heidegger's achievement in this respect lies in his reflections on *die Nähe* (the near-ing).[19] In Heidegger's later writings, the near-ing features as part of his reformulation of the ontological difference. It serves as a marker, in other words, for a renewed mode of attentiveness to the 'forgotten' question of the meaning of Being. At its bluntest, the near-ing indicates the manner in which Being in distinction from the totality of beings can make itself manifest in 'thought'. As such, it is represented in a mode of thought which both respects the *difference* of Being yet which brings Being *closer*. To think the near-ing is to articulate a form of fundamental proximity that is also a non-recoupable distance. The idea is of use for White's purposes because, as he interprets its role in Heidegger's reflections, it shows the way for an unprecedented awareness of the responsibility to otherness. In 'the gesture of the near-ing', as White puts it, 'bringing into one's presence, into one's world, must always be complemented by a letting go, an allowance of distance, a letting be in absence, thus bearing witness to our own limits, our own finitude'.[20] In the figure of the near-ing, then, Heidegger accomplishes an articulation of otherness which, as a moment of world-disclosure grounded in an acknowledgement of mortality, remains on the other side of intelligibility to the responsibility to act.

White's enthusiasm for this Heideggerian vocabulary of otherness is significantly qualified by his belief that it lacks critical edge when applied to moral and political problems of action-coordination. In order to make Heideggerian responsibility to otherness insightful at the level of ethics and politics, White argues, it needs transposition into the discourse of difference feminism – that is, a feminism, inspired by the work of Carol Gilligan, celebratory of simultaneous intimacy and distance, of the other as the subject of care. Only in this way, White thinks, does the postmodern concern for world-disclosure impinge critically on the discourse of justice. When it comes to questions of political ecology, however, the need for such a transposition, if necessary at all, is not so obvious.[21] Given his comment that 'nature' counts as an other to which responsibility is owed, it is surprising that White says nothing about the bearing his distinction has for the idea of ecological responsibility.[22] If White is right to think that Heidegger's great achievement is to show why the responsibility to act cannot exhaust responsibility, and if ecological politics is to be guided by a sense of responsibility in both its dimensions, then there might be more benign political significance to the Heideggerian thematization of otherness and its affinities with world-disclosure than White allows himself to admit.

THE TRUTH OF WORLD-DISCLOSURE

White's aim in invoking the distinction between responsibility to act and responsibility to otherness is to draw attention to two distinct dimensions of normative force and the modes of articulation appropriate to them. His strategy is to show how the nature of language opens up space for the intelligibility of both. By taking language as the medium of rationally binding intersubjectivity rather than the isolated subject as our point of departure, the responsibility to act can be put on a properly dialogical, rather than improperly monological, basis. In this manner, rationalist construals of the basis of responsibility can be purged of the objectivistic tendency associated with subject-centred responsibility. Responsibility to act need not be an objectivating responsibility, and it is part of White's achievement to show how Habermasian theory demonstrates this. Another virtue of the distinction between the two modes of responsibility is that it gives reason for those who are completely under the sway of the responsibility to act – even those who interpret it most dialogically – to think again about blanket charges of irresponsibility they may be tempted to launch at postmodern thinkers. The view White recommends thus promises to break down a serious obstacle to fruitful debate.

But how stable is White's distinction between the two kinds of responsibility? And how sound is it as the basis for a new understanding of responsibility that is at once post-metaphysical and sensitive to the voice of ecological conscience? I shall consider, in turn, three respects in which White's formulation stands in need of improvement. First, I shall take issue with the way White construes the context in which the need for a distinction between two kinds of responsibility emerges. Second, I question his representation of the central issues at stake in the critique of rationalist accounts of responsibility as coextensional with responsibility to act. Third, I point to confused and misleading aspects of his representation of the world-disclosive capacity of language, and therefore also of the corresponding dimension of responsibility.

First of all, recall that White's distinction arises in the first instance out of dissatisfaction with Habermas's early philosophical anthropology and its doctrine of knowledge-constitutive interests. This doctrine, according to White, with its exclusion of the constitutive significance of mortality, betrayed the structural deficit of the responsibility to act as a paradigm of responsibility as such. Even Habermas, the theorist responsible for the most advanced formulation of the principles of the responsibility to act, the theorist of the responsibility to act most sensitive to the structural deficit of subject-centred responsibility, is oblivious, seemingly endemically, to what is other in the constitution of responsibility.

White's argument for this thesis is that Habermas's deep-seated anthropological interests are arbitrarily selected and crucially incomplete. For White, the very fact that such a narrow, one-sided range of interests is chosen, is symptomatic of just how completely Habermas's thinking remains under the sway of the demands of the responsibility to act. But as should be clear from our discussion in chapter three, this reading of Habermas's early work, and its self-understanding as a kind of depth hermeneutics, is itself radically, and crucially, incomplete. For it takes no account precisely of the constitutive role of the other in critical theory's conception of the emancipatory interest. The human subject's interest in and claim to emancipation, as Habermas theorizes it, is in no way a reflection of the denial of mortality. It should not be regarded as the negation of human embodiment, contingency and finitude. Nor should it be seen as the liberation of the subject's will to dominate nature. These may indeed be characteristics of subject-centred emancipatory reason. But in what Habermas calls the causality of fate, freedom unfolds as a dialectic of recognition of self and other, and the emancipatory interest is made intelligible in terms of a cognitive, motivationally potent insight into the subject's debt to the other. At the very least then, White chooses an unfortunate point of departure for thinking beyond the responsibility to act.

This oversight would not matter so much if it were not for the fact that the causality of fate theme plays such a decisive role in Habermas's own way of thinking about responsibility. In *Knowledge and Human Interests*, Habermas maintains that emancipatory or 'depth hermeneutic' reflection, as contextualized paradigmatically in the psychoanalytic situation, fulfils its purpose by bringing the self to responsibility for its alienated other and *thereby* for itself. In the case of psychoanalytic reflection, this other is the unconscious alter-ego made manifest in the content of the analysand's symptoms. Habermas is clear that in order for responsibility, as the reverse side of emancipatory reflection, to count for anything, it must be motivationally rooted in a passion for self-transformation. The transformation at stake reconciles parties abstractly divorced from their 'common basis of existence'. In this sense, responsibility takes on an intersubjective, communal, rather than subject-centred character. In various places, Habermas explicitly draws attention to what he considers to be the failure of postmodernist conceptions of responsibility to accommodate this point.[23]

This leads us to the second problematic aspect of White's approach: his representation of the deficiency of the responsibility to act. In his early work, as we saw in chapter four, Habermas introduces the theme of the causality of fate in the course of elucidating the main thrust of the young Hegel's critique of Kant. According to one important strand of Hegel's critique, Kantian notions of self-responsible reason and universal justice impose an unacceptable psychological burden. In part, this is because the purity of the self-responsible will, together with the associated sanction of guilt, demands a sacrifice in terms of ordinary creaturely goods that is detrimental to the well-being of the whole moral personality. The ideal of self-responsible reason finds expression in juridical and moralistic practices that can harden the will against the contingent and spontaneous promptings of compassion, that can crush it under the burden of duty. Here, Hegel first exposes the notorious motivational deficit of Kantian constructions of the moral demand. Adapted to the terms of our present discussion, Hegel's insight is that the degree of abstraction required for processes of justification divorces the responsibility to act from the sources of motivation that might actualize it.

Yet there is no place for such considerations in White's representation of the deficiency of the responsibility to act, and consequently of the need for an alternative construction of responsibility. This is all the more surprising given the long-standing complaint – though perhaps not systematically thematized in postmodernist critiques – that theorists of the responsibility to act have failed to address in a satisfactory manner the issue of *why* one should act in a rationally justified way. Unless this is done, unless a substantive answer to the question 'why be responsible?' is non-contingently built into the alternative conception, *practically* intelligible responsibility remains precarious. But the problem with White's approach is not just that it neglects this major issue. It also risks *perpetuating* by other means the very motivational deficit of the Kantian approach. For on the one hand, it threatens to leave otherness split-off from action, thereby reproducing the kind of irrationalism that provokes the charge of irresponsibility, while on the other, it threatens to leave action split-off from otherness, thereby reproducing the insensitivities to context, embodiment and contingency of the responsibility to act. Otherness without action is empty; action without otherness is subject-centred.

In order for otherness to have the potency required for a successful critique of the responsibility to act, it must function, to borrow Taylor's term, as a moral source. A moral source is something contact with which empowers moral or good action from the person. To be in touch with a moral source, therefore, is to be motivated to responsible action. But sources can become remote. When they do, a special effort of reflection is required to retrieve their proximity. This, according to Gadamer's classical formulation, is the task of hermeneutic reflection: 'to let what seems far and alienated speak again'.[24] From the hermeneutic point of view, we can make sense of otherness as a marker of responsibility, in a sense irreducible to but not abstractly separated from the responsibility to act, as such a distanced and alienated moral source. By contrast to postmodernist conceptions of otherness, the hermeneutic idea of the *other-as-source* puts the responsibility to otherness in a space of intelligibility appropriate for beings engaged in and at the same time to some extent alienated from the natural world.

Before I pursue the implications of this thought for the problem of ecological responsibility, I should mention a third way in which White's approach runs aground. For the case for a hermeneutic transformation of the terms of White's distinction becomes all the more compelling in view of the ambiguous *content* of otherness in White's account. Who or what counts as other? White certainly accepts that this is a question deserving an answer: at one point, White speaks of the otherness to which we owe responsibility as 'other actors, external nature, or aspects of our own physical or psychological life'.[25] If, however, the other is other actors, the distinction between responsibility to otherness and responsible action is on the verge of collapse: what, after all, is *traditionally* meant by responsibility to act if not a responsibility grounded in duties to other agents or to non-transparent aspects of the self's well-being? If, on the other hand, our own physical or psychological life is to count as the other, it looks like an odd object of responsibility. This objection, that responsibility is an inappropriate attitude to take to alterity, holds just as much for the radical sense of an uncontainable energy or force disruptive of any appropriation by the self it has in much postmodernism.

The equivocality on content is reflected in White's representation of the capacity for world-disclosure. Just as there are distinct and incompatible notions of otherness operative in the idea of responsibility to it, so there are different and incompatible understandings of world-disclosive language that is supposed to voice the claims of the other. In the first instance, we saw, White highlights fictionality as such as the significant characteristic of world-disclosive language. Recognition of this and the 'deployment of new fictions against whatever fictions are socially in force' is supposed to involve 'a deep affirmation of the world-disclosive capacity'. But why should fictions be loosened rather than strengthened by more fictions? And more germanely, why should the deployment of new fictions not express an affirmation simply of the power to *create fictions* rather than the capacity to *disclose* a *world*? As we saw, White sets up the distinction between fundamental linguistic capacities in the context of post-structuralist scepticism about the rational foundation of norms. The operative function here is fictionality. But it is hard to see how otherness in this sense – as the correlate of this sense of world-disclosure – can be construed as a fit object of responsibility. In this respect the flaw in White's construction of the world-disclosive capacity of language mirrors that in his construction of responsibility to otherness.

But in his discussion of Heidegger and the near-ing, White invokes world-disclosure in the second of the above senses – not in postmodern celebration of the power to create fictions, but in acknowledgement of a capacity to uncover concealed significance. White is prevented from identifying any essential link between responsibility to otherness and this hermeneutic sense of world-disclosure because he has already committed himself, in introducing the two dimensions of language, to a conception of world-disclosure inspired by deconstruction. Hence, while White finds in Heidegger's conception of the near-ing a clue to responsibility to otherness appropriate to politics, he does so in spite of the distinction he himself rightly draws between the two dimensions of language. The near-ing and its horizon of responsibility remains an impossible horizon, it remains unintelligible, so long as the affirmation of world-disclosure celebrates the mere underlying fictionality of all discourse.

I have just argued that White's attempt at giving content to the other to which a peculiar kind of responsibility is owed either risks collapsing the distinction on which its peculiarity is based, or threatens to make responsibility in *any* sense an inappropriate attitude to it. If 'external nature' is to feature on the *other* side of the Kantian responsibility to act, and if it is to remain intelligible as a fit object of *responsibility*, it can not be by means of the postmodernist conception of world-disclosure. I have already suggested that White's distinction needs to be recast in hermeneutic terms if it is to have any chance of framing a post-metaphysically understood ecological responsibility. I urged that by way of rectifying the motivational deficit of the responsibility to act; the introduction of a notion of other-as-source would constitute one step in the right direction. But I must now link that idea to the world-disclosive dimension of language. How, if not by way of postmodernism, is responsibility to be rethought in relation to ecology through insights into the nature of world-disclosure?

I think a plausible answer can be teased from an alternative interpretation of the structure of Heidegger's thinking about the near-ing. Charles Taylor's reading of Heidegger is explicitly designed to show 'in what ways our status as language beings...lay us open to ecologically relevant demands'.[26] An important part of what it is to be a language being, *at least for language beings who have undergone or inherited the maturation processes of Enlightenment*, is to exist against a horizon of significance that only comes to light through creative acts of linguistic disclosure. In holding this view, Taylor observes, Heidegger belongs to a tradition of thought going back to Herder. Language, on analogy with the symbolic work of art, is regarded in this tradition as an inexhaustible power of creative expression, opening worlds of significance accessible only through linguistic mediation. Heidegger calls the space in which meaning presents itself the 'clearing'. The clearing is the name Heidegger gives to the possibility of there being beings made present at all.[27] So the question of the nature of the world-disclosive capacity of language and its relation to responsibility becomes, from Heidegger's point of view, a problem about the clearing and how human beings stand in relation to it.

Taylor distinguishes a series of different ways of making sense of the irruption of meaning in the space of the clearing. On the one hand, the irruption can be regarded as a 'manifestation', as a bringing to light of something otherwise concealed. In this case, the creative imagination serves as the medium for finding something out. On the other hand, the event of disclosure can be viewed merely as a linguistic 'effect', that is, as a bringing about of something which exists only in the individual or collective imagination. According to the latter view, there is no sense to the idea that linguistic invention might be for the purpose of discovery. But if the former view is adopted, a separate issue arises about whether what is made manifest is beyond and other to the generative powers of the human subject or just an expression of the self and its constitutive powers. Irrespective of the stance one takes on this matter, there is a further issue about whether the significant agent of expression in the clearing is an individual subject, a historical linguistic tradition, or some kind of impersonal linguistic structure.

Once the theoretical options raised by the acknowledgement of world-disclosure are broken down in such a way, the problematic role of the world-disclosive dimension of language as the basis of a postmodernist responsibility to otherness becomes still more evident. On the third issue, the issue of the agent of world-disclosure, all advocates of the paradigm shift to language – modern and postmodern – agree on an anti-subjectivist position. Neither Habermas nor Heidegger nor Derrida think that the clearing is the doing of an individual subject. But while White consistently adopts an anti-subjectivist stance on the agent of the clearing, there are points where, drawing more on Nietzsche and Derrida than Heidegger, he entertains a quite subjectivist reading of world-disclosure as a site of manifestation. This is evident in his depiction of the task of world-disclosure as a battle of fiction against fiction. To describe the effect of successful world-disclosure as loosening 'our world's hold upon us by confronting us with the ways in which it is structured by unrecognized or forgotten fiction' is to abstract the *telos* of the clearing from the happening of a manifestation, and therefore to commend a subjectivist reading of the capacity of the clearing to make things manifest at all. Or, if the postmodernist does acknowledge that the moment of world-disclosure brings something to light, it can only be the human generative power to create fictions. Moreover it is not clear why postmodern anti-subjectivism on the issue of the agent of the clearing, rather than hermeneutic anti-subjectivism on whether the clearing makes something beyond the self manifest, should hold out any promise for making sense of the moment of responsibility missing from the responsibility to act.

But if Heidegger, *pace* postmodernism, is anti-subjectivist on the issue of what happens in the clearing (as opposed to who makes it happen), and if, of the three issues raised by the world-disclosive power, this is the relevant one for making sense of an ecologically apposite responsibility to otherness, it is not because he thinks that the space of world-disclosure shows up an ontic order to which human beings stand accountable. As Taylor interprets the function of the ontological difference at least after *Being and Time*, Heidegger emphatically 'de-onticizes' the clearing: he denies any ontic grounding to the event of world-disclosure, like Platonic forms, Hegel's *Geist*, Schopenhauer's 'will', or Nietzschean 'will to power'. For Heidegger, the space of the clearing cannot be made intelligible in terms, say, of spirit coming to consciousness of itself or the satisfactions of unrepresentable will. This is the cardinal mistake of what Heidegger calls 'metaphysics'. Given that a responsibility which is on the other side of the responsibility to act is also on the other side of metaphysics, it cannot rely, according to Heidegger, on how humans stand to the ontic ground of the world-disclosive power, even assuming a manifestationist rather than subjectivist interpretation of the nature of that power. If world-disclosure is to help us make sense of ecological responsibility, it cannot be because it is grounded in an ontic representation of nature.[28]

On the Heideggerian, hermeneutic view, our nature as language beings is relevant for a new understanding of responsibility in virtue of the properties of 'the clearing itself, or language itself, properly brought to light ... in the event of disclosure'.[29] For if language, in its capacity for world-disclosure, is to fulfil its *telos*, it must disclose *itself* in the disclosure or showing up of something. If, as Taylor puts it, the goal of language is undistorted uncovering, then this uncovering itself can be no exception.[30] The *telos* of world-disclosure, when realized, is a disclosure of itself. Hence world-disclosure suggests a new paradigm for responsibility not by virtue of how it places human beings to what it shows up or discloses, but by the way it depicts how language beings stand in relation to language successfully disclosing its own disclosive powers. Being responsible to the essence of language is to relate responsibly to the clearing in a certain way, as in 'dwelling', which Heidegger describes as a 'unity of the fourfold'.[31] At this point, we can retrieve on a firmer basis the insights White himself takes from Heidegger's reflections on the near-ing. We can come to an understanding of what it means to be responsible in the requisite ecological sense – expressible in formulas like 'letting beings be', 'bearing witness to finitude', 'acknowledging otherness' – by getting clearer on what it is to be responsible to our own nature as language beings.

While admittedly sketchy, I think this proposal overcomes two difficulties inherent in attempts to rethink responsibility in a post-subject-centred paradigm by appeal to the world-disclosive dimension of language understood through postmodernist or post-structuralist theory. First, it helps bridge the gap between theory and practice – which opens up like an abyss in radical discourses abstracted from all sources of human motivation – by introducing the notion of the other-as-source and by aligning the requirements of world-disclosure with those of a caring, non-instrumental stance to nature. Second, and relatedly, it takes the modern ontological predicament seriously, in that it gives due acknowledgement to our own contribution to the existence of meaning in a disenchanted universe. These two qualities also commend it as a first step towards making sense of a more than prudential ecological responsibility without appeal to an imagined normatively instructive ontic order.

POLITICS, LANGUAGE AND CRITICISM

The acknowledgement of non-human goods through the resonance carried in their disclosure, Taylor asserts, is a key moral challenge of our time. It is a challenge that can only be met by the invention of new languages that keep non-human goods alive. Taylor claims that in making non-human goods matter, the new interpretive language can help to motivate ecologically attuned action: 'It would greatly help in staving off ecological disaster', Taylor states, 'if we could recover a sense of the demand that our natural surrounding and wilderness make on us'.[32] So far in this chapter I have defended a strong hermeneutic analysis of the intelligibility of ecological conscience. But the *political* significance of these hermeneutic insights is still not transparent. In the remainder of the chapter I will indicate why, at the political level, there is something instructive about Habermas's critical distanciation from hermeneutics.

As a way of approaching the intelligibility of ecological conscience discourse ethics soon falls short. Habermas himself concedes that the 'anthropocentric way of looking at things' built into discourse ethics cannot make sense of moral intuitions made manifest in compassion for 'the pain caused by the destruction of biotypes'.[33] His response is to delimit the domain of philosophical ethics 'to clarify the universal core of our moral intuitions and thereby to refute value scepticism'. 'By singling out a procedure of decision making', discourse ethics 'seeks to make room for those involved, who must then find answers on their own to the moral–practical issues that come to them, or are imposed upon them, with objective historical force'.[34] But like most self-limiting manoeuvres, Habermas's looks suspiciously *ad hoc*. Nothing is explained about the *specific* intuited wrong of biotype destruction by making it external to the imputed universal core of morality. Similarly, from the point of view of an opponent who has that intuition of wrong, Habermas's response will just beg the question of what constitutes the core of what are properly called moral intuitions.[35] Neither is it self-evident that the intuited wrong of biotype destruction is a manifestation of *compassion*. It at least remains an issue whether the intuited demands that the natural environment might make on us are based on something more than the suffering of sentients.

The *content* of the moral–practical issues that come to the participants in the dialogical decision-making procedure depends partly on what *matters* to the participants themselves. And what counts as mattering depends upon the moral world that is disclosed to them. The task of the 'subjective' critic is to *sensitize* us to dimensions of an intersubjectively *non-actualized* moral reality. This activity of sensitization – the creative imaginative undertakings of the subjective critic – corresponds to what might be called the politics of world-disclosure. To a certain extent, Habermas seems to concur with this point when he ascribes 'green' protest to sensitivity to those industrial developments that 'noticeably affect the organic foundations of the life-world and make one drastically aware of standards of livability, of inflexible limits to the deprivation of sensual/aesthetic background needs'.[36] This view *need* not be interpreted in anthropocentric terms. Something can only matter to a human being if, in some sense, it satisfies a need. But it doesn't follow from this that the satisfaction of a need is *why* something matters. Individual need satisfaction is a condition of the recognition of a good, but not necessarily that in virtue of which it is a good. The politics of world-disclosure concerns just this recognition: the rendering articulate of actually unrecognized or muted moral claims. It seeks to make this attack more visible, to make us even more drastically conscious of criteria of livability, where what it is to live a fully human life covers the acknowledgement of non-sentient claims made vocal *through* the overcoming of aesthetic deprivation. If we think of inflexible limits to the deprivation of sensual/aesthetic needs as signifying something about the state of the moral world through subjectivity, rather than signifying something about subjectivity through the state of the objective world, then the anthropomorphic locus of world-disclosure can be combined with intuitions about its more-than-anthropocentric content.

Political ecology, then, has this world-disclosive character. It seeks to transform, as we might say, the mattering of the world. To this end it attempts to show the inadequacy of discourses that represent the natural environment as relating to humans as a 'standing resource' by way of a contrasting language with deeper subjective resonance.[37] Only *given* this resonance or sensitivity can green issues matter in a non-instrumental way; it must be *prior* to any decision-making process about human dealings with the environment. There is something in this kind of will-formation that the strong hermeneutic focus on qualitative contrasts captures more satisfactorily than the discourse ethical grounding of philosophical critique on the idea of unconstrained intersubjectivity or *democratic* will-formation.

Once the decision-making process has begun, however, we move beyond the orbit of world-disclosure to the politics of problem-solving. The critical labour of deconstructing the 'world picture',[38] or of disclosing a world of deeper personal resonance, is essentially a preliminary task: problems might be redefined, reprioritized or rediscovered; the relationship of the individual to the whole might be transfigured, but particular intramundane problems of action-coordination remain. If we can call the imaginative re-workings of world-disclosure to be the task of the subjective critic, the purpose of the 'objective' critic is to identify those public or intersubjective constraints on what counts as normatively valid problem-solving practices. *At this level*, Habermas's discourse ethics offers itself as a plausible model for how individuals aspiring to autonomy might have that autonomy respected simultaneously to coordinating their actions in a rational manner. For the institutionalization of the presuppositions of communicative action, to the degree of structuring the public order of references, does not suffer from the difficulties facing the conception of nature as a moral source *under conditions of modernity.* Leaving aside the strong claims Habermas makes for discourse ethics – that it articulates the common core to all moralities, and reconstructs the essence of strictly 'moral' intuitions – is it so cripplingly anthropocentric as to be of *no* relevance for an understanding of the environmental crisis that motivates political ecology?

Although practical problems have a meaning that is partly determined by the best available language of self-interpretation, they are also imposed on agents, as Habermas reminds us above, by an 'objective historical force'. This is the force not only, in Habermas's vocabulary, of the symbolic *a priori* of an intersubjectively shared lifeworld, but of the material *a priori* of the state/economic system. To focus exclusively on the politics of world disclosure, in the manner of subjective critique, is to open oneself to the 'idealist' charge that one is tacitly presupposing that a particular horizon of world interpretation is the *cause* of the environmental crisis. It is to neglect, that is, action-consequences the meaning of which is graspable not from the point of view of the lifeworld, but from the vantage point available to the theorist of the historical forces arising from the self-perpetuating mechanism of the prevailing socio-economic system. The crucial point is that the proper object of critique is here the *lack* of accountability of action-consequences to decision-making procedures circumscribed by the normative content of the modern lifeworld, rather than actions that are themselves thought to be expressions or manifestations of that lifeworld. This is not necessarily to say, as Habermas is forced into advocating, that the source of accountability for environmentally destructive action-consequences is the procedure of decision making, but it is to give due focus on the *de facto* threat to the environment consequent upon the bypassing of communicatively reached solutions to problems of action-coordination.

Of course, there can be no guarantees in this domain. It is logically possible that communicative problem-solvers will continue that 'rage against Being' wrought by the systemic imperatives of profit and control. But it seems hardly unwarranted to claim that processes of genuine (non-systemically distorted) democratic will-formation are less likely to generate self-undermining conditions of environmental devastation. Though not a guarantee, three rather obvious considerations can give us confidence that democratic problem-solving, theorized along Habermasian lines as action-coordination governed by the rational principles of a communicative ethic, would turn the tide against environmental destruction, and hence support the view that discourse ethics is of *some* relevance for grasping the philosophical basis of a normatively secure political ecology. First, and most obvious, the control exercised by communicative actors over decision-making processes concerning technology is not to be confused with unfettered technological control over nature. Second, since only norms which lead to the satisfaction of *universalizable* interests pass through the legitimating communicative procedure, then maxims which when institutionalized frustrate the satisfaction of the interest in a healthy environment that *everyone* has will not do so. Here, indeed, the problem of reaching a rational consensus over incommensurable interests that in other contexts beleaguers communicative ethics does not arise. Third, the interference of democratic problem-solving processes by the profit imperative at the level of production gives an eminently plausible explanation of that which provokes the need for critique.[39]

To be sure, even if we acknowledge that the environmental consequences of communicative action are less likely to be as destructive as those of actions mediated by money and power, it still does not account for the intelligibility of ecological conscience. But even the subjective critic cannot escape the nexus of action-coordinative problems that need to be solved under the material constraints of a social world. Furthermore, the believability and desirability of worlds disclosed through subjectivity is partly conditioned by their *uncoerced* resonance. If this point is neglected an awkward question looms: what distinguishes the subjective critic from the propagandist? On the task of articulating moral sources, Taylor himself notes that 'the whole thing may be counterfeited', and continues:

> This is not to say that words of power themselves may be counterfeit. But the act by which their pronouncing releases force can be rhetorically imitated, either to feed our self-conceit or for even more sinister purposes, such as the defence of a discreditable status quo. Trite formulae may combine with the historical sham to weave a cocoon of moral assurance around us which actually insulates us from the energy of true moral sources. And there is worse: the release of power can be hideously caricatured to enhance the energy of evil, as at Nuremburg.[40]

But how are we to tell the difference between the wholesome act of pronouncement and the rhetorical imitation, the caricature and the real thing, the counterfeit and the genuine article? Not of course simply by the degree of subjective resonance – as the powers of the propagandist or charismatic dictator amply testify. As a subjective critic, Taylor can only pit the power of his pronouncements against those of others. He does not have the critical conceptual resources available to distinguish the *pragmatics* of subjectively resonant philosophy and propaganda. After acknowledging the need to make a distinction between genuine and counterfeit contact with moral sources, and the dangers of forgetting it, he offers nothing by way of justifying such a distinction.

The objective critic balks at the subjective critic's quietism on this issue. More specifically, Habermas can argue for the need to establish intersubjective constraints on the project of world-disclosure. The argument would look something like this. The pronouncements of the poet exploit the world-disclosive powers that are intrinsic to language in its capacity to mediate rationally coordinated action, even though the capacity for world-disclosure is enhanced by the bracketing of illocutionary obligations. The speech act pragmatics of propaganda, on the other hand, exploit extra-linguistic coercive forces for the purpose of persuading the hearer of the acceptability of what is disclosed in the propaganda. Of course, Habermas elaborates an argument of this kind in his construction of the conditions of the intelligibility of systematically distorted communication, and thereby of the intelligibility of a critique of ideology. This kind of critique thus falls within the province of objective criticism. We can agree with Habermas that the non-coercive pragmatics of epiphanic poetry or philosophy implicitly presuppose the symmetrical intersubjective structure of communicative action. But this does not commit us to the claim that the legitimate task of the subjective critic is limited to the raising and redeeming of validity claims to authenticity. Nor does it commit us to the assertion that the validity of subjective criticism is criterially constrained by the possibility of reaching a consensus. As I have argued, Habermas's taxonomy of validity claims, as well as his views on the consensual orientation of communicative action, must be rejected. But these claims are adventitiously related to the model of democratic will-formation represented in the dialogical situation of communicative problem-solvers, a situation that it is not unreasonable to suppose can structure the public order of references under conditions of modernity.

Finally, I want to stress that the tasks of objective and subjective criticism as I am offering them here are neither 'objectivist' nor 'subjectivist', in so far as these terms have accrued pejorative connotations. The reason becomes manifest by considering their contribution to critical political ecology. Subjective criticism, as a moment of strong hermeneutics, has a realist core: it is *about* subjectivity only in the sense that the world is disclosed only under certain conditions of intentionality, but in articulating these conditions, its critique is directed towards the world; it is subjective in '*manner*', not in '*matter*'.[41] To say that the natural environment, as a world disclosed in languages with various potentials for personal resonance, must matter *to* human beings, is not necessarily to claim that human beings are the only things that matter. The pejorative force of 'subjectivism' is attendant first upon the *ontological* claim that value exists in the world just to that extent to which a subject's *de facto* desires are satisfied, and following from this, upon the *ethical claim* that the best world is one in which all of these (compossible) desires are in fact satisfied. Since subjective criticism is neither ontologically nor evaluatively subjectivist, it is not a fit object of the pejorative force associated with the term 'subjectivism'. It is, however, *semantically* subjectivist, but only with respect to a restricted domain of discourse. This is the domain in which meaning has an irreducibly experiential core, which in turn is an apt object of phenomenological exploration. This is the domain of 'private' language only to the extent that, as a matter of fact, the claims expressed in it are not recognized in what Taylor calls the public order of references. The language of subjective criticism is not private in the empiricist sense, attacked by Wittgenstein, of being meaningful in virtue of referring to a private ontology of internal mental states. I see no reason why this limited semantic–phenomenological subjectivism should offend the anti-anthropocentric sensibilities of the radical ecologist.[42]

Just as the innocence of subjective criticism from the charge of 'subjectivism' is testified by its link with the politics of world-disclosure, so the connection between objective criticism and the politics of democratic problem-solving can relieve worries about the complicity of such critics with 'objectivism'. The objectivity secured by intersubjective agreement under communicative constraint concerns a problem-solving capacity for rational action-coordination. Again, the pejorative force of objectivism is directed towards certain ontological, epistemological and ethical commitments: that the world is nothing but an aggregate of atomic objects interacting according to mechanistic laws; that knowledge of it is exclusively a function of a method of the kind that modern physicists are supposed (by objectivist philosophers) to follow; and that it is good to follow it – both as an expression of human excellence in intellectual conduct, and in its utility. But if we think of the objective critic, along Habermasian lines, as clarifying the public or intersubjective conditions of rational action-coordination, the objectivist charge has no real force. Indeed, objective criticism comes into play when the intersubjectively binding presuppositions of communicatively rational action-coordination are violated by the pseudo-objectifications of science.

How, then, can it come into play in the kind of critique that is relevant to our ecological predicament? One suggestion that has been made goes like this: the critical thrust of communicative reason can be salvaged from its anthropocentric bias by including the rich diversity of life-forms – and even the earth itself – as virtual *participants* in the dialogue situation.[43] But it is extremely difficult to see how this idea could be sustained, and impossible to see how it could fit with anything remotely resembling communicative ethics.[44] A much more plausible idea is hinted at, but not followed through, by Habermas himself. As I said, objective criticism comes into play when the intersubjectively binding presuppositions of communicative action are violated. But communicative action presupposes the integrity of a background lifeworld horizon. Further, as Habermas remarks above, the integrity of the *organic foundations* of the lifeworld can come, indeed are, under threat. The violation of these organic foundations, it follows, is a suitable object for objective criticism; their breakdown is criticizable (objectively) in virtue of being inconsistent with the presuppositions of unconstrained communicative action as a medium of will-formation. This doesn't tell us *why* the environment itself might be intrinsically worth preserving. But then to *show* that is the task of world-disclosure.

The critical thrust of political ecology can thus be understood as standing at the interface of the politics of world-disclosure and problem-solving. This point parallels, but is not identical with, Habermas's understanding of green politics as a border conflict between system and lifeworld. According to Habermas, green protest is a reaction from the point of view of the lifeworld to an environmental crisis that manifests itself as a visible attack upon the organic foundations of the lifeworld. But it also generates 'a new category of literally invisible risks that can only be grasped from the vantage point of the system'.[45] These are risks the responsibility for which is offset by their 'uncontrollable magnitude'. They are problems that must be tackled with the resources of the lifeworld, yet, as Habermas remarks, they go beyond the level of complexity that can be experienced within it.

While the politics of world-disclosure struggles to expand and deepen the resources of the lifeworld, the politics of democratic problem-solving pursues means of putting a heightened sense of responsibility into effect by way of a particular form of decision making. From this double-perspective, the challenge facing criticism is to create new languages of personal resonance – to disclose matterings in the world and to voice previously inarticulate moral claims – which are capable of *motivating collectively coordinated action* constrained by the social and ecological imperative of effective democratic problem-solving.

Notes

INTRODUCTION

1 See Freud, 'Introductory Lectures on Psychoanalysis', trans. James Strachey, *The Standard Edition of the Complete Psychological Works of Sigmund Freud* (London: Hogarth, 1963), vol. 16, pp. 284–5.

2 Ibid., p. 285.

3 See Richard Rorty, 'Freud and Moral Reflection', in Rorty, *Essays on Heidegger and Others* (Cambridge: Cambridge University Press, 1991).

4 Rorty, *Contingency, Irony and Solidarity* (Cambridge: Cambridge University Press, 1989), p. 22. It is important to see here that Rorty is not merely reminding us of the trivial truth that all things human occur in time and in ways not fully pre-determined from the beginning of time. Rather, he is making the much more controversial claim that there is ultimately *nothing more* to human phenomena – like language, conscience and community – than the contingencies of their occurrence.

5 See Gilles Deleuze, *Nietzsche and Philosophy*, trans. Hugh Tomlinson (London: Athlone, 1983); and Jean-Francois Lyotard, *Libidinal Economy*, trans. Ian Hamilton Grant (London: Athlone, 1993).

6 For a statement of deconstruction's 'reduction of meaning' to a structure 'which in itself has no meaning', see Jacques Derrida, 'The Ends of Man', in Derrida, *Margins of Philosophy*, trans. Alan Boas (London: Harvester, 1982), p. 134. For systems theory, which reduces meaning to the adaptive exigencies of social systems, see Niklas Luhmann, *The Differentiation of Society*, trans. Stephen Holmes and Charles Larmore (New York: Columbia University Press, 1982).

7 Barbara Herrnstein-Smith, *Contingencies of Value: Alternative Perspectives for Critical Theory* (Cambridge, Mass.: Harvard University Press, 1988).

8 Habermas's main statements on discourse ethics are *Moral Consciousness and Communicative Action*, trans. Christian Lenhardt and Shierry Weber Nicholson (Cambridge: Polity, 1990); *Justification and Application: Remarks on Discourse Ethics*, trans. Ciaran Cronin (Cambridge: Polity, 1993); and *Between Facts and Norms: Contributions to a Discourse Theory of Law and Democracy*, trans. William Rehg (Cambridge: Polity, 1996). The discourse ethics research programme owes as much to the work of Karl-Otto Apel as Habermas, but I shall only be dealing with Habermas's contributions here.

9 Habermas's criticisms of Rorty and post-structuralism are in Habermas, *The Philosophical Discourse of Modernity*, trans. Frederick Lawrence (Cambridge: Polity, 1987). For more observations on the convergence between Habermas and his 'postmodern' opponents, see Peter Dews, *The Limits of Disenchantment: Essays on Contemporary European Philosophy* (London: Verso, 1995), p. 7.

1 THE VARIETY OF HERMENEUTICS

1 It is conventional to approach the subject of hermeneutics with an overview of the main phases of its history, but I shall not add to the many already available. For general summaries, the following anthologies are useful: Josef Bleicher ed., *Contemporary Hermeneutics: Hermeneutics as Method, Philosophy and Critique* (London: Routledge, 1980); Kurt Müller-Vollmer ed., *The Hermeneutics Reader: Texts of the German Tradition from the Enlightenment to the Present* (Oxford: Oxford University Press, 1985); and Gayle L. Ormiston and Alan D. Schrift eds, *The Hermeneutic Tradition: From Ast to Ricoeur* (Albany: SUNY Press, 1989). For a more detailed introduction to the history of hermeneutics, see Jean Grondin, *Introduction to Philosophical Hermeneutics*, trans. Joel Weinsheimer with foreword by Hans-Georg Gadamer (New Haven: Yale University Press, 1994). By far the most influential interpretation of the sources of the hermeneutic tradition is Gadamer, *Truth and Method*, trans. Joel Weinsheimer and Donald G. Marshall (London: Sheed and Ward, 1993), first published in German as *Wahrheit und Methode* (1960). But Gadamer's view is contested in Manfred Frank, *Das individuelle Allgemeine: Textstrukturierung und Textinterpretation nach Schleiermacher* (Frankfurt am Main: Suhrkamp, 1977). Drawing on Frank's work, Andrew Bowie attempts to correct what he believes to be Gadamer's misrepresentation of hermeneutic thought stemming from Schleiermacher in *From Romanticism to Critical Theory: The Philosophy of German Literary Theory* (London: Routledge, 1996). For a sympathetic study of Schleiermacher that takes a different direction to Frank's, see Gunther Scholtz, *Ethik und Hermeneutik: Schleiermacher's Grundlegung der Geisteswissenschaften* (Frankfurt am Main: Suhrkamp, 1995). For a more comprehensive list of works on hermeneutics, see the bibliography to Grondin, *Introduction to Philosophical Hermeneutics*, pp. 169–228.

2 See Joel Weinsheimer, *Philosophical Hermeneutics and Literary Theory* (New Haven: Yale University Press, 1991); and David C. Hoy, *The Critical Circle: Literature and History in Contemporary Hermeneutics* (Berkeley: University of California Press, 1978), for good discussions of hermeneutics in this context.

3 See Ernest Gellner, *Postmodernism, Reason and Religion* (London: Routledge, 1992), p. 75. The position I call Enlightenment fundamentalism is not identical to the one described by Gellner as 'Enlightenment rationalist fundamentalism', but it is based on ideas defended by Gellner in that text and elsewhere, especially his main philosophical work, *Legitimation of Belief* (Cambridge: Cambridge University Press, 1974).

4 Perhaps the most upfront attack on hermeneutics to have appeared since Gellner's book on postmodernism is Hans Albert's *Kritik der reinen Hermeneutik* (Tübingen: Mohr, 1994). Albert laments the 'hermeneutic wave' he perceives to have flooded the sciences, a fact he attributes not to the intellectual compulsion of hermeneutics, but to 'the fascination of a word, whose inflationary use simply conceals the confusions brought about by means of it' (p. vii). According to Albert, advocates of hermeneutics like Heidegger and Gadamer attempt to undermine the objectivity of the modern natural sciences by making them relative to some contingent cultural background or horizon of interpretation. Albert, by contrast, endeavours to reassert the primacy of the modern scientific method even for dealing with problems of meaning and understanding. Fittingly, the book is dedicated to Gellner.

5 Gellner, *Legitimation of Belief*, p. 207.

6 Ibid., p. 27.

7 Ibid., p. 174. See also Albert, *Kritik der reinen Hermeneutik*, p. 227.

8 Gellner, *Legitimation of Belief*, p. 180.

9 Ibid., p. 63.
10 Ibid., p. 100.
11 John McDowell, *Mind and World* (Cambridge, Mass.: Harvard University Press, 1994), p. 71.
12 Ibid., p. 76. McDowell calls the view I am ascribing here to the Enlightenment fundamentalist 'bald naturalism'. McDowell himself opposes it to two rival positions. First, one based on Davidson's supervenience thesis; and second – his own preferred view – a 'naturalized Platonism', according to which concepts suitable to the realm of meaning (rather than the disenchanted realm of law) constitute an openness to the world. In his defence of the latter position, McDowell makes a major contribution to what I am calling here strong hermeneutics.
13 Gellner, *Legitimation of Belief*, p. 106.
14 Ibid., p. 37.
15 Ibid., p. 196. For further discussion of the cultural implications of the antagonistic relation between the languages of science and common sense, see C. P. Snow, *The Two Cultures and a Second Look* (Cambridge: Cambridge University Press, 1964); Wilfrid Sellars, *Science, Perception and Reality* (London: Routledge and Kegan Paul, 1967); and Tom Sorell, *Scientism: Philosophy and the Infatuation with Science* (London: Routledge, 1991).
16 As Gellner explains, 'The more general or fundamental features of the world, though now demoted to the status of mere hypotheses, often elude rational assessment because they are unique or *sui generis* or very fundamental. They become relativised, optional, and deprived of their privileged, entrenched status – but without becoming, for all that, eligible for rational, instrumental evaluation' (Gellner, *Relativism and the Human Sciences* [Cambridge: Cambridge University Press, 1985], pp. 81–2).
17 In these respects, weak hermeneutics is heavily indebted to Thomas S. Kuhn's critique of algorithmic notions of science in *The Structure of Scientific Revolutions*, 2nd edn (Chicago: University of Chicago Press, 1970). See Richard Rorty, *Philosophy and the Mirror of Nature* (Princeton: Princeton University Press, 1979); and Lyotard, *The Postmodern Condition: A Report on Knowledge*, trans. Geoff Bennington (Manchester: Manchester University Press, 1984). For a reading of Kuhn in a more 'strong hermeneutic' tone, see Richard Bernstein, *Beyond Objectivism and Relativism: Science, Hermeneutics and Praxis* (Philadelphia: University of Pennsylvania Press, 1983). I draw on MacIntyre's and Taylor's response to Kuhn myself in chapter three.
18 'Introduction' to Gianni Vattimo, *The End of Modernity: Nihilism and Hermeneutics in Post-modern Culture* (Cambridge: Polity, 1988), by Jon R. Snyder, p. xiii. Author's emphasis.
19 The pre-discursive constitutive forces operative in Nietzsche's philosophy have been appropriated in various ways by Deleuze, Foucault, Derrida and Lyotard. For a critique of post-structuralism that revolves precisely around its Nietzschean elements, see Peter Dews, *Logics of Disintegration: Post-structuralist Thought and the Claims of Critical Theory* (London: Verso, 1987). For an attempt at dispelling the reductionist appearance of weak hermeneutics, see Richard Rorty, 'Non-reductive Physicalism', in *Objectivity, Relativism and Truth* (Cambridge, Cambridge University Press, 1991), pp. 113–25.
20 Nietzsche, 'On Truth and Falsity in their Ultramoral Sense', in *The Complete Works of Friedrich Nietzsche*, ed. Oscar Levy (London: Allen and Unwin, 1911), vol. 2, p. 180.
21 Nietzsche, *The Will to Power*, trans. Walter Kaufmann and R. J. Hollingdale (New York: Random House, 1968), sec. 552.

22 Stephen K. White, in *Political Theory and Postmodernism* (Cambridge: Cambridge University Press, 1991), argues that postmodernism is best thought of precisely as an attempt at articulating a different kind of responsibility – one wholly lost on Enlightenment fundamentalism – which he designates 'responsibility to otherness'. I give a critique of White's view in chapter seven.

23 Lyotard, *The Postmodern Condition*, p. xxv.

24 Derrida, 'Differance', in *Margins of Philosophy*, p. 3.

25 John D. Caputo, *Radical Hermeneutics: Repetition, Deconstruction and the Hermeneutic Project* (Bloomington: Indiana University Press, 1987), p. 209. A case for the view that democracy would be served better by a 'post-philosophical culture' self-conscious of its own contingency than by a philosophical culture aspiring to transcend it is also made by Rorty in *Consequences of Pragmatism* (Minneapolis: University of Minnesota Press, 1982).

26 Caputo, *Radical Hermeneutics*, p. 264.

27 Rorty, *Essays on Heidegger and Others*, p. 6.

28 This objection does not so much apply to Gellner's explicit doctrine, as to a direction which Enlightenment fundamentalism can easily take. It happens when *meaning* is theorized through truth conceived according to the ethic of cognition. For if meaning is bound to the conditions of truth, then where conditions of truth do not obtain, neither does meaning. This of course is the way statements of moral (apparent) significance are analysed by logical positivists. I by no means want to suggest, incidentally, that the prima facie objections to Enlightenment fundamentalism's moral anti-realism I am putting here need end up with strong hermeneutic realism. Indeed, it may well be the case, as Crispin Wright has suggested in *Truth and Objectivity* (Cambridge, Mass.: Harvard University Press, 1992), that the old paradigms of anti-realism, like logical positivism, are an inappropriate basis for thinking about the realism or otherwise of discourses. I will consider Wright's own proposals in chapter three.

29 Enlightenment fundamentalism sees itself as following Kant in wanting to emphasize the contribution of human subjectivity to knowledge without thereby forfeiting the objectivity of knowledge. Reflecting this Kantian strategy, Gellner comments: 'There is a reason why the world is made up of machines, and that reason lies not in the world but in our practices of explanation' (*Legitimation of Belief*, p. 107).

30 Admittedly, the idea of primary qualities is closely connected to that of public and repeatable verification procedures. The epistemological significance of primary qualities is, of course, that in being measurable and quantifiable, the verification procedure for truth claims in which they feature is minimally vulnerable to sceptical objection. At this point Enlightenment fundamentalism assumes a conspicuous empiricist form. On the significance of the distinction between primary and secondary qualities for empiricism, see Colin McGinn, *The Subjective View: Secondary Qualities and Indexical Thoughts* (Oxford: Oxford University Press, 1983); and for its implications for morality, see J. L. Mackie, *Ethics: Inventing Right and Wrong* (Harmondsworth: Penguin, 1977).

31 On these notions of absolute description and objectivity, see Bernard Williams, *Descartes: The Project of Pure Enquiry* (Harmondsworth: Penguin, 1978); and Thomas Nagel, *The View from Nowhere* (Oxford: Oxford University Press, 1986).

32 Put otherwise, strong hermeneutics keeps the logic of the human and the natural sciences distinct, whereas weak hermeneutics collapses the distinction. It should be stressed that the distinction itself can be formulated in various, sometimes incompatible ways. The distinction maintained by Gadamer and

Taylor, for instance, is far from that advocated by Weber, which in turn deviates from Dilthey's formulation of it. For an exchange between advocates of weak and strong hermeneutic positions on this issue, see the contributions of Richard Rorty and Charles Taylor to *Review of Metaphysics*, 1980, 34, pp. 25–55; and James Tully ed., *Philosophy in an Age of Pluralism: The Philosophy of Charles Taylor in Question* (Cambridge: Cambridge University Press, 1994). While Ricoeur distances himself from Gadamer for opposing understanding (the putative goal of the human sciences) to explanation (the putative goal of the natural sciences), it is not clear that Gadamer really does subscribe to the understanding/explanation dichotomy Ricoeur ascribes to him, or for that matter the radical separation of truth and method. Cf. Paul Ricoeur, *Hermeneutics and the Human Sciences: Essays on Action, Language and Interpretation*, trans. John B. Thompson (Cambridge: Cambridge University Press, 1981), p. 36 and p. 131; and Gadamer, foreword to the second edition, *Truth and Method*, p. xxix.

33   See 'Interpretation and the Sciences of Man', in Taylor, *Philosophy and the Human Sciences* (Cambridge: Cambridge University Press, 1985). For parallel criticisms applied to the scope for absolute description in historical explanation, see Arthur C. Danto, *Analytic Philosophy of History* (Cambridge: Cambridge University Press, 1965).

34   See Taylor, 'Rationality', in *Philosophy and the Human Sciences*; and 'Comparison, History, Truth', in Taylor, *Philosophical Arguments* (Cambridge, Mass.: Harvard University Press, 1995).

35   See Taylor, *Hegel* (Cambridge: Cambridge University Press, 1975), chapter one. In deploying this argumentative strategy, Taylor borrows from Hegel's own model of immanent critique.

36   Cf. Gadamer's Hegelian reconstruction of the notion of *Bildung* as 'rising to the universal' in *Truth and Method*, p. 14ff.

37   Taylor calls this the 'Best Account' principle. It is elaborated in *Sources of the Self: The Making of the Modern Identity* (Cambridge, Mass.: Harvard University Press, 1989), p. 69ff. The kind of epistemological and metaphysical considerations I have in mind here are those making up the 'natural attitude' bracketed by classical phenomenology.

38   For the idea of philosophical anthropology at work in strong hermeneutics, see Taylor, *Philosophy and the Human Sciences*, Introduction; and Ricoeur, 'The Question of the Subject', in Don Ihde ed., *The Conflict of Interpretations: Essays in Hermeneutics* (Evanston: Northwestern University Press, 1974). As Taylor reminds us, we have to use the expression 'philosophical anthropology' with special caution. On the one hand, there is hardly any official recognition of philosophical anthropology as a legitimate academic discipline in the English-speaking world. And where it does constitute a recognized strand of philosophical knowledge – in continental Europe – it is often associated with a particular brand of anti-democratic, 'culturalist' politics. For an intriguing account of the different strands of philosophical anthropology from a disillusioned enthusiast, see Habermas's 1958 encyclopedia article 'Philosophische Anthropologie', reprinted in Habermas, *Kultur und Kritik* (Frankfurt am Main: Suhrkamp, 1973). For a more extensive account of the pertinence of the tradition of philosophical anthropology, see Axel Honneth and Hans Joas, *Social Action and Human Nature*, trans. Raymond Mayer with a foreword by Charles Taylor (Cambridge: Cambridge University Press, 1988).

39   Ricoeur, 'On Interpretation', in *From Text to Action: Essays in Hermeneutics II*, trans. Kathleen Blamey and John B. Thompson (London: Athlone Press, 1991), p. 15ff.

40 Cf. Taylor, 'The Opening Arguments of the Phenomenology', in A. MacIntyre ed., *Hegel: A Collection of Critical Essays* (New York: Doubleday, 1972).

41 Ricoeur, 'On Interpretation', p. 16.

42 See Ricoeur, *The Rule of Metaphor: Multi-Disciplinary Studies of the Creation of Meaning in Language*, trans R. Czerny (Toronto: University of Toronto Press, 1977); and *Time and Narrative* (3 vols) (Chicago: University of Chicago Press, 1984–1988).

43 Ricoeur, 'On Interpretation', p. 19.

44 Ibid. For a comparative analysis of Ricoeur's account of metaphor and Derrida's weak hermeneutic approach that is favourable to the former see Peter Dews, *The Limits of Disenchantment*, pp. 99–105.

45 Ricoeur, 'On Interpretation', p. 18.

46 For instance, both Ricoeur and Taylor take an investigation of the 'social imaginary' to be an essential part of their inquiries, one that obviously requires significant input from outside philosophy (see Ricoeur, *Hermeneutics and the Human Sciences*, p. 39; and Taylor, *Philosophical Arguments*, p. x). But whereas Ricoeur leans considerably on structuralist theories of symbolism and discourse, the extra-philosophical input to Taylor's hermeneutics comes more from historical studies.

47 See Taylor, 'Overcoming Epistemology', in *Philosophical Arguments*.

48 Taylor, *Sources of the Self*, p. 520. Gadamer offers a similar formulation when he writes that hermeneutics aims 'to let what is alienated by the character of the written word or by the character of being distanciated by cultural or historical distances speak again. This is hermeneutics: to let what seems to be far and alienated speak again' (Gadamer, 'Practical Philosophy as a model of the Human Sciences', *Research in Phenomenology*, 9, p. 83).

49 Habermas, *Knowledge and Human Interests*, trans. Jeremy Shapiro (London: Heinemann, 1972).

50 Besides *Truth and Method*, Gadamer's main contributions to the debate are 'The Universality of the Hermeneutical Problem' and 'On the Scope and Function of Hermeneutic Reflection', both in Gadamer, *Philosophical Hermeneutics* (Berkeley: University of California Press, 1976). Important presentations of Habermas's counter-claims include *On the Logic of the Social Sciences* (Cambridge: Polity, 1988); 'The Hermeneutic Claim to Universality', in Bleicher ed., *Contemporary Hermeneutics*; two articles in *Inquiry*, 13, 1970, 'On Systematically Distorted Communication', and 'Towards a Theory of Communicative Competence'; and the essay 'Interpretive Social Science vs. Hermeneuticism' in N. Haan et al. eds, *Social Science as Moral Enquiry* (New York: Columbia University Press, 1983). The key texts are collected in Ormiston and Shrift eds, *The Hermeneutic Tradition: From Ast to Ricoeur*. Extensive secondary literature occasioned by the debate is documented in Robert C. Holub, *Jürgen Habermas: Critic in the Public Sphere* (London: Routledge, 1991), pp. 193–4.

51 See Ricoeur, *Freud and Philosophy: An Essay on Interpretation*, trans. D. Savage (New Haven: Yale University Press, 1970), p. 26. Ricoeur's distinction has been very influential in shaping subsequent appraisals of the exchange between Habermas and Gadamer, but I do not mean to suggest that it adequately captures the full range of issues at stake. Nor should the distinction be absolutized. Even Gadamer's hermeneutics requires a certain distance from tradition and is perfectly compatible with a profound suspicion of it. Habermasian ideology critique, for its part, cannot do without some kind of appropriative relation to the past. For Ricoeur's own response to the Gadamer–Habermas debate, which incidentally is much more nuanced than a simple

invocation of the conflict between suspicion and retrieval, see his 'Hermeneutics and the Critique of Ideology' in *Hermeneutics and the Human Sciences*.

52 Besides *Moral Consciousness and Communicative Action* and *Justification and Application*, Habermas works out the beginnings of a discourse theory of ethics in the two volumes of *The Theory of Communicative Action*, trans. Thomas McCarthy (Cambridge: Polity, 1984 and 1987), developing it into a theory of law in *Between Facts and Norms*. For a more concise statement of the basic principles of Habermas's moral theory, see now Habermas, 'On the Cognitive Content of Morality', *Proceedings of the Aristotelian Society*, vol. XCVI, pt 3, 1996, pp. 335–58.

53 See Habermas, *Theory of Communicative Action*, vol. 1, *Reason and the Rationalization of Society*, p. 48ff.

54 See ibid., p. 64.

55 Ibid., p. 70.

56 Habermas, *Theory of Communicative Action*, vol. 2, *Lifeworld and System: A Critique of Functionalist Reason*, p. 130.

57 Ibid., p.126.

58 See Gellner, *Spectacles and Predicaments: Essays in Social Theory* (Cambridge: Cambridge University Press, 1979), Introduction.

59 Habermas, *The Theory of Communicative Action*, vol. 1, p. 100; vol. 2, p. 120.

60 Ibid., vol. 1, p. 340.

61 Ibid., p. 10.

62 Habermas, *The Philosophical Discourse of Modernity*, p. 315.

63 Furthermore, Habermas's reformulation and radicalization of the validation imperative enables him to distinguish two senses of rationalization: the 'communicative' rationalization of the lifeworld and the 'functional' rationalization of the 'system'. The lifeworld concept gets its distinctive meaning in Habermas's theory not only from its complementary relationship to communicative action but also in its distinction from social reality considered as a 'system'. According to the social theory which backs up discourse ethics, society *qua* system is rational to the degree that it integrates action consequences according to criteria of efficiency in performing functions necessary for its self-preservation. In the sub-systems of the economy and the bureaucratic state, action integration is mediated not communicatively, but by the 'delinguistified steering media' of money and power which react back and subsequently colonize the symbolic reproduction of the lifeworld. Accordingly, the main cause of lifeworld erosion is not so much disenchanting cognition as the 'pseudo-communicative' or delinguistified media of system integration. Habermas acknowledges that cognitive claims become increasingly rarefied and split-off from everyday discourse in the domain of scientific expert spheres, but the specialized training required to understand these claims also conditions competence for participation at the highest level of discourse in which other validity claims are thematized – moral and aesthetic discourse also get separated from the horizon in which everyday life is led. But this impoverishment of identity is of secondary significance to the 'colonization' of identity wrought when the horizon within which identities are forged becomes mediated by money and power. It is the latter which 'de-worlds' the lifeworld, not cognition. But a symptom of colonization is a one-sided rationalization of the lifeworld in its cognitive/technological dimension. And herein lies the *imbalance* between being and knowing characteristic of the times. Furthermore, if what is 'de-worlding' about money and power is that they are 'delinguistified', Habermas will have to extract from language as such a model of normativity that explains the vulnerability of human identity to this kind of corrosion. He needs to establish not only that the claims of morality have as

good a place in argumentative procedures as scientific/cognitive claims. He must also show that there is good reason for abiding by these procedures – that doing so satisfies the requirements of human identity.

2 STRONG HERMENEUTICS AND THE CONTINGENCY OF SELF

1 Zygmunt Bauman, *Intimations of Postmodernity* (Oxford: Blackwell, 1992), p. 134.
2 Rorty, *Contingency, Irony and Solidarity*, p. 32.
3 I do not mean to suggest that Rorty's is the only way of remodelling ethical reflection around the acknowledgement of contingency. While heavily indebted to Rorty in his understanding of anti-foundationalism, Bauman finds Levinas most instructive for thinking about morality in a postmodern age. In his recent explorations of 'postmodern ethics', Bauman accentuates the *existentialist* moment of the encounter with contingency: 'The denizens of the postmodern era', he writes, are 'forced to stand face-to-face with their moral autonomy, and so also their moral responsibility' (Bauman, 'Morality without Ethics', *Theory, Culture and Society*, 1994, 11, 4, pp. 1–34). Such a stance courageously affirms the moral in its very groundlessness; it acknowledges the claims of the other in its very otherness, 'face-to-face'. Another influential but very different way of bringing the contingency of value to self-consciousness, one which accentuates the *systemic dissolution* of moral autonomy, is offered by Herrnstein Smith in *Contingencies of Value*.
4 Taylor, *Human Agency and Language* (Cambridge: Cambridge University Press, 1985), p. 3.
5 Taylor, *Sources of the Self*, p. 34.
6 See ibid., pp. 14–19.
7 Ibid., p. 27.
8 Ibid., p. 30.
9 See Martin Löw-Beer, 'Living a Life and the Problem of Existential Impossibility', *Inquiry*, 1991, 34, pp. 217–316.
10 Taylor, *The Ethics of Authenticity* (London: Harvard University Press, 1992), p. 39.
11 The 'emotivist self' is MacIntyre's term. See *After Virtue* (London: Duckworth, 1981), p. 30.
12 Rorty, *Objectivism, Relativism and Truth*, p. 109.
13 Rorty, *Essays on Heidegger and Others*, p. 147.
14 Ibid., p. 155.
15 Rorty, *Objectivism, Relativism and Truth*, p. 110.
16 In *Sources of the Self*, Taylor takes on board the idea – owed of course to MacIntyre's *After Virtue* – of a life quest, which Rorty is disputing here.
17 Rorty, *Essays on Heidegger and Others*, p. 161.
18 Rorty, *Contingency, Irony and Solidarity*, p. 31.
19 Taylor, *Sources of the Self*, p. 480.
20 See Derrida, 'Signature, Event, Context', in *Margins of Philosophy*, p. 323.
21 Williams, *Ethics and the Limits of Philosophy* (London: Fontana, 1985), p. 177.
22 Ibid., p. 193.
23 Habermas, *Knowledge and Human Interests*, p. 234.
24 See Jay Bernstein, 'Self-knowledge as Praxis: Narrative and Self-narration in Psychoanalysis', in Bernstein, *Recovering Ethical Life: Jürgen Habermas and the Future of Critical Theory* (London: Routledge, 1995), pp. 58–87.

25   See Taylor, *The Ethics of Authenticity*; and Axel Honneth, *The Struggle for Recognition: The Moral Grammar of Social Conflicts*, trans. Joel Anderson (Cambridge: Polity, 1995).

26   See Charles B. Guignon and David R. Hiley, 'Biting the Bullet: Rorty on Private and Public Morality', in Alan Malachowski ed. *Reading Rorty* (Oxford: Blackwell, 1990), pp. 339–64. For an overview of the sociological literature, see Axel Honneth, *Desintegration* (Frankfurt am Main: Fischer, 1994), the theoretical assumptions of which are explored by the same author in 'Pathologien des Sozialen. Tradition und Actualität der Sozialphilosophie', in Honneth ed., *Pathologien des Sozialen* (Frankfurt am Main: Fischer, 1994), pp. 9–69. For a psychoanalytical perspective, there is Stephen Frosh, *Identity Crisis: Modernity, Psychoanalysis and the Self* (London: Macmillan, 1991).

27   Rorty occasionally gives ground on this issue. Describing Taylor's anti-subjectivist characterization of modern art as taking up the task of seeing ourselves as part of a larger order that can make a claim on us, Rorty writes that it 'did not quite convince me that we need to worry about subjectivism and to be aware of anthropocentrism, but it came close. It unsettled some of my previous convictions' (Rorty, 'In a flattened world', review of *The Ethics of Authenticity* by Charles Taylor, *London Review of Books*, 1993, 8, April, p. 3). See also Rorty, 'Taylor on Self-celebration and Gratitude', *Philosophy and Phenomenological Research*, 1994, LIV, 1, pp. 197–202.

28   Ricoeur, *Oneself as Another*, trans. Kathleen Blamey (Chicago: Chicago University Press, 1992).

29   Ricoeur defines 'philosophies of the subject' broadly as those that formulate the subject 'in the first person – *ego cogito* – whether the "I" is defined as an empirical or a transcendental ego, whether the "I" is posited absolutely (that is, with no reference to another) or relatively (egology requiring the intrinsic complement of intersubjectivity)' (ibid., p. 4). For this reason Ricoeur takes 'philosophies of the subject' to be equivalent to 'philosophies of the cogito'.

30   Ibid., p. 2.

31   Ibid., p. 19ff.

32   Ibid., p. 22.

33   Bernard P. Dauenhauer does a good job in bringing out other convergent trajectories of Taylor's and Ricoeur's recent work on selfhood in his review essay of *Sources of the Self* and *Soi-même comme un autre*, 'Taylor and Ricoeur on the Self', *Man and World*, 1992, 25, pp. 211–25.

34   On Ricoeur's account, Parfit's oversight in answering the question 'who narrates itself or herself?' has parallels in discourses addressing the other who?-questions. Although Ricoeur maintains that the senses of self-identity answering to the questions 'who speaks?' and 'who acts?' are most fully explored in analytic philosophy, particularly in Strawson's philosophy of language, speech act theory, and Anscombe's and Davidson's theories of action, he is so critical of the grounding assumptions of these discourses it is difficult to see what warrants the long detour in his reflections. Strawson is found wanting for failing to reconcile the mode of being that allows of referential designation with that of active, reflective subjectivity. Davidson's account of 'actions without agents', for its part, is criticized for relying on a taken-for-granted ontology of impersonal events, one that makes sense only of the 'ascription' of action in terms of sameness, not its 'imputation' in terms of selfhood. According to Ricoeur, neither Strawson nor the speech act theorists, neither Anscombe nor Davidson, address in anything like a satisfactory manner the *amphibian* ontology of self-identity, its ipse/idem mode of existence.

35   See Derek Parfit, *Reasons and Persons* (Oxford: Clarendon, 1984).

36 Taylor's terse response to Parfit (*Sources of the Self*, p. 49) chimes with Ricoeur's but is less developed.
37 Ricoeur, *Oneself as Another*, p. 132.
38 Ibid., p. 150.
39 Ibid.
40 Ibid., p. 140.
41 This idea is explored further in chapter four, where it provides the guiding theme for our discussion of 'deep hermeneutic' reflection.
42 Ibid., p. 138.
43 See Hegel, *Phenomenology of Spirit*, trans. A. V. Miller (Oxford: Oxford University Press, 1977), p. 365ff.
44 Ricoeur, *Oneself as Another*, p. 342. See '"Guilt", "Bad Conscience", and the Like', in Nietzsche, *On The Genealogy of Morals*, trans. Walter Kaufmann and R. J. Hollingdale (New York: Vintage, 1967).
45 Ricoeur, *Oneself as Another*, p. 351.
46 Ibid.
47 Ibid., p. 355.
48 Ibid.

3 INTERPRETATION, PRACTICAL REASON AND TRADITION

1 See Taylor, *Sources of the Self*, and 'Explanation and Practical Reason', in *Philosophical Arguments*. See also MacIntyre's, 'Epistemological Crises, Dramatic Narrative and Philosophy of Science', *The Monist*, 1977, 60, pp. 453–72; MacIntyre, *Whose Justice? Which Rationality?* (Notre Dame, Ind.: University of Notre Dame Press, 1988); and Ernst Tugendhat, *Self-Consciousness and Self-Determination*, trans. Paul Stern (Cambridge, Mass.: MIT Press, 1986).
2 See Crispin Wright, *Truth and Objectivity*.
3 See Taylor, *Sources of the Self*, p. 47ff.
4 Taylor, like Bernard Williams, takes the idea of a 'basic reason' to be a common presupposition of the two main opponents of traditional moral theory, Kantianism and utilitarianism. See Taylor, *Sources of the Self*, p. 76ff; and Williams, *Ethics and the Limits of Philosophy*.
5 Taylor, *Sources of the Self*, p. 72.
6 See Taylor, 'Explanation and Practical Reason'.
7 See Thomas Kuhn, *The Structure of Scientific Revolutions*; and I. Lakatos and A. Musgrave eds, *Criticism and the Growth of Knowledge* (Cambridge: Cambridge University Press, 1970).
8 I am not assuming that this *is* enough to establish a sound interpretation. Matters are much more complex. Account must be made, for instance, of the ambiguities to the transition famously brought to light by Foucault. See Foucault, *Discipline and Punish: The Birth of the Prison*, trans. Alan Sheridon (New York: Pantheon, 1977).
9 Taylor invokes this formulation of moral anti-realism – namely, that 'concerning strong evaluations, there is no truth of the matter' – in Taylor, 'Understanding and Explanation in the *Geisteswissenschaften*', in S. L. Holtzman and C. Leich eds, *Wittgenstein: To Follow a Rule* (London: Routledge, 1981), p. 200.
10 Here I follow Taylor, 'Interpretation and the Sciences of Man', in *Philosophy and the Human Sciences*.
11 Ibid., p. 24.
12 Ibid., p. 19.

13   For further criticisms of this approach to political science, and a brilliant exposition of the inescapable reliance of political and social theory on some evaluatively 'thick' philosophical anthropology, see Taylor's 'Neutrality in Political Science', in *Philosophy and the Human Sciences*.

14   'Understanding and Explanation in the *Geisteswissenschaften*', p. 192.

15   The point that the meaning of strong evaluations does not withstand division into 'fact-stating' and 'value-projecting' components is worth bringing to the attention of partisans of a 'value-free', 'scientific' reading of Marx. Their efforts to purify Marx's concept of exploitation of evaluative residue, by translating its objective component into a neutral term like 'pumping out' results in failure to pick out something in the world which is essential to what Marx identifies; namely *exploitative* practices.

16   Not altogether fairly, this position is often associated with the work of Peter Winch. See Winch, *The Idea of a Social Science and its Relation to Philosophy* (London: Routledge and Kegan Paul, 1958).

17   See Taylor, *Sources of the Self*, p. 69.

18   Ibid.

19   Ibid., p. 58.

20   For concerns about the motivation of Taylor's avowed moral realism that take a different direction to those raised here, see Michael Rosen, 'Must we Return to Moral Realism?', *Inquiry*, 1991, 34, pp. 183–94.

21   Taylor, *Sources of the Self*, p. 57.

22   Ibid., p. 81.

23   See A. J. Ayer, *Language, Truth and Logic* (London: Victor Gollancz, 1936); and J. L. Mackie, *Ethics*.

24   Wright, *Truth and Objectivity*, pp. 28–9.

25   Ibid., p. 75.

26   Ibid., p. 93.

27   Ibid., p. 147.

28   Ibid., p. 91.

29   Ibid., p. 146.

30   Ibid., p. 92.

31   Ibid., p. 148. Wright's term for the other key test for realism is 'wide cosmological role'.

32   Ibid., p. 76.

33   Compare Wright's comment, for instance, with Taylor's remark about the 'mind-numbing relativism' of the 'Vulgar Wittgensteinian' view in 'Understanding and Explanation in the *Geisteswissenschaften*', p. 205. John Divers has pointed out to me, if I understand him correctly, that my concern that interpretive truth gets contorted under Wright's grid of minimal truth and cognitive command should be ameliorated by refinements in Wright's account that allow us to think of interpretation as *mediating* minimally truth-apt and metaphysically more substantive discourses. While this is a fascinating idea to explore further, my present view is that the picture of the subject engaged in belief-formation that goes with cognitive command misrepresents the basic cognitive predicament facing self-interpreting subjects.

34   See Taylor, 'Cross-purposes: The Liberal–Communitarian Debate', in *Philosophical Arguments*, p. 181.

35   See Taylor, *Hegel and Modern Society* (Cambridge: Cambridge University Press, 1979). For a Wittgensteinian critique of justifications of conservatism in these terms, which I shall turn to presently, see Sabina Lovibond, *Realism and Imagination in Ethics* (Oxford: Blackwell, 1983).

36   The limits to contingency that constitute our defining or transcendental situation, as noted in our discussion of Ricoeur at the end of chapter two, do

not constrain freedom but provide the conditions for its real possibility. As Taylor puts it in a discussion of Hegel, 'all the varied notions of situated freedom...see free activity as grounded in the *acceptance* of our defining situation. The struggle to be free – against limitations, oppressions, distortions of inner and outer origin – is powered by an affirmation of this defining situation as ours. *This* cannot be seen as a set of limits to be overcome, or a mere occasion to carry out some freely chosen project' (Taylor, *Hegel and Modern Society*, p. 160).

37 S. Lovibond, *Realism and Imagination in Ethics*, p. 217. Lovibond constructs her distinction in the context of a discussion of Wittgenstein. In recontextualizing it, I will modify it slightly.

38 For this distinction between comprehensive and revisionary critique, see Taylor, 'The Motivation behind a Proceduralist Ethics', in Ronald Beiner and William James Booth eds, *Kant and Political Philosophy: The Contemporary Legacy* (New Haven: Yale University Press, 1993). This article is reprinted with slight modifications as 'Justice after Virtue', in John Horton and Susan Mendus eds, *After MacIntyre: Critical Perspectives on the Work of Alasdair MacIntyre* (Cambridge: Polity, 1994).

39 Taylor, 'The Motivation behind a Procedural Ethics', p. 355.

40 If I may summon one final image to ward off the spectre of conservatism, this time borrowing from McDowell (*Mind and World*, p. 81), the person engaged in hermeneutic reflection is in the same predicament as the sailor in Neurath's boat. Just as the sailor must overhaul the boat from within to remain afloat, so critical reflection must take place in 'the midst of the way of thinking one is reflecting about'. Properly understood, immanence holds no solace for the moral conservative.

4 DEEP HERMENEUTICS, EMANCIPATION AND FATE

1 Habermas, *The Philosophical Discourse of Modernity*, p. 316.

2 Ibid., p. 306.

3 See J. Bernstein, *Recovering Ethical Life*, especially pp. 177–96. Besides Bernstein's book, the only interpretation of Habermas to do justice to the causality of fate theme is Anne Créau, *Kommunikative Vernunft als 'entmystifizierte Schicksal': Denkmotive des frühen Hegel in der Theorie der Jürgen Habermas* (Frankfurt am Main: Anton Hain, 1991).

4 Included in G. W. F. Hegel, *Early Theological Writings*, trans. T. M. Knox (New York: Harper and Brothers, 1961) pp. 182–301.

5 Ibid., p. 226.

6 Ibid., p. 238.

7 Hegel considers the fate to remain external even if law is self-willed. His underlying point seems to be that the avenging force of the ethical stands outwith the autonomy of the isolated rational will. And to the degree to which it is therefore heteronomous, the Kantian opposition between the autonomous and the heteronomous breaks down.

8 Ibid., p. 232. This reference holds for the remaining quotations in this paragraph.

9 Ibid., p. 228.

10 See Williams, *Ethics and the Limits of Philosophy*, pp. 174–96.

11 Admittedly this formulation is slightly misleading. The universality of the moral law has its foundation in the necessity of practical reasoning, as Williams explains in chapter four of his book.

12 Ibid., p. 191 (my emphasis).

13 Ibid., p. 195.
14 Ibid., p. 193.
15 Williams gives us reason for thinking *that* the oppositions between duty and inclination and between volition and force need to be reconciled but he offers little by way of indicating *how* they might be. Elsewhere, in *Moral Luck* (Cambridge: Cambridge University Press, 1981), p. 30, n. 2, he acknowledges that an answer might lie in a tragic conception of agency; a thought that is taken somewhat further, though in an indirect fashion, in *Shame and Necessity* (Berkeley: University of California Press, 1993). Hegel, on the other hand, develops such a conception more systematically.
16 Hegel, *Early Theological Writings*, pp. 230–1. The feeling of a life disrupted 'must' become a longing for what has been lost if there is to be reconciliation. But the force of this 'must' is not categorical, it is not determined by the moral law.
17 Ibid., p. 231.
18 Ibid., p. 238.
19 Ibid., p. 230.
20 Ibid., p. 229.
21 Habermas, *Theory and Practice*, trans. J. Viertel (London: Heinemann, 1974), p. 148. See also *Knowledge and Human Interests*, p. 56.
22 In the following remark, Habermas makes explicit his strategy of theorizing 'life', the source of moral injunction, as the site where communicative *rationality* is deposited: 'Any violation of the structures of rational life together, to which all lay claim, affects everyone equally. This is what the young Hegel meant by the ethical totality which is disrupted by the deed of the criminal and that can only be restored by insight into the indivisibility of suffering due to alienation' (Habermas, *The Philosophical Discourse of Modernity*, p. 324). The problem Habermas now faces is that of making Hegel's insight intelligible within a general account of the emergence of structures of rational life. Habermas takes this to be equivalent to the task of accounting for the evolution of the different kinds of communicative competence within a *theory of rationalization*. But bringing Hegel's model of moral identity to bear on the problematic of rationalization is bound to face difficulties, since the latter is organized around the Weberian conception of modernity as instantiating formal or procedural norms of rationality only.
23 Habermas, *Knowledge and Human Interests*, p. 229.
24 Ibid., p. 226
25 Ibid., p. 227.
26 Ibid., p. 228.
27 Ibid., pp. 216–17.
28 Habermas, 'The Hermeneutic Claim to Universality', in Bleicher ed., *Contemporary Hermeneutics*, p. 194.
29 Habermas, *Knowledge and Human Interests*, p. 218.
30 Ibid., p. 256.
31 Ibid.
32 Ibid., p. 271.
33 Ibid., p. 245.
34 Ibid., p. 257.
35 Habermas, 'The Hermeneutic Claim to Universality', p. 193.
36 Habermas, *Knowledge and Human Interests*, p. 234.
37 Ibid., pp. 235–6.
38 In a footnote to 'Some Difficulties in the Attempt to Link Theory and Praxis' (*Theory and Practice*, p. 285, n. 38) Habermas expresses vexation that his doctrine of human interests should be accused both of naturalism (by Michael

Theunissen) and anti-naturalism (by Hans Albert), but he does not directly address the issues that will concern us here.

39 R. Keat, *The Politics of Social Theory: Habermas, Freud and Positivism* (London: University of Chicago Press, 1981).

40 Ibid., p.108.

41 Ibid., p. 107.

42 Habermas, *Knowledge and Human Interests*, p. 271.

43 Keat, *The Politics of Social Theory*, p. 108.

44 Habermas, *Knowledge and Human Interests*, p. 220.

45 Habermas acknowledges that for Freud, this is an inevitable part of human psycho-social development

46 Keat, *The Politics of Social Theory*, p. 179. After making this comment, Keat turns to Habermas's attempt to clarify the rational foundation of norms in discourse. Keat fails to appreciate that the model of communicative action through which Habermas attempts to do this is *already* central to his interpretation of psychoanalysis. However, Habermas's substantive anthropological and formal pragmatic arguments do sit uneasily together, as we will see in chapter six.

47 Ibid.

48 Habermas, *Knowledge and Human Interests*, p. 232.

49 See Habermas's account of the pathologies of the modern lifeworld in *The Theory of Communicative Action*, vol. 2.

50 J. Bernstein, *Recovering Ethical Life*, p. 66.

51 Ibid., p. 68.

52 The anthropological foundations of critical theory are stressed by Axel Honneth in *The Struggle for Recognition*. Thus, despite the affinity Bernstein notes between his own work and Honneth's (*Recovering Ethical Life*, p. 8), there is in fact some latitude between their positions.

5 COMMUNICATION AND THE CONTINGENCY OF LANGUAGE

1 Postscript to Habermas, *Knowledge and Human Interests*, p. 314.

2 For a clear commentary on the three functional aspects of Habermas's concept of communicative action, see Maeve Cooke, *Language and Reason: A Study of Habermas's Pragmatics* (Cambridge, Mass.: MIT Press, 1994), chapter 1.

3 See Habermas, *The Theory of Communicative Action*, vol. 1, p. 286. In a later work, 'A Reply', Habermas denies that communicative action and strategic action differ 'primarily in terms of the attitude of the actors'. Rather, Habermas asserts, there are differences in the underlying 'structural characteristics' of the two types of action that compel different attitudes on the part of communicative and strategic actors. See Habermas, 'A Reply', in Honneth and Joas eds, *Communicative Action: Essays on Jürgen Habermas's The Theory of Communicative Action*, trans. Jeremy Gaines and Doris L. Jones (Cambridge: Polity, 1991), p. 242.

4 Habermas, *The Theory of Communicative Action*, vol. 1, p. 288.

5 Ibid. The conflation of 'indirect communication' and strategic language use in this passage is suspect, since it leads to a problematically broad and diffuse category of strategic action. However, the main criticism I make of Habermas in the immediately following discussion turns not on this ambiguity in Habermas's classification, but on infelicities arising through the modifications Habermas is forced to make to Austin's distinction for the sake of grounding language in its communicative use. For the original formulation of Austin's

distinction, see J. L. Austin, *How to Do Things with Words*, 2nd edn, J .O. Urmson and M. Sbisà eds, pp. 98–103.

6　See Jonathan Culler, 'Communicative Competence and Normative Force', *New German Critique*, 1985, 35, pp. 133–44; and, more tellingly, Allen Wood, 'Habermas's Defence of Rationalism', *New German Critique*, 1985, 35, pp. 145–64. Habermas acknowledges the force of Wood's objections in 'Toward a Critique of the Theory of Meaning', in Habermas, *Postmetaphysical Thinking: Between Metaphysics and the Critique of Reason*, trans. William Mark Hohengarten (Cambridge: Polity, 1994), pp. 86–7.

7　Habermas, *The Theory of Communicative Action*, vol. 1, p. 293.

8　Ibid., p. 292.

9　Since *The Theory of Communicative Action*, Habermas has modified his characterization of perlocutionary acts. See 'A Reply', pp. 240–3; and 'Toward a Critique of the Theory of Meaning', pp. 73–84.

10　Culler, 'Communicative Competence and Normative Force', p. 137.

11　Habermas, *The Philosophical Discourse of Modernity*, p. 196.

12　Ibid., p. 198.

13　Ibid., p. 199.

14　I discuss the difference between deconstructivist and strong hermeneutic understandings of world-disclosure in chapter seven.

15　Lyotard, *The Postmodern Condition*, p. 10.

16　Ibid., p. 57.

17　Ibid., p. 16.

18　Ibid., p. 17.

19　Ibid., p. 65.

20　See Peter Dews ed., *Autonomy and Solidarity: Interviews with Jürgen Habermas*, rev. edn (London: Verso, 1992), p. 21. But also compare the position outlined in Lyotard's *The Differend: Phrases in Dispute*, trans. G. Van Den Abbeele (Minneapolis: University of Minnesota Press, 1988), which offers a more Weberian analysis of the unavoidable antagonism between illocutionary aims. For a discussion of the debate between Lyotard and Habermas that focuses on Lyotard's work after *The Postmodern Condition*, see David Ingram, *Reason, History and Politics: The Communitarian Grounds of Legitimation in the Modern Age* (Albany: SUNY Press, 1995), pp. 321–42.

21　If, indeed, Wittgenstein really takes consensus to be requisite of meaning at all.

22　Habermas, *The Theory of Communicative Action*, vol. 2, p. 16.

23　Ibid., p. 18. The same reference holds for the rest of the citations in this paragraph.

24　Ibid., p. 17.

25　K. O. Apel, *Towards a Transformation of Philosophy*, trans. Glyn Adey and David Frisby (London: Routledge, 1980), p. 280.

26　Compare David Rasmussen, *Reading Habermas* (Oxford: Blackwell, 1990), p. 31.

27　G. P. Baker and P. M. S. Hacker, *Wittgenstein: Rules, Grammar, and Necessity* (Oxford: Blackwell, 1985), p. 248.

28　See L. Wittgenstein, *Remarks on the Foundations of Mathematics*, trans. G. H. Von Wright, R. Rhees and G. E. M. Anscombe, 3rd edn (Oxford: Blackwell, 1978), p. 365.

29　'If language is to be a means of communication there must be agreement not only in definitions but also (queer as it may sound) in judgements. This seems to abolish logic but does not do so' (Wittgenstein, *Philosophical Investigations*, trans. G. E. M. Anscombe, 3rd edn [Oxford: Blackwell, 1967], sec. 242).

30　Wittgenstein, *Remarks on the Foundations of Mathematics*, p. 323.

31　Habermas, *The Theory of Communicative Action*, vol. 1, p. 17.

32 McDowell, *Mind and World*, p. 125.
33 See Habermas, 'A Reply', especially pp. 215–22, where Habermas responds to Taylor, 'Language and Society', in the same volume.
34 See Habermas, 'A Reply', p. 221.
35 Ibid., p. 222.
36 Habermas insists on keeping his contributions to the theory of action and the theory of meaning distinct – indeed he chastises himself for not always respecting their boundaries (see Habermas, 'Toward a Critique of the Theory of Meaning', pp. 86–7). But given the particular approach he takes to the theory of meaning – namely, formal pragmatics – there is bound to be considerable overlap. Moreover, Habermas seeks to consolidate the same basic convictions in the two regions of discourse. The most basic of these is the thesis that language is non-contingently – or non-derivatively or non-parasitically – oriented to the reaching of understanding with an other on the basis of reasons. For if Habermas can establish the validity of that thesis, he will be on course for showing that 'the human interest in autonomy and responsibility is not mere fancy' without needing to resort to a philosophical anthropology.
37 As Anne Créau (*Kommunikative Vernunft als 'entmystifiziertes Schicksal'*) also observes, this is how the young Hegelian theme of an ethical totality – the appropriation of which, we have noted, shapes Habermas's self-understanding of his transformation of Critical Theory – finds its way into the central thesis of formal pragmatics.

6 STRONG HERMENEUTICS AND DISCOURSE ETHICS

1 Habermas, *Legitimation Crisis*, trans. T. McCarthy (London: Heinemann, 1976), p. 120.
2 This idea gains mature expression in the colonization thesis of the theory of communicative action. See chapter one, note 63, above.
3 See Mackie, *Ethics*, p. 36ff.
4 See Habermas, 'On the Cognitive Content of Morality', pp. 346–7. For commentary on the difference between discourse ethics and the allegedly 'monological' deontological theories of Kant and Rawls, see Seyla Benhabib, *Situating the Self: Gender, Community and Postmodernism in Contemporary Ethics* (Cambridge: Polity, 1992); Kenneth Baynes, *The Normative Basis of Social Criticism: Kant, Rawls and Habermas* (Albany: SUNY Press, 1991); William Rehg, *Insight and Solidarity: The Discourse Ethics of Jürgen Habermas* (Berkeley: University of California Press, 1994); and Shane O'Neill, *Impartiality in Context* (Albany: SUNY Press, 1997). For criticism of the view that the discourse ethical version of deontology really does constitute a significant move away from monological accounts of morality, see J. Bernstein, *Recovering Ethical Life*.
5 See Habermas, 'Philosophy as Stand-In and Interpreter', in *Moral Consciousness and Communicative Action*; and Habermas, 'Questions and Counterquestions', in Richard Bernstein ed., *Habermas and Modernity* (Cambridge, Mass.: MIT Press, 1985), pp. 210–11.
6 See Habermas, *Moral Consciousness and Communicative Action*, p. 106.
7 For Habermas's early recognition of these problems, see his 'Some Difficulties in the Attempt to Link Theory and Praxis', in *Theory and Practice*, especially pp. 22–4. For a lucid summary of the shift in Habermas's research programme, see Richard Bernstein's 'Introduction' to *Habermas and Modernity*; and Axel Honneth, *The Critique of Power: Reflective Stages in a Critical Social Theory*, trans. Kenneth Baynes (Cambridge, Mass.: MIT Press, 1991), pp. 280–5.

8   For a general treatment of the epistemological difficulties facing the claims of reconstructive science, see Seyla Benhabib, *Critique, Norm and Utopia* (New York: Columbia University Press, 1986), pp. 263–70.

9   See Habermas, 'On the Cognitive Content of Morality', p. 351.

10   Habermas, *Moral Consciousness and Communicative Action*, p. 197.

11   For systematic and sympathetic treatments of Habermas's anti-sceptical arguments see William Rehg, *Insight and Solidarity*; and Tony Smith, *The Role of Ethics in Social Theory: Essays from a Habermasian Perspective* (Albany: SUNY Press, 1991).

12   Habermas, *Moral Consciousness and Communicative Action*, p. 104.

13   Habermas, 'Questions and Counterquestions', p. 210.

14   Habermas, *Moral Consciousness and Communicative Action*, p. 108.

15   Ibid., p. 178.

16   Ibid., p. 109.

17   Ibid.

18   Ibid., p. 206.

19   Habermas uses the term 'therapeutic discourse' for critical reflection on evaluative statements because he considers them to be judgements of ways in which a form of life *as a whole* can go well or badly. As we saw in chapter four, this is an issue which arises for the analysand undergoing psychoanalytical therapy. The emancipatory 'deep hermeneutic' reflection called for by the raising of the question of the course of one's life as a whole, which Habermas also terms 'methodically carried out self-critique', aims at self-realization but only by removing sources of disturbance. It is because psychoanalytical reflection provides Habermas with a paradigm case of self-reappropriation that he coins the terms 'therapeutic' discourse and 'clinical' intuition to cover evaluative reflection and judgement.

20   For more thoughts on the paradigmatic status of modern natural science even in Habermas's communicative model of 'gains in rationality', see J. Bernstein, *Recovering Ethical Life*, p. 105ff.

21   Habermas, *Justification and Application*, p .4.

22   Ibid.

23   Ibid., p. 9.

24   Ibid., p. 10. But on Habermas's account the ethical use of practical reason – or hermeneutic self-clarification – is not just a matter for individuals: it also applies to deliberations concerning group or collective identity. Habermas elaborates more upon the notion of an ethical employment of practical reason in the latter sense in *Between Facts and Norms*.

25   Ibid., p. 5.

26   I think that William Rehg understates the difference between Habermas and Taylor when he writes that 'Taylor's analysis of the internal relation between description and evaluation does not differ radically from our own [discourse ethical] account of the internal link between moral norms and values' (*Insight and Solidarity*, p. 116). The difference is understated because Taylor's disagreement with Habermas's differentiation of the validity claims gives him a radically different perspective on the logic and ontology of strong evaluation. I shall consider Rehg's reconstruction of the Habermas/Taylor debate in more detail later in the chapter.

27   Habermas, *The Philosophical Discourse of Modernity*, p. 145.

28   See Benhabib, *Situating the Self*, p. 72.

29   Habermas, *Moral Consciousness and Communicative Action*, p. 201.

30   See Taylor, 'Inwardness and the Culture of Modernity', in A. Honneth et al. eds, *Philosophical Interventions in the Unfinished Project of Modernity* (Cambridge, Mass.: MIT Press, 1992).

31 See Taylor, *Sources of the Self.*

32 Habermas, *The Philosophical Discourse of Modernity,* p. 7

33 A third way of bringing about mediation, Habermas contends, is prefigured in works of art which show how the 'entangled' differentiated moments of a whole can be reconciled in a freely moving, harmonious or 'balanced' totality (see Habermas, 'Philosophy as Stand-in and Interpreter'). However, Habermas does not believe that this undertaking should be understood as an act of reason. For further discussion of the untapped mediating potential of art and aesthetic judgement in Habermas's theory of rationality, see Martin Seel, *Der Kunst der Entzweiung: Zum Begriff der ästhetischen Rationalität* (Frankfurt am Main: Suhrkamp, 1985); by the same author, 'The Two Meanings of Communicative Rationality', in Honneth and Joas eds, *Communicative Action*; and David Ingram, *Reason, History and Politics.* We shall return to the role of art in Habermas's theory in the concluding section of this chapter.

34 See Habermas, *Justification and Application,* pp. 36–9.

35 For a fuller elaboration of the difficulties facing the discourse ethical separation of justification and application, see Albrecht Wellmer, 'Ethics and Dialogue', in Wellmer, *The Persistence of Modernity: Essays on Aesthetics, Ethics, and Postmodernism,* trans. David Widgley (Cambridge: Polity, 1991). Habermas's response to Wellmer (see previous note) does not pick up on the general problems that concern me here.

36 Habermas, *Moral Consciousness and Communicative Action,* p. 182.

37 See Carol Gilligan, *In a Different Voice: Psychological Theory and Women's Development* (Cambridge, Mass.: Harvard University Press, 1982); Benhabib, *Critique, Norm, and Utopia,* pp. 340–3, and *Situating the Self.* Habermas replies to Benhabib's objection in an interview entitled 'Discourse Ethics, Law and *Sittlichkeit*', in Habermas, *Autonomy and Solidarity,* pp. 251–2. Habermas's defence turns on the idea that in real discourses of application, as opposed to the idealized context of justification, the other must always be concretized. But this response will only be convincing if one has already accepted the strong distinction between justification and application.

38 Habermas, *Moral Consciousness and Communicative Action,* p. 108.

39 Habermas, *Autonomy and Solidarity,* pp. 166–7.

40 Habermas's comments in this interview might be given a different interpretation. In *Kommunikative Vernunft als 'entmystifiziertes Schicksal',* Créau argues that the absence of any systematic theoretical reflection on the standard of 'health' applicable to ethical life is not the result of neglect or failure on Habermas's part; rather it is an expression of the quasi-religious, 'dogmatic core' of his theory. For Habermas, as Créau reads him, the normative content of ethical life, the standard of intact intersubjectivity on which the theory of communicative action ultimately relies, has an intuitive, non-demonstrable character. Habermas's conviction, inspired by the young Hegel, that communicative reason operates in history as an avenging force, is in the last analysis a matter of faith. But while this interpretation accurately reflects Habermas's scepticism regarding the ontological competence of reason, his distrust of philosophical anthropology, and a certain Kantian agnosticism in his outlook, none the less it does not fit well with other aspects of Habermas's theory, nor with other concerns Habermas clearly displays. First, it is not clear how the formalization and proceduralization of Hegel's model helps avoid an untenably 'theorized' appropriation of ethical life. Second, Habermas does want to retain the notion of rational transitions in forms of life as a whole – a task which, as Gadamer's hermeneutics shows, can be achieved without positing a philosophically determinable end to history. But most important, the load carried by the core notion of intact intersubjectivity is simply too weighty to be left to a

dogma. As I suggested in chapter four, the causality of fate theme can only really carry conviction once it is integrated into a philosophical anthropology. It has to find expression in a strong hermeneutics that makes perspicuous the damaged, but potentially self-surpassing, life of broken intersubjectivity.

41   Habermas, *Moral Consciousness and Communicative Action*, p. 206.

42   Ibid., p. 214, n. 15.

43   See Habermas, *Justification and Application*, p. 122ff. In a broader political context, Habermas suspects that 'neo-Aristotelianism' seeks to deactivate the 'explosive force of universalistic principles of morality', thereby minimizing 'the burden of moral justification incumbent upon the political system' (Habermas, *The New Conservatism: Cultural Criticism and the Historians' Debate*, trans. Shierry Weber Nicholson [Cambridge: Polity, 1989], pp. 41–2).

44   It should be stressed that this is not equivalent to Habermas's idea that the differentiated truth and normative rightness validity claims are always raised *simultaneously*.

45   Cited in Habermas, *Justification and Application*, p. 123.

46   Ibid., p. 124.

47   Or, in the terms Wright lays down for realism vs anti-realism debates, hermeneutically retrieved 'clinical intuitions' have a validity that breaks out of minimal truth without entering cognitive command. Put otherwise, Wright's framework is unsuitable for making sense of the idea of excellence in the ethical employment of practical reason.

48   Ibid., p. 122.

49   Ibid., p. 125.

50   Habermas, *Autonomy and Solidarity*, p. 162.

51   See Taylor, 'Language and Society', in Honneth and Joas eds, *Communicative Action*, especially pp. 29–34; and Taylor, 'The Motivation behind a Procedural Ethics'.

52   See Rehg, *Insight and Solidarity*. Habermas responds to this specific point indirectly in 'A Reply' (pp. 215–22) via an excursus on Humboldt, and in *Justification and Application* (pp. 69–75) by way of counter-criticisms of Taylor's own project as elaborated in *Sources of the Self*. We encountered the former discussion at the end of chapter five and we will cover the latter in the reflections that follow. However, I will not discuss Habermas's lengthy critical response to Taylor's essay 'The Politics of Recognition', entitled 'Struggles for Recognition in Constitutional States' (both collected in Amy Gutmann ed., *Multiculturalism: Examining the Politics of Recognition* [Princeton: Princeton University Press, 1994]), nor will I discuss his brief critique of Taylor in *Between Facts and Norms* (pp. 498–9). The interested reader may wish to know that I do explore the issues raised by these texts elsewhere, in my forthcoming book, *Charles Taylor*.

53   See Habermas, 'A Reply to my Critics', in John B. Thompson and David Held eds, *Habermas: Critical Debates* (Cambridge: Polity, 1982), p. 227.

54   Rehg, *Insight and Solidarity*, pp. 143–4.

55   Ibid., p. 154.

56   Ibid., p. 159.

57   Ibid., p. 170.

58   Habermas, *Justification and Application*, p. 75.

59   Ibid., pp. 75–6.

60   'As soon as one links the validity of a particular conception of morality with its acceptability to other groups, one has committed oneself at some level to a formal–procedural moral theory' (Rehg, *Insight and Solidarity*, p. 158).

61   Although 'transcendental structure' does not have the same meaning in the two cases. For Habermas, the transcendental structures of linguistic action are

properly investigated by way of universal pragmatics. But the transcendental structures that interest Taylor – the formal characteristics of beings ontologically constituted through disclosure in language – can only be approached by way of hermeneutic reflection. In the next chapter, we consider the possibility of an ethics of nature grounded in the latter – in world-disclosure – rather than in the procedural presuppositions of communicative linguistic action.

62 See Habermas, 'On the Cognitive Content of Morality', p. 341.
63 Habermas, *The Philosophical Discourse of Modernity*, pp. 315–16.
64 Taylor, *Sources of the Self*, p. 171.
65 See Habermas, *The Philosophical Discourse of Modernity*, pp. 297–301.
66 Taylor, 'Comments and Replies', *Inquiry*, 34, 1991, p. 252.
67 Habermas, 'A Reply', pp. 225ff.
68 See Ingram, *Reason, History and Politics*, pp. 298–320.
69 Ibid., p. 318.
70 Habermas, *The Philosophical Discourse of Modernity*, p. 139.
71 Taylor, *Sources of the Self*, pp. 509–10.
72 Ibid., p. 510.

7 THE ECOLOGICAL POLITICS OF STRONG HERMENEUTICS

1 I owe the expression 'ecological conscience' to the title of John Llewelyn's difficult book, *The Middle Voice of Ecological Conscience* (London: Macmillan, 1991). His reflections on the topic, which are shaped mainly by a 'chiasmic' reading of Levinas and Heidegger, take a very different course to my own.

2 The literature on the topic tends to reflect the polarized positions I have just briefly introduced. On the one hand, 'deep ecologists' take the Enlightenment project and its disenchanted view of nature to be inseparably bound to an egocentric conception of responsibility (what I shall call 'subject-centred responsibility'). By way of exposing this interconnection, deep ecology invites us to imagine an alternative, re-enchanted vision of nature, one more in tune with a sense of responsibility to and for nature. It encourages us to think of modern mechanistic science either as an obsolete paradigm, superseded by a more holistic scientific world view, or as an ideology of nature that we can choose to replace by another. Defenders of the Enlightenment are typically appalled by what they regard as the cognitive naïvety of such claims. They too see the issue of a more than prudential responsibility for nature as bound up with projects of re-enchantment, which they dismiss as metaphysical. For an introductory survey of the current debate surrounding 'deep ecology', see Andrew McLaughlin, *Regarding Nature: Industrialism and Deep Ecology* (Albany: SUNY Press, 1993). Other useful guides on these general matters include Robin Eckersley, *Environmentalism and Political Theory: Toward an Ecocentric Approach* (Albany: SUNY Press, 1992) and Andrew Brennan, *Thinking about Nature* (London: Routledge, 1988). On the more specific question of responsibility, John Passmore's *Man's Responsibility for Nature: Ecological Problems and Western Traditions* (London: Duckworth, 1980) inclines to the latter of the aforementioned poles; Hans Jonas's *The Imperative of Responsibility: In Search of an Ethics for the Technological Age*, trans. Hans Jonas with the collaboration of David Herr (Chicago: University of Chicago Press, 1984), though politically astute and theoretically provocative, does not really fit into the debate that presently concerns us. For the beginnings of a formal analysis of the concept of responsibility in relation to the natural

environment, see C. C. Hooker, 'Responsibility, Ethics and Nature', in David E. Cooper and Joy A. Palmer eds, *The Environment in Question: Ethics and Global Issues* (London: Routledge, 1992), pp. 147–64.

3 Stephen K. White, *Political Theory and Postmodernism* (Cambridge: Cambridge University Press, 1991).

4 On subject-centred reason, see Habermas, *The Philosophical Discourse of Modernity*. For Taylor on self-responsible reason, see *Sources of the Self* and 'Overcoming Epistemology' in *Philosophical Arguments*.

5 Habermas, *The Philosophical Discourse of Modernity*, p. 7.

6 See T. W. Adorno and M. Horkheimer, *Dialectic of Enlightenment*, trans. John Cumming (New York: Herder and Herder, 1972); and M. Foucault, *The Order of Things: An Archaeology of the Human Sciences* (London: Tavistock, 1970).

7 White, *Political Theory and Postmodernism*, p. 20.

8 Ibid.

9 Ibid.

10 See Habermas, 'What is Universal Pragmatics?' in *Communication and the Evolution of Society* (Boston: Beacon Press, 1979).

11 White himself carefully reconstructs the argument behind this claim in White, *The Recent Work of Jürgen Habermas: Reason, Justice and Modernity* (Cambridge: Cambridge University Press, 1988), pp. 48–66.

12 See Derrida, *Margins of Philosophy*, p. 323.

13 White, *Political Theory and Postmodernism*, p. 27.

14 Ibid., p. 30.

15 See Habermas, *Knowledge and Human Interests*.

16 White, *Political Theory and Postmodernism*, p. 56.

17 Ibid., p. 57.

18 Ibid., p. 60.

19 White himself draws heavily from Emile Kettering, *NÄHE: Das Denken Martin Heideggers* (Pfullingen: Neske, 1987).

20 White, *Political Theory and Postmodernism*, p. 67.

21 I agree with White that, defined in purely Heideggerian terms, responsibility to otherness is at best irrelevant to matters of justice. On a less generous, and probably more truthful, interpretation of Heidegger's thought, the demands of justice are not only beyond Heideggerian provenance but occluded by it. But while the legacy of Heidegger for a renewed and improved 'environmental ethics' is far from uncontroversial, it does not suffer the same difficulties it does regarding justice, and many more philosophers and social critics have been drawn to Heidegger on account of his insights about ecology than the (non)sense he makes of justice. On the general question of Heidegger's relevance to modern, ecologically troubled, political thought, see Michael A. Zimmerman, *Heidegger's Confrontation with Modernity: Technology, Politics and Art* (Bloomington: Indiana University Press, 1990).

22 White, *Political Theory and Postmodernism*, p. 19. White considers the ecological problematic briefly in his own book on Habermas and in White and Luke, 'The Information Revolution and an Ecological Modernity', in J. Forrester ed., *Critical Theory and Public Life* (Cambridge, Mass.: MIT Press, 1985), but neither discussion is informed by the model of language and responsibility he proposes here. His hypothesis that the framework for thinking about justice laid out in *Political Theory and Postmodernism* can be applied to other areas of political theory (p. xii) will be tested in the reflections that follow.

23 See Habermas, *The Philosophical Discourse of Modernity*, p. 14 and p. 316. See also Habermas, *The New Conservatism*, pp. 262–3. My point here is only that Habermas has recourse to a more complex conception of responsibility

than White allows, one that does not fit readily into White's analytical framework. Admittedly, this understanding of responsibility is often dormant in Habermas's more recent work. I take up the question of the relevance of Habermas's theory for ecological politics later.

24 Gadamer, 'Practical Philosophy as a Model for the Human Sciences', *Research in Phenomenology*, 9, 1980, p. 83.

25 White, *Political Theory and Postmodernism*, p. 19.

26 Taylor, 'Heidegger, Language and Ecology', in *Philosophical Arguments*, p. 101.

27 'Beings can be as beings only if they stand within and stand out within what is cleared in this clearing.... Thanks to this clearing, beings are unconcealed in various degrees' (Heidegger, 'The Origin of the Work of Art', in Heidegger, David Farrell Krell ed., *Basic Writings* [London: Routledge, 1993], p. 178).

28 Taylor's reading of Heidegger dovetails with his critique of Hegel in *Hegel*, and his interpretation of the modernist movement in *Sources of the Self*. In *Hegel* (p. 476), Taylor expresses dissatisfaction with the ontological closure implicit in Hegel's understanding of art as an imperfect form of absolute knowledge. He also praises Heidegger for refusing to countenance such a move. Schopenhauer and Nietzsche pose a different kind of problem. In *Sources of the Self* (p. 448) they are described as helping to establish the idea of nature as an amoral source, a notion which in turn occasions a post-romantic 'crisis of affirmation'. Such a vision of nature, if conceived as the ontic ground of the clearing, is as hard to fit with ecological conscience as the disenchanted view (which leaves no room for the clearing at all).

29 Taylor, 'Heidegger, Language and Ecology', p. 120.

30 Ibid., p. 121.

31 See Heidegger, 'Building, Dwelling, Thinking', in *Basic Writings*.

32 Taylor, *Sources of the Self*, p. 513.

33 Habermas, *Moral Consciousness and Communicative Action*, p. 211. For an assessment of Habermas's views on ecological matters in general, see Peter Dews, 'Lifeworld, Metaphysics and the Ethics of Nature in Habermas', in *The Limits of Disenchantment*; Joel Whitebrook, 'The Problem of Nature in Habermas', *Telos*, 1979, 40, pp. 41–69; Henning Ottman, 'Cognitive Interests and Self-Reflection', in Thompson and Held eds, *Habermas: Critical Debates*, pp. 79–97; T. McCarthy, 'Reflections on Rationalization', in R. Bernstein ed., *Habermas and Modernity*. For more sympathetic readings of Habermas's approach to an ethics of nature, see John S. Dryzek, 'Green Reason: Communicative Ethics for the Biosphere', *Environmental Ethics*, 1990, 12, pp. 195–210, and in a much more anthropocentric vein, Stephen Vogel, *Against Nature* (Albany: SUNY Press, 1996).

34 Habermas, *Moral Consciousness and Communicative Action*, p. 211.

35 As a philosophical doctrine, discourse ethics seeks to refute scepticism concerning the validity of justice claims. But this is done without considering the role that might be played by prima facie moral intuitions of the kind at issue here: they simply do not feature in the rational reconstruction of the moral point of view attempted in discourse ethics.

36 Habermas, *The Theory of Communicative Action*, vol. 2, p. 394.

37 See Heidegger, 'The Question Concerning Technology', in *Basic Writings*, p. 322.

38 I mean 'world picture' here in the sense given to it by Heidegger in 'The Age of the World Picture', in Heidegger, *The Question Concerning Technology and Other Essays*, trans. William Lovitt (London: Harper and Row, 1977).

39 That said, if a critique of the instrumentalization of nature is to avoid hermeneutic idealism, it must be rooted in a more democratic model of

economic activity than the one Habermas himself is prepared to countenance. Plenty of sympathetic critics of Habermas have objected to his compromise to systems theory on this score. See for instance T. McCarthy, 'Complexity and Democracy, or The Seducements of Systems Theory', *New German Critique*, 1985, 35, pp. 55–82.

40 Taylor, *Sources of the Self*, p. 97.

41 Taylor, *The Ethics of Authenticity*, pp. 81–2.

42 But, for a 'subjectivist' interpretation of Taylor that does leave such sensibilities offended, see Stephen R. L. Clark, 'Taylor's Waking Dream', *Inquiry*, 1991, 34, pp. 195–215.

43 This suggestion is made by John S. Dryzek in 'Green Reason: Communicative Ethics and the Biosphere'.

44 Dryzek writes, 'Intersubjective discourse presupposes some ecological – and not just linguistic – standards. Although it is easy to forget, our communications with one another can proceed only in and through the media made available by the natural world . . . if Lovelock is right, the atmosphere in which we live, talk, hear, write, read, smell, and touch is composed and regulated by the planet's biota acting in concert. This biota makes possible and maintains a physical environment fit for itself – and for us, and our communications. . . . Because any such [communicative] act is made possible by this ecological system, it can be called to account in accordance with ecological standards. If indeed nature is a silent participant in every conversation, then perhaps it deserves a measure of the respect that we accord to human participants. If critical communication theorists argue that only entities capable of entering into communication can be assigned value, then there is a sense in which Gaia passes their test' (ibid., p. 205).

In this passage, Dryzek shifts from the interesting and eminently plausible idea that there are 'ecological standards' that are presupposed in intersubjective discourse to the much less plausible suggestion that these presuppositions should be considered as unheard participants in discourse. The latter view is wholly adventitious to the first and requires the addition of the speculative Gaia hypothesis. The former point can be upheld without relying on such speculation, which in any case betrays a misunderstanding of the nature of communicative ethics. Critical communication theorists need not claim that only beings capable of speech and action are assigned value, but only that such beings, in their capacity for world-disclosure and rational problem-solving, can meaningfully assign it. Since the procedural test does not function as a mechanism for selecting candidates for participation, it is misleading to propose that Gaia can either pass or fail it.

45 Habermas, *The Theory of Communicative Action*, vol. 2, pp. 394–5.

Index